Diocletian and the Military Restoration of Rome

Diocletian and the Military Restoration of Rome

Lee Fratantuono
(with photographic illustration by Kate McGarr)

Pen & Sword
MILITARY

First published in Great Britain in 2023 by
Pen & Sword Military
An imprint of
Pen & Sword Books Ltd
Yorkshire – Philadelphia

ISBN 978 1 52677 183 4

A CIP catalogue record for this book is
available from the British Library.

Typeset by Mac Style
Printed in the UK by CPI Group (UK) Ltd, Croydon, CR0 4YY.

Pen & Sword Books Limited incorporates the imprints of Atlas,
Archaeology, Aviation, Discovery, Family History, Fiction, History,
Maritime, Military, Military Classics, Politics, Select, Transport, True
Crime, Air World, Frontline Publishing, Leo Cooper, Remember
When, Seaforth Publishing, The Praetorian Press, Wharncliffe Local
History, Wharncliffe Transport, Wharncliffe True Crime, White Owl
and After the Battle.

For a complete list of Pen & Sword titles please contact

PEN & SWORD BOOKS LIMITED
47 Church Street, Barnsley, South Yorkshire, S70 2AS, England
E-mail: enquiries@pen-and-sword.co.uk
Website: www.pen-and-sword.co.uk

Or

PEN AND SWORD BOOKS
1950 Lawrence Rd, Havertown, PA 19083, USA
E-mail: Uspen-and-sword@casematepublishers.com
Website: www.penandswordbooks.com

For David Rowland Sweet, with gratitude

Contents

Preface and Acknowledgements

The present book seeks to fill a gap in the Pen & Sword collection of biographies and studies of Roman emperors. Diocletian is an interesting figure in Roman military history, not only because of the superlative accomplishments of his long tenure in power, but also because of the paltry remains of literary sources for his reign and exploits. To study his age is a challenge of a very different sort from that posed by periods where we have an abundance and even surfeit of riches from surviving evidence. From purple to a pension, from conquest to cabbages, Diocletian is one of the most intriguing and simultaneously enigmatic figures from the annals of ancient Rome. Precision in chronology is often impossible; details about how he won appreciable military victories are usually wanting. The first forty or so years of his life were spent in near total obscurity. He may have been born a slave. And yet for over twenty years, he managed one of the most extraordinary episodes in Roman renewal, restoration, and recovery with skill and vigour, and bequeathed a far more stable empire to his successors than that which he had inherited.

Diocletian has been the subject of a wide range of fine scholarly studies, many if not most of them devoted to technical considerations of the various problems posed by his reign. We cannot emphasize sufficiently strongly how the chronology of events for his rule is deeply vexed, especially with respect to the dates for many of the military operations against border incursions. We cannot be certain even of such basic dates as the year of Diocletian's death, let alone of his birth. Other works have focused on Diocletian's relationship with Christianity, or on the economic history of his reign. Numismatic scholars have contributed impressive work by close study of the extensive coinage from the tetrarchal period. Archaeologists have provided the answers to many questions, not least via the study of Diocletian's monumental palace at Split – even as answers often yield challenging new questions. The bibliographical references in the present study aim at providing a guide to further study, and make no pretence whatsoever of being comprehensive or exhaustive. Anglophone sources have been prejudiced over continental for the sake of the convenience of a general readership; Seston's 1946 French study of Diocletian and the tetrarchy remains the most important relevant continental work in terms of comprehensive usefulness, at least in my experience and estimation. Stephen Williams' *Diocletian and the Roman Recovery* and David Potter's *The Roman Empire at Bay, AD 180–395* are particularly outstanding guides to the period in question.

This volume is a popular history, not a scholarly one in the strict sense. It does not seek so much to add new knowledge to the study of Diocletian's reign, as to provide an introduction for non-specialists that is both reliable and accessible. It aims to be readable by a wide range of audiences, including those with relatively little knowledge of Roman history. Throughout, there is analysis and comment on the main problems of the period, but always with the caveat that detailed appraisal of controversies will require the reader to pursue further study, for which the notes and bibliography are meant to provide an initial map. Given the nature of the times under study and the history of the Diocletianic tetrarchy, it is necessary to devote attention to those men with whom our imperial subject shared power, and to those who succeeded him. The survey and study of the history of the period ends after Constantine's defeat of Licinius, which seems to provide a convenient end point. Constantine in particular has been the subject of a vast bibliography, and no attempt has been made to go into much detail regarding the events of his life after the death of Diocletian. The history of Rome before Diocletian is sketched with brutal brevity, so as to provide both a refresher for those with some familiarity of the monarchy, Republic, and earlier ages of the empire, and a primer for those who will be interested in pursuing the study of other periods. Military and political interests are given more consideration throughout than economic.

In short, readers will find herein new explorations of old problems, even if the conclusions are not so much novel as judicious reassessments, with agreement and disagreement with predecessors livened with occasional independent speculation. Throughout, then, the emphasis has been on responding to the question, why should a student of ancient Roman history (or of early Christianity) want to learn more about Diocletian? He may be the most important emperor about whom the least, relatively speaking, is known. Spending more than a year studying him closely has been a humbling experience: those who have worked on his reign have laboured largely in dark and shadowy areas of literary evidence in particular. Coins and archaeological remains provide their own lights, oftentimes raising two questions for every answer they provide. The reader of this book, it is hoped, will leave the volume with great interest to pursue this or that topic in the life of Diocletian and tetrarchal studies via further, scholarly research. Diocletian's is a very different world from that of the late Republic and early Empire, one poised on a precipice before matters became more or less doomed in terms of the administration of the Roman west. One point of occasional controversy should be noted: the present study is not sympathetic to the view that the tetrarchy is a mere construct of scholarly inventiveness.

As ever, I am indebted to the help and patience of my editor, Phil Sidnell. Kate McGarr once again contributed much appreciated photographic images to enhance and illustrate the volume, the fruits of her extensive travel and labour especially in Croatia, Turkey, and elsewhere in the eastern Mediterranean and along the Adriatic coast, as well as the Catalonian haunts of one of the more celebrated victims of Diocletian's persecution, the martyr Eulalia. My time in Serbia, Croatia, and elsewhere in the Balkans has been unfailingly delightful through many visits, and I am indebted to the generous friendship of Anka and Bogdan Bazalac. This book would not have been possible without the resources and help of my academic home, The Department of Ancient Classics of the National University of Ireland-Maynooth. I am grateful in particular to the head of the department, Professor William Desmond.

Lastly, this book is dedicated to Professor David Rowland Sweet of the Department of Classics of the University of Dallas, in grateful appreciation for all his help to me for more than twenty years.

Lee Fratantuono
27 June 2022
In Festo Protomartyrum Romanae Ecclesiae

Chapter 1

Reconstructing an Imperial Life

What follows in these pages is modest in aims, if not in scope. There will be no attempt to argue some innovative thesis or explanation for historical events, or to critique in detail the important work done by predecessors. This is a book for a general reader more than for a specialist. It seeks to provide an introduction to the life of the Roman emperor Diocletian, situating him within the troubled history of his own age, as well as within the broader picture of Roman history. It seeks to make Diocletian more familiar to audiences curious about ancient history, and not to enter headlong into the myriad scholarly debates about aspects of his reign. Besides his obvious importance to those interested in Roman history (especially military), Diocletian is of particular interest to students of early Christianity because of his infamous persecution of the faith near the end of his reign; this book may be of some use in providing a brief introduction to the man whose name is associated with the martyrdoms of so many celebrated heroes and heroines from the annals of hagiography. He is a key figure in the history of the security of the frontiers of the Roman empire, especially with respect to what is usually described as Rome's (at least western) 'decline and fall'. He is of inestimable importance to the study of the late Roman government and economy, and of the development of the imperial office.

The title of this chapter is 'reconstructing an imperial life', with obvious enough reference to the sources that are utilized by historians in determining the events of an age. 'Reconstruction' is limited by the quantity and quality of those sources, and in the case of Diocletian we have less rather than more, certainly by the former criterion, and arguably by the latter as well. In military affairs, often we know that there may have been a clash with a particular barbarian foe, but we are uncertain of such details as exact date and place for the engagement, let alone for the strategy and tactics employed by the two sides. In my *Battle of Actium* volume, it was possible to assemble a significant range of sources with specific details about the naval clash. In the present study, vague information about battles is not the fault of the student of the period, but an inevitable consequence of the silence or spottiness of the record.

Diocletian reigned for a very long time by third century standards. For more than twenty years, he responded to crisis after crisis on multiple fronts of the empire, and engaged in extensive reorganization and consolidation efforts in areas both military and economic, as well as political and social. Tremendously appreciated while he was alive, he died unable even to secure the courtesy of a reply to a request to a successor that his imprisoned daughter be sent home to him. Dead either of natural causes or suicide, he would be buried in a splendid tomb in his massive, glorious retirement seaside residence, a better fate than many of the rulers of his age, even if by then he had become something of a living fossil, a discarded relic. For countless reasons, his life deserves and repays close study, if only to understand how he managed to do so much to help Rome to recover from a long nightmare.

The tradition of writing imperial biographies is a long and venerable one, a tradition perhaps most familiar to contemporary readers by the popular *Vitae Caesarum* or 'Lives of the Caesars' by Suetonius.[1] Roman imperial history, not surprisingly, became defined by the lives of the men who governed and ruled the often unwieldy, far-flung provinces and territories of the empire. Some of those men were remembered almost universally for being extraordinary, outstanding rulers who deserved the simple yet profound epithet 'good': men like Trajan or Marcus Aurelius.[2] Others are vilified in our sources, remembered even by those with the most passing familiarity with ancient history as 'bad' or even 'monstrous': men like Caligula or Nero. The diverse personalities of the emperors sometimes seem to define the age in which they lived, such that the history of 37–41 CE becomes indelibly associated with the life of Caligula, just as 79–81 is defined by Vespasian's son Titus. For earlier emperors, the question of the relationship of offices like the principate to the republican traditions of Rome was of paramount importance. For rulers like Diocletian, republicanism long ago had been all but buried. The senate will figure in our story, but to nothing like the extent that was the case earlier in imperial history.

Biography is not the same as history, though the two genres overlap and share much in common. Like historians, biographers have diverse goals in mind in the production of their works. Plutarch's parallel approach, with a famous Greek and a famous Roman in studied contrast (complete with an essay to explore the commonalties and differences), shades more toward the philosophical than the sensational or the lurid. Roman emperors provide a potent mix of material for comparison, not least in the matter of their relative success and failure in responding to the challenges of their ages. In the case of Diocletian, those challenges were compelling, indeed of such a degree of severity that even competent and skilled men may have found them to be overwhelming. Emperors like Aurelian and Probus were recent predecessors of Diocletian who had done outstanding work in resolving the crises that beset Rome, only to find themselves assassinated. Diocletian had witnessed many a tumultuous episode of upheaval and chaos at the highest levels of government. Survival alone was a difficult challenge, and one that Diocletian met ably.

Our imperial subject has been treated in diverse ways by history.[3] Some today know Diocletian only because of his infamous persecution of Christianity, with his name being notorious as a virtual Antichrist of the early history of that religion, far worse even than Nero in his savagery towards Christians. His name is repeated almost daily in the liturgy of Roman Catholics, as the names of the martyr victims of his *Magna Persecutio* are identified temporally as having died 'under Diocletian' or 'in the reign of Diocletian'. Others vaguely recall that he was one of the stronger and more accomplished emperors in an age in which quality stood in sharp relief to the mediocrity and incompetence that dominated the political and martial landscape. Those with more familiarity with Roman history are aware that he was responsible for a major development (more accurately, perhaps, 'refinement') in Roman political history and the oversight of empire, as the progenitor of the tetrarchy and of what would come to be known as the 'Dominate',[4] and, perhaps, that he was a Roman emperor who could legitimately (we might whimsically think) apply for the pension benefits that we would associate with retirement from one's career.

Diocletian is less remembered in some circles for his foreign military campaigns, though he conducted many successful engagements against a wide range of barbarian and other foes, and with appreciable, often impressive success. Indeed his greatest successes, it could be argued, were in foreign policy, not domestic. Throughout his life, there was an untiring practicality that motivated his responses to crises. In foreign affairs that attention to practicality and reality meant near constant military campaigns and the maintenance of a vast array of armed forces. As for domestic concerns, standardization of taxation and government organization were seen as pressing matters.

Diocletian could be called a millennial man. He was born very close to the time when Rome celebrated its thousandth birthday. An ancient horoscope writer or astrologer – and astrology was a popular hobby and avocation in the imperial Rome of Diocletian's day – might have been tempted to associate the emperor's auspicious birth, so close to the Roman millennium, with his future success and high office.[5] For, after a thousand years, Rome was in an extremely precarious position, her very survival as an empire called into question. The millennial child would do much to secure her future for many more years. Rome was in a frightful state at the time of her thousandth birthday, and while there was a tremendous celebration and glorious festival to commemorate the event, there was also a palpable sense of crisis and chaos. The fabric of empire seemed to be unravelling.

The decade before Diocletian's birth had been fraught with troubles, and the first half of his life would prove to be even more difficult. In what can only be considered a savage blow of fortune, Diocletian would meet his death well aware that the system that he had put into place with such success and acumen was already at serious risk of total collapse, though the very strength of his achievements meant that even times of crisis and the undermining of the social and political order were able to be withstood and endured. And for all the trouble that beset Rome in the wake of Diocletian's arrangements for retirement, there would be another saviour figure in the mix, in the person of the man known to history as Constantine the Great. At the end of the third century, Diocletian would emerge as the man most responsible for the recovery of Rome. Early in the fourth century, Constantine would become the new, larger than life imperial potentate. It is of special interest to note that Diocletian had envisaged a system of shared governance, of efficient collegiality, while Constantine would revert more to a model of monarchy – the inevitable pendulum swings in response to current and recent events relative to one's reign.

Diocletian would be responsible for a profound reorganization of the provincial system, a work that was significant for its coming centuries after the last such major effort that had taken place under Augustus.[6] The contemporary map of Europe is not without its debt to Diocletian. Just as the Augustan system would endure fundamentally unaltered for centuries, so too would the Diocletianic division of the empire into dioceses and other units of administrative oversight remain in place for centuries.[7] Diocletian's tetrarchy may not have done well in its first succession process, but his arrangement of the empire's vast territories did. One of the advantages of his system was that it succeeded in helping to avoid the problem of having too much power concentrated into the hands of any one individual – the perennial source of civil war and internecine conflict. We are fortunate to have a list of Diocletian's imperial divisions, which is known as the *Laterculus Veronensis* or 'Verona List', so named because it survives in a seventh century manuscript that was preserved at Verona.[8] The text may be found in the standard collection of Roman geographical works, the so-called *Geographi Latini Minores* volume edited by Alexander Riese in 1878. There is a Diocese of the East; of Pontus; of Asia; of Thrace; of the Moesias; of the Pannonias; of the Britains;[9] of the Gauls; of Viennensis; of Italy; of the Spains and of Africa – a dozen in all, subdivided into provinces. Again, we see here the future of European maps both political and ecclesiastical, and the indefatigable work of a man who laboured in many parts of the empire, in an age in which cartography was a primitive and inexact art.

In addition to the *Laterculus*, we possess also an invaluable document from the early fifth century, the so-called *Notitia Dignitatum*. It is a notoriously problematic text, for all its invaluable information – not least because of how many of its points of information date to the late third/ early fourth centuries.[10] It outlines the divisions of government and the organization of military units. While of inestimable use, it also has marked limitations, not least the absence of information on numbers of men, for example, in different divisions of the army. The text is challenging not least for the risks of using it to reconstruct the situation in early periods, especially given the turmoil of the intervening decades. What is certain is that there were more *legiones* by the time of the *Notitia* than there were in earlier Roman history, which, coupled with archaeological evidence in particular, attests to the smaller size of late imperial legions. Estimates vary as to the size of the Roman armed forces in Diocletian's time. Figures as high as 645,000 have been proposed, which is probably too large; half a million might be a better estimate, though the truth is that we have more evidence for the size of the army during the principate than for the dominate. Legions traditionally had 5,500 men, which is part of what has led to some scholars assuming that the army of the tetrarchy had a million-man force. In reality the size of the legions was almost certainly reduced, but we do not know by how much – it is possible that the size was not so very different, but that the emphasis was on greater dispersal and field mobility.[11] Like the *Laterculus*, the *Notitia* offers evidence that can help to answer some questions about Diocletian's reign, so long as extreme caution is exercised in interpreting its data.

As for specific units and what we can learn about them, the *Notitia*, for example, mentions the storied *Legio VI Victrix*, a distinguished unit that had been established probably by Octavian. Later based in Eboracum (modern day York), it is listed as part of the forces of the *Dux Britanniarum*, and was the legion that proclaimed Constantine emperor in 306 on the death of his father.[12] Conversely, the *Notitia* does not mention *Legio XX Valeria Victrix*, referred to on coins of the usurper Carausius, which has led to the conclusion that the legion may have been disbanded.[13]

What we can say is this: Diocletian did not only restore Rome's existing legions (often seriously weakened as they were by near constant warfare), but he also created an unprecedented number of new ones.[14] Quantity was the watchword, perhaps, but not necessarily more than quality.[15]

For all his significance in both military and political history, Diocletian remains something of an enigma. The present study aims to provide an overview (in detail) of the life and career of an emperor who is, perhaps, one of the more neglected of those who may fairly be counted among the outstanding rulers of Rome. Certainly we might think of Antoninus Pius as a 'forgotten' emperor, a man who ruled for many years in a time of stability and appreciable prosperity. Diocletian oversaw the Roman Empire in a period of crisis and chaos, and he succeeded both in improving the condition of the empire's stability and in developing a novel, theoretically sound mechanism for the future governance of the empire.

How did he manage what successes he enjoyed? Diocletian did not benefit from coming to power in a time of peace and serenity. He did not have the advantages of family name or wealthy pedigree. He had in all likelihood the most basic of educations, with nothing of the training and study of those who could boast of rhetorical expertise and familiarity with Greek and Latin literature. He was, in fact, a figure of virtually no noteworthy report for much of his life. And yet in appreciable and outstanding ways, he was a saviour for Rome in an hour of supreme peril. If nothing else, he was a testament to the superior training and value of the Roman military, such that a man who likely began his career as a common soldier was able to rise to the highest of positions, with the competence and practicality that have been traditionally and stereotypically associated with the behemoth that was Rome's military might. That said, there had been a series of many emperors in the years preceding Diocletian's rule whose origins were in Rome's army.

Diocletian would prove to be one of the most accomplished and successful of these men, a testament not only to the institution that reared him and gave him an upbringing, but also to his personal ability and talent. He was radically different in origins from most of those storied figures of the fall of the Republic and the birth of empire. And yet, in the final analysis, he was probably the right man for the task that confronted him. His failures included the dark fact that his wife and daughter would be sentenced to death by one of his successor tetrarchs, after he retired, with Diocletian probably unable even to win a response to his request for his family's safety. His successes included the impressive system of fortification and defence (both static and mobile) with which he would guard the vast borders of the empire. Diocletian oversaw one of the most massive military expansions in Roman history.[16] For him, Rome needed to be a militarized state, a vast army juggernaut in which the legions were a permanent guarantee of the security of the state. The money that was needed to maintain them would come from a complex and detailed standardized system of taxation. The economy would be supported by extensive agricultural development, including in border areas where the farms would be manned by transplanted barbarians and immigrants to the empire. Above it all would loom the distant person of the emperor, a divine figure at a remove from lowlier society, a mystical ruler who managed everything as Jupiter on earth. In some ways, he was more Roman than the Romans, raised as he was in a Balkan milieu that prided itself on its embrace of traditional Roman virtues. Indeed, at the height of power when he finally visited Rome for the first and only time in his life, we shall see that he was deeply uncomfortable with the way in which the reality that confronted him did not match a lifetime of accumulated dreams.

Diocletian's reign of some two decades is inextricably associated with early Christian history, in particular with the notorious persecution of Christians that he inaugurated near the end of his tenure.[17] The persecution was responsible for something of the preservation of more records about his rule than we would otherwise possess. Diocletian presents a case in Roman imperial history where we lack extensive surviving histories of his age, notwithstanding his long service in office and the weighty and dramatic events thereof. If we exclude those sources that were authored by Christians, our extant literary evidence becomes exceedingly jejune. And those Christian works oftentimes are in the nature of polemics, with a strong criticism of the man who was responsible for the attempted suppression of their faith and the martyrdom of so many adherents to the religion. There is no *Vita Diocletiani*, and no long narrative history that tells the story of his time.

It will be of profit to review something of the history of the world into which Diocletian was born. We know nothing of his early education or life, beyond that which may be inferred from our knowledge of Roman pedagogy and the typical upbringing of children in the empire. Even this, as we shall see, is fraught with peril – Diocletian may even have been born a slave, if the tradition that he was a freedman of a senator can be believed. It is possible that in the case of Diocletian a reverse of the usual practice of embellishing one's origins was at play. Diocletian may have emphasized humble roots precisely in order to appear all the more successful and great in his achievements. At best in terms of his social standing, Diocletian may have been the son of a manumitted slave (certainly of a man of very low status), a man for whom the army represented the only realistic avenue for social advancement and success. Humble origins of this sort meant that education was rudimentary at best. We have no knowledge of when later in life (if ever) Diocletian would have acquired more learning. What mattered for his upbringing and future success was his entry into the army. The military opened every door for the future successful emperor.

Diocletian was born close to the midpoint of the third century CE – one of the most harrowing, confused and confusing, and altogether momentous periods of the long centuries of Roman history. Diocletian was born into a chaotic world that may well have survived its third century crisis in part by virtue of the strong foundations of the political and military institutions that made Rome both famous and feared. There was no assurance that the empire was going to endure the problems of the third century, and every likelihood that it would collapse (or at least that it would break apart into at least two separate realms). But first, then, a look back in survey at how Rome passed its first thousand years.

The study of the history of ancient Rome is conventionally divided into three major periods: the Monarchy; the Republic; and the Empire. Rome was traditionally founded on 21 April 753 BCE; the monarchy endured for some two and a half centuries until the expulsion of the last king and the establishment of a republican government in 509 BCE. These dates, we should note, are more traditional than strictly exact. Our evidence and knowledge for the first centuries of Roman history is notoriously problematic, and there is little that has not been the topic of significant scholarly debate and argument. What is certain is that Rome developed a strong antipathy for monarchy and the notion of the solitary rule of a potentially despotic figure, and a corresponding passion for republican government. The story of how that republican system would prove less than stable, and of how Rome would eventually become a de facto monarchy, is one of the most researched and debated facets of classical studies. Once Rome became an empire, she would experience the reigns of vastly different imperial heads, some of whom behaved in such an autocratic fashion so as for one rightly to think that Rome had reverted to monarchy. Indeed, in some regards Diocletian would prove to be one of the more monarchical of emperors, choosing to follow in the footsteps of those predecessors who were more given to the trappings of power and rule by dictate than those who espoused more republican views – even as he was willing and eager to share power with colleagues.

The transition from Roman Republic to Roman Empire is a change more difficult to date precisely. We often think of Augustus as the first Roman emperor, and the date of his coming to power is sometimes fixed in 31 BCE, the year of his victory over Antony and Cleopatra at the naval battle of Actium.[18] That triumph in the waters off north western Greece was the culmination of a long period of seemingly interminable civil wars that plagued the Republic and brought Rome to the brink of ruin amid constant turmoil and upheaval both social and military. The names of the antagonists of those bloody conflicts are familiar to students and scholars of ancient Rome: Marius and Sulla; Caesar and Pompey. In some ways these men were like proto-emperors or at least would-be emperors of Rome. Each was larger than life, with military might as a tool to achieve political ends. All of them, beyond question, would deny vigorously that they were seeking to overthrow the Roman Republic. On the contrary, they would have cast their actions in terms of the preservation of the Republic against a foe who was seeking to destroy it. Further, all of them were working at least in principle to preserve Rome from one of the most regular threats to her security – the looming spectre of civil war. Ambitious men with command of military forces had proven time and again all too prone to the temptation to make a bid for power.

Gaius Julius Caesar was considered by his foes (and even some of his friends and partisans) to have monarchical designs on Rome.[19] His deeds and exploits defined his age, whether in the business of his military and political achievements in Gaul and Britain, or in his wide-ranging activities across theatres as diverse as Spain, Greece, the Roman Near East, and north Africa. Towards the end of his life he became involved in his fateful affair with the Egyptian monarch Cleopatra VII Philopator (better known to history simply as Cleopatra); with her he would have an ill-fated son Caesarion (literally, 'Little Caesar' in Greek). Finally, he would be assassinated on the Ides of March in 44 BCE, the victim of a senatorial, aristocratic conspiracy that was rooted in the fear that he intended to take complete possession of the mechanisms of government. Some would say that Caesar was the first Roman emperor, an argument that may be supported by the fact that his *cognomen* 'Caesar' became a title in itself for later emperors of Rome, a title that endured even into twentieth century world history in the German *Kaiser*. Caesar has probably won the popularity contest of men of the Roman Republic, perhaps earning even the title of the most famous Roman of them all. He would be deified after his death, a fitting culmination of a career for the man whose lineage was traditionally traced back to the goddess Venus. One achievement of his is certain – he would become arguably the most famous Roman for subsequent generations, known even to those who might struggle if asked to name another.

The death of Caesar was accompanied by a political reality that has been all too often repeated in the annals of government and public administration: there was no firm or detailed plan as to what to do in the wake of the stabbing of Caesar. Today, from the vantage point of centuries and the detached perspective of those who can benefit from hindsight, the Caesarian assassins seem naïve. It is as if they expected that the Roman Republic would resume its operation and productive course, as if Caesar had been something of an aberration that simply needed to be eliminated. Rome's larger than life military and political hero lay dead, and no one – either friend or foe – seemed to know exactly what should happen next.

The senators who collaborated in Caesar's death may not have comprehended fully just how enervated and weak the republican system was by their day. The relationship between the so-called patricians and plebeians in Roman society – the 'Struggle of the Orders' – had never been definitively resolved. Rome faced significant and pressing threats on numerous borders, not least the problem of what to do in the face of threats from Rome's mighty eastern neighbour, the Parthian Empire. Indeed one of the reasons for the selection of the Ides of March as the date of Caesar's assassination was the fact that the great military genius was due to embark on a major operation against Parthia, one which would mean his absence for some time from Rome – and the chance for him to achieve a lasting fame and glory, should he succeed in silencing Rome's most dangerous foreign enemy. Rome in some ways had sleepwalked into empire, and now the empire – or republic – needed direction and leadership in the wake of the assassination of the man who had dramatically expanded and solidified the Roman state.

Caesar died in middle age, having achieved much in the course of life, and yet living all too conspicuously in the shadow of Alexander the Great. Having conquered so much of the known world of his day, Alexander died at thirty-three. Caesar had another twenty and more years of life in which to work out his destiny. The story is told that when he was in his thirties, Caesar wept at the sight of a statue of Alexander in Spain. Caesar was sorrowful and rueful of the fact that he had done nothing to match the peerless deeds of the Macedonian monarch.

But therein lies part of the problem of our story. Alexander had the great fortune of being born a prince, the son of the Macedonian king Philip, a hero storied in his own right. Macedonia was a kingdom, not a republic. Alexander was born heir to kingship, and ultimately his death would come from illness or alcohol, most probably – not from poison or any sort of assassination machinations. At the very least, if Alexander was the victim of some fatal, poisonous plot, the plotters were far less dramatic than the senators of the Ides. And Alexander would die prematurely, at a young age – all the better for the development of his legend, with its justifiable pride in how he had done so much by his early thirties.

Alexander likely died of natural causes. Caesar was certainly assassinated. Chaos followed in the wake of both deaths. Our story, in contrast, is focused on someone who did not leave office by either the Alexandrian or the Caesarian route. Diocletian would be that great rarity: a Roman emperor who would abdicate from his imperial power, something that before him had been done only by Nerva (and in very different circumstances). Diocletian would resign from the job of being Rome's sovereign, and he would die in retirement, either of natural causes, or by suicide. Before that death he would enjoy the pleasure that comes from being invited to take back one's position and power – an offer that he would refuse.

Diocletian took power 270 years after the death of Augustus. We have observed that in the wake of Caesar's assassination, the senators of Rome had lacked a clear vision of what should follow, other than a hopeless wish that Rome might revert to normal republican government. Indeed it is not clear that anyone remembered what 'normal' republican government was, so long and so profound had been the crises that had crippled the political and military institutions of Rome. In the end, the winner of the political contest and rivalry that ensued in the wake of Caesar's death would be his heir.

Like Alexander in the matter of his royal birth, the man who would be best known to history as 'Augustus' had a happy bit of fortune in his pedigree: he would be Caesar's adopted heir, entitled under Roman law to use the name of Caesar as his own. Gaius Octavius became a member of the Julian family or *gens*, a Gaius Julius in his own right. Certainly this pedigree brought with it significant threats. Caesar's heir was but 18 when his benefactor and patron was assassinated. There were powerful men in the senate who distrusted anyone connected too closely to Caesar. There were equally powerful Caesarian partisans and allies who were resentful of the young heir – prominent among them Caesar's long-time partner in arms, Marcus Antonius (better known to us as Mark Antony). And there was the queen of Egypt with her child by Caesar, the notorious Cleopatra.

Caesar's heir was a man of many names. History books often refer to him in the crucial years of his rise to and consolidation of power as 'Octavian', since after his adoption by Caesar he was often distinguished from him by the addition of the clarifying appellation 'Octavianus' to his new legal name, such that he became Gaius Julius Caesar Octavianus. He was eventually granted the honorific title 'Augustus' by the senate on 16 January 27 BCE, and thenceforth he is usually referred to simply by that name.

The thirteen years from 44 to 31 BCE were almost guaranteed to be a baker's dozen of tumultuous, violent and dramatic years. There would be civil wars between the supporters of Caesar and his assassins. There would be conflict with Egypt's queen, who soon enough took up a new paramour in her relationship with Mark Antony (who followed in Caesar's steps even in the matter of his mistress). There would be further domestic troubles and challenges, problems rooted in the notion that Rome was, after all, supposed to be managed in a more egalitarian, republican fashion.

By a combination of luck, fortune, talent and skill, Octavian won his conflict against all possible foes, not least the double threat of Antony and Cleopatra. The naval battle of Actium in 31 BCE was one of those battles that mattered, an engagement that inaugurated a year that would culminate with Octavian's triumphal entrance into Alexandria in the late summer of 30, with Antony and Cleopatra destined to commit suicide.[20] Caesar's son Caesarion was one of the casualties of war – killed, history records, on the orders of Octavian. 'Too many Caesars', as we are told – Octavian recognized that a brutal expedient was necessary to ensure his own freedom from sources of potential opposition.

But Caesar's heir nevertheless faced a question in 31–30 that was not dissimilar to that of the assassins of 44: what to do in the wake of victory? Unlike the senatorial conspirators, the man we know best as Augustus managed a brilliant political and social revolution. From 31 BCE until his death in 14 CE, there was no question that Caesar's heir was the supreme figure in Roman government and administration. He benefited, to be sure, from the Republic's exhaustion with civil war and seemingly perennial conflict. He profited from his family link to Caesar and the rich network of allies that it afforded him. He succeeded in casting his civil conflict with Mark Antony into an eminently foreign light by focusing his venom more on Cleopatra of Egypt than on his onetime colleague and associate Antony.

He also mastered the art of making it seem that what he was doing was not so much the establishment of some nascent monarchy, but rather the restoration and preservation of the Republic of old. In short, if he had monarchical ambitions he knew how to conceal them with just enough political and legal sleight of hand so as to appear honest enough when he spoke in defence of his renewal of the venerable old institutions of traditional Rome. Even today, scholars of Roman political and social history debate the exact nature of Augustan reforms and legislation. It can be difficult, if not impossible, to determine precisely what powers Augustus had at any given moment of his reign – if reign is the appropriate word to use (he would no doubt object to it). Image and reality converged in the Augustan Age, in a veritable kaleidoscope that could both dazzle and mislead. Augustus was a master of blending appearance and substance.

And whatever he was doing, he succeeded in his efforts to bring peace and prosperity to Rome. There is good reason why Saint Luke in his gospel speaks of the birth of Christ as coming in the Augustan Age, 'when the whole world was at peace.' Augustus Caesar had a marvellous machine of propaganda (literary and otherwise) that ensured that the message of his accomplishments would be preserved for the ages. This propaganda can be appreciated most readily in the work of such men as the poets Virgil and Horace. Virgil's *Aeneid* is a lasting epic monument to the glory of the Augustan regime. Literary scholars have long debated whether or not Virgil's epic displays any attitude of ambivalence toward the nascent Augustan regime. Some would argue that the *Aeneid* is, on the whole, a striking defence and championing of Augustus' achievement, and that any seemingly negative, pessimistic passages are more the result of overly subtle modern literary interpretations than of any deliberate intention on the poet's part. Others would say that while Virgil was undoubtedly supportive and appreciative of the Augustan renaissance that had stabilized Roman life and which, more personally, was responsible for his livelihood and career, he was also deeply troubled by the problem of what might happen should Augustus no longer be alive and in power. The Augustan system worked best while Augustus was alive, just as the system inaugurated by Diocletian would work best while Diocletian was at the helm. In the case of Augustus, death in the summer of 14 would test the stability of the political edifice. Diocletian would abdicate, with the same test of stability in the wake of his resignation as had been the case almost three centuries earlier. Both men would enjoy success tempered by the harsh reality that things were not nearly as well managed or peaceful when they were not in power.

The Augustan system and regime – for better or worse – endured for the long life of its founder. The problem that plagued it, however – a problem known early on, to be sure – was what would happen in the case of Augustus' death in terms of the succession. The *princeps* or 'first citizen' needed a replacement or heir. There were two obvious sources for heirs in the Roman system: one's biological children, or one's children by adoption and inheritance. A ruler might have a son who could be trusted to take over the reins of government for his father. A ruler might also seek out the person who would be the best possible successor from the ranks of the great and worthy men of political and military life. Such a 'best man for the job' could then be adopted by the ruler, ready to carry on for him with the legal benefit and approbation of the family name and familial inheritance. This problem of the succession is one that would remain a critical threat to Roman stability for centuries. Our subject Diocletian would be noteworthy if only because he fashioned something of a solution to the problem, even if ultimately it would prove untenable or unworkable. One thing is certain: while Augustus was scrupulous in his careful management and cooperation with the Roman senate, Diocletian was more inclined to ignore it. The autocracy level had increased dramatically in Rome, and for much of the reign of the tetrarchs the senate was side lined from any serious participation in the affairs of state – at least in comparison to the emperor.

Augustus was not blessed in the matter of children, and in the end the long culmination of the process for finding a successor devolved on the son of his wife Livia from her previous marriage – the man known to history as the future emperor Tiberius.[21] Partly in consequence of Augustus' own long life, Tiberius would be in middle age when he could finally assume control of the state apparatus. Augustus' death was the occasion of significant concern – this was the first time that his system would be tested, as it were, in the always delicate matter of the succession question.

To a greater or lesser extent, every subsequent transition of power in Roman imperial history would be fraught with the same anxiety regarding the succession. In some cases, imperial reigns would end violently – the assassinations of Caligula and Domitian come to mind. In other instances, there would be relatively calm transfers of power – one thinks of the peaceful death from natural causes of the emperor Vespasian, and the succession of his son Titus; of the death of Trajan and the accession of Hadrian; and of the similar case of Hadrian's reign giving way to that of Antoninus Pius.

The system that Augustus had instituted remained more or less stable for almost two centuries. When we say 'more or less', admittedly we gloss over both extraordinarily felicitous and unimaginably challenging and difficult circumstances. But until what came to be known as the crisis of the third century, the Augustan regime displayed a remarkable vitality that is a testament to the strength of Roman institutions alongside the success of the Augustan model or paradigm. Rome throughout her history was able to endure periods of true crisis with fortitude and reserves of strength and discipline. There were also moments of splendid management in times of significant power and prosperity, such as that which emerged in the wake of the reign of terror of Domitian and his assassination in 96.

For some students of ancient Rome, the pinnacle of Roman glory came during this period, in the long period of the rulers who became known to history by a simple and elegant appellation: the 'Good Emperors'. From Nerva to Trajan to Hadrian to Antoninus Pius to Marcus Aurelius, Rome would know almost a century (96–180 CE) of relatively stable and highly prosperous circumstances. This is not to say that the century was devoid of strife both foreign and domestic; indeed, there were significant conflicts and threats to Rome in this period. It is also true that under Trajan, Rome reached the greatest territorial expanse in her long history. For good reason, textbooks of both Roman history and the Latin language often include a frontispiece map that illustrates Rome c. 120 CE, at the zenith of her success and glory.[22]

The death of Marcus Aurelius in 180 was followed by the coming to power of another of the notorious 'bad' emperors of Rome, his son Commodus. If there is any surprise about the reign of Commodus, it is that it lasted a dozen years until his assassination in 192. That assassination set into motion one of Rome's most devastating periods of crisis and near collapse. As in previous periods of instability, a dynasty would emerge that would play a salvific role as a bringer of order and restorer of (relative) calm: the Severan Dynasty, centred on the great African emperor Septimius Severus. Hauntingly, like Marcus Aurelius, the father would prove to be exceedingly ill served by the son. Septimius Severus was one of Rome's greatest and most accomplished leaders (especially in military matters), with victories to his credit literally from one corner of the empire to the other (he would die in Britain).[23] His son Caracalla was, in some regards at least, everything that his father was not. Like Commodus, Caracalla would be assassinated.[24] The Severan Dynasty would face even steeper decline in the person of the notorious Elagabalus or Heliogabalus, who figures often in lists of the worst emperors Rome produced.[25] Like Caracalla, Elagabalus was assassinated. His cousin Alexander Severus would succeed him, and he, too, would face death by assassination.[26]

The Severan Dynasty had ended, like the Antonine and the Flavian and the Julio-Claudian before it. Once again there was a dramatic difference in quality between different representatives of the family. The death of Alexander Severus would usher in a period of chaos, however, such that Rome had never known – at least not for so sustained a length of time. The year 235 was the beginning of what would be decades of ever worsening problems, an era of disasters and upheavals that would afflict the empire for half a century. These crises were both domestic and foreign, allowing no respite on any front for the men brave enough to aspire to be emperors. In less than a century, Rome had declined significantly, and it would be due to the interventions and success of several powerful men of military talent and origins that the empire would be saved from the threat of collapse.

We see something of a pattern here: periods of crisis that were punctuated by the appearance of an outstanding figure who would stabilize matters. Some might argue that the Augustan imperial system was inherently flawed, and that the problem stemmed from its studied ambiguity about the succession. The Augustan plan had been in part to obfuscate about the status of the Republic versus the empire. As time went on, the masquerade was more or less difficult to maintain. Augustus at least for a while could claim with some credibility that what he was doing was to preserve order in time of extraordinary crisis. Rome did after all have a tradition from her early history of a *dictator*, a man who would assume total power for the sake of resolving an existential threat to the Republic. The ideal dictator was a man like the famous Cincinnatus, who would exit office after the crisis had been resolved. Augustus was a master of defining and arranging the powers of office that he would and would not maintain, arrogating now this or now that privilege to himself or to the senate. He clearly envisioned that his principate system would endure, ideally with as successful a new *princeps* at the helm as he had been. Diocletian's system introduced a new fundamental refinement – the two *principes*, as it were – the two Augustuses – would be able to know when it was time to vacate office.

All of these concerns were domestic and internal. But existentially, the seemingly insurmountable problem that Rome faced in the late second and early third centuries was the problem of her relationships with neighbouring tribes and empires, notably the incessant strife to the north with the Germans, and to the east with both Parthia and (later) Persia.[27] The army was of obvious enough paramount importance in quelling disturbances and maintaining order, as well as being an extremely expensive and potentially dangerous feature and entity of empire. Alexander Severus was assassinated in a military coup, and his death in 235 CE ushered in what is known as the period of the Soldier or Barracks Emperors, that aforementioned half century of significant instability and crises. Instability was such that the year 238 is known to historians as the 'Year of the Six Emperors'. To put into sharp relief just how terrible the problems of the age were, in 260 the emperor Valerian would be the first emperor in Roman history to be captured by a foreign power (Persia); he would die in ignominious captivity. It was arguably the nadir of Roman foreign policy episodes.

A half century of chaos, then, is what the subject of our story inherited when he became emperor. We may ask how the Rome of Diocletian in 284 was different from that inherited by Tiberius in 14. One significant difference has not yet been mentioned: the spread of Christianity.[28] We do not know when exactly Christianity was introduced to Rome, but the historical record attests to the presence of the apostles Peter and Paul in Rome during the reign of Nero, and there were Christian martyrs under the reign of his predecessor Claudius. By Diocletian's day, Christianity had spread throughout the empire, and for long periods of time it was more or less tolerated. Some evidence for this tolerance or lack thereof survives in such works as the correspondence of the emperor Trajan with Pliny the Younger, in which one can read about the question of how Roman officials dealt with Christianity – a religion that was viewed as a challenge to the Roman state in large part because of its monotheistic character. A good emperor of Rome could expect to be deified after his death. Vespasian's dying words are humorously related to have been that he was becoming a god. Rulers like Caligula affected divinity even while still alive. Christianity, to be sure, denied that there were any such imperial gods, and so the religion could easily enough become identified with threats to the stability of the imperial system.

Today, if one opens an edition of the volume known as the *Martyrologium Romanum* or 'Roman Martyrology', one will find an unusually high number of citations of the emperor Diocletian, as the man responsible for the deaths of countless Christians.[29] Throughout the lands formerly controlled by the empire, his was the age of martyrs – in Britain, we may recall Saint Alban.

For Diocletian is famous in Christian history for his inauguration of what became known as the Great Persecution, the period of violence against adherents to Christianity that led to violent upheaval throughout the empire. One of the relatively few works of classical literature that survives from the reign of Diocletian is a lengthy treatise in five books ascribed to one Arnobius, usually under the title *Adversus gentes* or 'Against the Nations'.[30] Arnobius writes what is not so much an apology for Christianity as a blistering attack on Roman religion and classical mythology. Indeed, Arnobius is read today more for the lore that he preserves incidentally about pagan Roman religious practices and obscure mythological variants than for any summation of Christian doctrine or liturgy. Some have even decided that Arnobius was not a very good Christian in terms of his knowledge of Christian beliefs and teachings, given the poor job he does in his treatise at explicating the dogmas and doctrines of the faith. Arnobius spends many pages decrying the recorded stories of gods like Jupiter and Apollo, recalling the notorious tales of the peccadilloes of the immortals and of their shameful exploits. Readers of his books will not learn very much about what Christians believed in the days of Diocletian, but they will discover something of how a learned man could make mockery of the traditional Roman religion – not least in response to persecution of monotheistic Christianity. Arnobius, we might note, was a teacher of Lactantius, who would write his own work of Christian apologetics, the *Institutiones Divinae*, which dates to the period around the end of Diocletian's life.[31] The *Institutiones* has goals broadly similar to the *Adversus gentes*, with a concern for highlighting the logic and reasonable nature of Christianity in comparison to pagan religion. Lactantius is important as an historical source for the reigns of the tetrarchs in particular because he also wrote a treatise devoted to the deaths of the persecutors of Christianity (a work that offers something of a history of the tetrarchy), while Arnobius provides information of immense use to students of Roman religion, with little in the way of value for a student of Diocletian's reign.

By Diocletian's day, the Romans were notably tolerant when it came to the question of introducing new gods – one of the advantages of polytheism is that in theory there is always room for another deity. To oversimplify, it could be said that the Romans were accepting of the idea of adding new deities to the roster of gods who were the object of cult worship, at least of worship by non-citizens. But Christianity posed the problem of demanding adherence to only one god, with no room for any others. Diocletian, we shall see, found in this a threat to the stability and identity of the Roman state. It was clearly at variance with any promotion of the idea of Diocletian as a god or quasi-god.

In short, many a Christian who was raised with stories of the early history of the religion knows the name of Diocletian, if only in the context of his being one of the notorious opponents of Christian practice and worship. If religious persecution were all that Diocletian were remembered for, his actions would prove the veracity of a statement written decades before his anti-Christian edicts: *semen est sanguis Christianorum*, 'blood is the seed of Christians.' The author Tertullian had made that famous comment on the question of martyrdom, and indeed within just a few brief years of Diocletian's death, Christianity would become the state religion of the Roman Empire. There would be additional imperial persecutions of Christians and attempts to restore the pagan worship of Rome as the official religious practice of the Empire – but Diocletian's great venting of fury against Christianity would not succeed in destroying the faith that he found so detestable and problematic. Early Christianity, we might note, was focused on the apocalyptic notion that the world would be ending sooner rather than later – the anticipated return of Christ was supposed to be heralded by increasing disasters, and the troubles of the third century seemed to be exactly the sort of doom that it had been foretold would occur before the advent of Christ as judge of the world. It is easy enough to discern how non-Christians might acquire the idea that Christians were to blame for the empire's problems: not only did they disavow and denigrate traditional Roman religious practices, but they were also viewed with suspicion by some as being all too eager for the world to come to its end, so as to usher in the reign of Christ. The increased frequency of barbarian incursions was interpreted by some Christians as evidence of the decline of the age and the approach of the end times. The same trouble was viewed by some pagans as a sign of how the traditional gods of the Olympian pantheon were unhappy with their neglect and with the tolerance of Roman officials for the affront to the pagan gods that was Christianity. In short, both pagans and Christians could interpret upheaval as being evidence of the veracity of their views.

We may now focus in on the period in which our subject was born. Diocletian was a man who was not bred for power and prominence. One proof of this fact is that we are not certain of the year of his birth – nobody, after all, could have predicted that it would be worth remembering or recording. It can be estimated as being c. 242 to 245, working backwards from evidence we have about his age.[32] We know where he was born – the Roman province of Dalmatia, a vast region that dominated much of the Balkans.[33] Today the countries of Croatia, Serbia, Montenegro, Bosnia and Herzegovina, and Albania all include territory that once was part of Dalmatia, a locale that took its name from the Dalmatae, an Illyrian tribe. What is perhaps most extraordinary about the life of Diocletian is that well over half of his life is shrouded in almost total obscurity. We think that he died not too long before he would have turned 70, with 68 cited as his age. We are ignorant of much of the detail of the first forty-some years of his life. We may recall here the story of Caesar and his tears on account of the statue of Alexander. Diocletian lived for decades with no fame or achievement that history has recorded. He would make his name and prove his worth only in middle age. Diocletian thus poses a curious case in Roman history, given the utter change in status that he underwent from living in obscurity to inhabiting the purple and gold bedecked palaces of imperial power.

Mention has already been made in passing of the problem of our relative lack of sources to chronicle the life of Diocletian. There are essentially three bodies of literary evidence that we possess: 1) surviving histories and epitomes of histories of Rome and her emperors; 2) surviving panegyrics that were designed as laudatory works in honour of imperial achievements; and 3) the works of Christian apologists and polemicists, who serve as something akin to anti-panegyrists, focusing on the persecution of Christians under Diocletian and his colleagues in the tetrarchy.[34] These three bodies of material constitute the bulk of the written records that we may employ in reconstructing Diocletian's life and times, not counting the vast number of surviving inscriptions and the evidence from coinage.

The author Eutropius composed a work entitled *Breviarium historiae romanae*, or the 'Abridgment of Roman History', sometime in the latter half of the fourth century. He is one of our few surviving historical sources for Diocletian, in this case providing coverage for the emperor's life and reign at a relatively close remove in time. Eutropius records the variant traditions that Diocletian was perhaps the son of a scribe, or perhaps a freedman of a senator – in either case, exceedingly humble origins for the future emperor. His birth name (if he were born free) was Gaius Valerius Diocles. If he were a slave, he was simply Diocles.

Eutropius' shorter Roman history is a problematic source for the study of imperial reigns. Traditionally Eutropius was a popular author in the Latin language curriculum on account of the relatively simple and lucid character of his writing. His history commences with the founding of Rome and proceeds to his own time (i.e. the reign of Jovian in 364). He is tantalizingly brief (in accordance with the parameters of his work). Eutropius' *Breviarium* is one of a handful of similar fourth century CE shorter Roman histories and imperial biography collections that focus in particular on the wars of Rome and the lives of the emperors. We may compare the *De Caesaribus* or 'Book of the Caesars' of Sextus Aurelius Victor, and the *Epitome de Caesaribus* that is attributed to the same author. There is also a fourth century *Breviarium* of Roman history ascribed to Festus, a work that does not match Eutropius for quality of prose style and diction. All of these are necessary works for our knowledge of Roman imperial history in the chaotic fourth century. All are also highly problematic. There has been scholarly study and consideration of the idea that these works are the descendants of a common, lost ancestor. The so-called *Enmannsche Kaisergeschichte* is the intellectual offspring of the German Alexander Enmann, who developed the hypothesis that there has been a common source for such works as those of Aurelius Victor, Eutropius, and the biographers of the *Historia Augusta*. The work is thus entirely hypothetical; we cannot be certain that it existed, and certainly there is no surviving evidence to indicate that anyone in antiquity thought that it did. There are those – present author included – who are suspicious of the soundness of the thesis. It possesses real elements of persuasive, common sense logic that explain real mysteries. But all we can say is that it is a brilliant explanation for something that cannot be resolved definitively in the absence of new evidence.

The *Breviarium* and related works offer a snapshot of imperial lives and Roman history, with a basic narrative seasoned with occasional snippets of key information that either confirms or challenges what is cited elsewhere. We shall consider Eutropius and related works, before exploring the material they preserve in more detail. If anything, Eutropius offers a concise account of the period, without ornamentation or editorializing. Here is the passage in which Diocletian is first mentioned, followed by the rest of the coverage of his reign, in Latin and in English translation with brief commentary (the text is from the Budé edition). We may utilize it to give a brief overview of our subject's life:

Interea Carinus, quem Caesarem ad Parthos proficiscens Carus in Illyrico, Gallia, Italia reliquerat, omnibus se sceleribus inquinavit. Plurimos innoxios fictis criminibus occidit, matrimonia nobilia corrupit, condiscipulis quoque, qui eum in auditorio vel levi fatigatione taxaverant, perniciosus fuit. Ob quae omnibus hominibus invisus non multo post poenas dedit. Nam de Perside victor exercitus rediens, cum Carum Augustum fulmine, Numerianum Caesarem insidiis perdidisset, Diocletianum imperatorem creavit, Dalmatia oriundum, virum obscurissime natum, adeo ut a plerisque scribae filius, a nonnullis Anullini senatoris libertinus fuisse credatur.

'Meanwhile Carinus (whom Carus had left behind in Illyricum, Gaul, and Italy when he set out for the Parthians) defiled himself with every iniquity. He killed many innocent people on account of false charges, he corrupted noble marriage, and he was pernicious to his fellow pupils who annoyed him in the auditorium by some minor irritation. On account of all of these things he was hateful to men, and not long after paid the penalty. For the army – now victorious over the Persian – created Diocletian as emperor when it had lost Carus Augustus by lightning and Numerian Caesar by treachery. Diocletian was a Dalmatian by birth, born in utter obscurity, so much so that by most he was believed to be the son of a scribe, and by some to be the freedman of Anullinus the senator.'

The imperial scion Carinus had been left behind by his father Carus to manage Illyricum, Gaul, and Italy while the emperor proceeded against the Persian threat. The son did not manage affairs at all well; he was given over to all manner of crimes, including charging people with false accusations (always a good route to ensuring that one will be overthrown). Among other vices and exhibitions of bad behaviour, he corrupted the wives of noblemen – another swift path to self-destruction. Diocletian experienced the death of two emperors, after Carus had been lost on account of lightning, and Numerian (Carus' other son and successor) on account of treachery. As for Diocletian, he was a Dalmatian, most obscure in his origins – so obscure that by many he was said to be the son of a scribe, and by some to be a freedman of the senator Anullinus. In other words, the only noteworthy detail about Diocletian on his entry into the pages of history is that he was virtually unknown. If Diocletian were a freedman, it means that slavery was his lot at birth: 'From Slave to Emperor/God' could be the subtitle for a study on his reign. If most believed that he had been the son of a scribe, it is possible that this was proposed as a narrative to conceal the real story of his servile origins. Certainty is impossible.

Is prima militum contione iuravit Numerianum nullo suo dolo interfectum, et cum iuxta eum Aper, qui Numeriano insidias fecerat, constitisset, in conspectu exercitus manu Diocletiani percussus est. Postea Carinum omnium odio et detestatione viventem apud Margum ingenti proelio vicit, proditum ab exercitu suo, quem fortiorem habebat, aut certe desertum, inter Viminacium atque Aureum montem. Ita rerum Romanarum potitus cum tumultum rusticani in Gallia concitassent et factioni suae

Bacaudarum nomen inponerent, duces autem haberent Amandum et Aelianum, ad subigendos eos Maximianum Herculium Caesarem misit, qui levibus proeliis agrestes domuit et pacem Galliae reformavit.

'In his first assembly with the soldiers, Diocletian swore that Numerian had not died because of any treachery on his part. Aper was standing next to him – the one who had crafted the plot – and Diocletian struck him down in the sight of the soldiers. After this he conquered Carinus in a great battle at Margus. Carinus was living with the extreme hate of everyone, and he was betrayed by his army, which was stronger than Diocletian's, certainly deserted by it between Viminacium and Mount Aureus. So Diocletian obtained power over Rome, and he sent Maximian Herculius to subdue the peasants who had incited a disturbance in Gaul, having given the name of "Bagaudae" to their faction. Maximian defeated them in light battles and restored peace to Gaul.'

Eutropius blames Aper for the assassination, and the regicide is soon enough struck by Diocletian's own hand (this was a man who did his own killing, we might say). Diocletian proceeded to defeat Carinus, who was now hated by all, indeed to the point of detestation. Not only did Diocletian have nothing to do with the death of Numerian, but his clear enough act of rebellion against Carinus was sanctioned, as it were, by the fact that everybody hated him. This was the best way in which anyone could dispense with what would otherwise be the charge of imperial betrayal and murder. Diocletian won his battle at the Margus because Carinus' army betrayed him. Despite having a larger force than his adversary, Carinus did not have their loyalty. The defeat is localized between Viminacium and Mount Aureus. The former place is located some dozen miles from Kostalac in modern Serbia – it was the capital of the province of Moesia Superior, and the site of a major military camp. When Diocletian reorganized the provinces, Viminacium became the capital of Moesia Superior Margensis.

Viminacium was the base of *Legio VII Claudia*, which had a distinguished history from Caesar's Gallic wars through the engagements on the Danube in the third century. It is listed in the *Notitia*.[35] Other Balkan legions, we may note, included *XI Claudia* at Durostorum (cited in the *Notitia*); *IIII Flavia Felix* at Singidunum (also still in the *Notitia*); *I Italica* at Novae (again with the usual attestation). Diocletian probably served first in one of the Claudian legions, most probably VII, though both VII and XI sometimes had units at Tilurium, which was likely the closest military base to his childhood home.

Diocletian's first actions after taking power are cited as seeing to the response to a rustic revolt in Gaul, the so-called Bagaudae uprising. His colleague Maximian was sent to resolve the problem, which was ended with 'light battles' (*levibus proeliis*) by which peace was restored.

Anyone in Diocletian's position would have underscored his innocence in any conspiracy. As for the victory at the Margus, the historical record has its emphasis on the fact that Carinus' army was inclined to desert. This solves one problem – the absolution of Diocletian from the charge of open rebellion against a legitimate emperor – while introducing a new (albeit arguably less serious) one: Diocletian cannot be credited with any brilliant tactic or strategy at the Margus. The most that could be argued is that he defeated a significantly larger army.

Per haec tempora etiam Carausius qui vilissime natus strenuae militiae ordine famam egregiam fuerat consecutus, cum apud Bononiam per tractum Belgicae et Armorici pacandum mare accepisset, quod Franci et Saxones infestabant. Multis barbaris saepe captis nec praeda integra aut provincialibus reddita aut imperatoribus missa cum suspicio esse coepisset consulto ab eo admitti barbaros, ut transeuntes cum praeda exciperet atque hac se occasione ditaret, a Maximiano iussus occidi purpuram sumpsit et Britannias occupavit.

'After these events Carausius, who had been born in quite poor circumstances, had obtained a noble reputation by strenuous service in the military. At Bononia he received an assignment to bring peace to the sea by Belgica and Armorica, which had become infested by Frankish and Saxonian pirates. Many barbarians were often captured, but the entire loot was not returned to the provincials or sent to the emperors. The suspicion arose that Carausius was deliberately allowing the barbarians to pass through, so that he could intercept them for their plunder and thereby enrich himself. Ordered to be slain by Maximian, he assumed the purple and seized Britain.'

The rebellion of Carausius is introduced next, with a brief summation of the genesis of the problem: the pirate hunter's own piracy and Maximian's order for him to be slain, followed by his becoming a usurper in Britain. Carausius' original role in connection to pirate actions in response to the Franks and the Saxons is referenced.[36] Carausius is introduced as if he were on the same path as Diocletian, with a mean upbringing that was followed by exemplary military service, not to mention a bid for imperial power. This is classic Eutropius: a laconic account of a dramatic set of events.

Ita cum per omnem orbem terrarum res turbatae essent, Carausius in Britanniis rebellaret, Achilleus in Aegypto, Africam Quinquegentiani infestarent, Narseus Orienti bellum inferret, Diocletianus Maximianum Herculium ex Caesare fecit Augustum, Constantium et Maximianum Caesares, quorum Constantius per filiam nepos Claudii traditur, Maximianus Galerius in Dacia haud longe a Serdica natus. Atque ut eos etiam adfinitate coniungeret, Constantius privignam Herculii Theodoram accepit, ex qua postea sex liberos, Constantini fratres, habuit, Galerius filiam Diocletiani Valeriam, ambo uxores, quas habuerant, repudiare conpulsi. Cum Carausio tamen, cum bella frustra temptata essent contra virum rei militaris peritissimum, ad postremum pax convenit. Eum post septennium Allectus, socius eius, occidit atque ipse post eum Britannias triennio tenuit. Qui ductu Asclepiodoti, praefecti praetorio, oppressus est. Ita Britanniae decimo anno receptae.

'Thus when all things were disturbed throughout the world, with Carausius rebelling in Britain, Achilleus in Egypt, the Quinquegentiani in Africa, and with Narseus bringing war to the east, Diocletian promoted Maximian Hercules from Caesar to Augustus, and named Constantius and Maximian [Galerius] Caesars. Constantius was said to be the grandson of Claudius [i.e. Claudius II Gothicus] by a daughter, while Maximian Galerius was born in Dacia, not far from Serdica. And in order that he might join them by affinity as well, Constantius received Theodora, the stepdaughter of Herculius, from whom later he had six children, the brothers of Constantine; and Galerius received Valeria, the daughter of Diocletian. Both Caesars repudiated their former wives. Peace was at last arranged with Carausius, when battles had been attempted in vain against a man who was so skilled in military science. After seven years Allectus, his comrade, killed him and then held Britain for three years. He was besieged by the efforts of Asclepiodotus, the praetorian prefect. And so Britain was restored to the empire in the tenth year.'

In addition to a significant British problem, there were revolts in Egypt and Africa, as well as renewed conflict with Persia. The tetrarchy was established (in Eutropius' narrative, there is an implicit connection between the need to resolve all of these frontier problems, and the expansion of the imperial office). Marriage bonds were employed to tie the four men together more closely. Carausius was soon enough defeated, and in turn his successor Allectus. Britain had been recovered after a decade. Eutropius' account gives balanced attention to the military exploits of all of the tetrarchs. Diocletian almost fades into the background, save for the key detail that he was responsible for setting up the tetrarchy.

Per idem tempus a Constantio Caesare in Gallia bene pugnatum est. Circa Lingonas die una adversam et secundam fortunam expertus est. Nam cum repente barbaris ingruentibus intra civitatem esset coactus tam praecipiti necessitate, ut clausis portis in murum funibus tolleretur, vix quinque horis mediis adventante exercitu sexaginta fere milia Alamannorum cecidit. Maximianus quoque Augustus bellum in Africa profligavit domitis Quinquegentianis et ad pacem redactis. Diocletianus obsessum Alexandriae Achilleum octavo fere mense superavit eumque interfecit. Victoria acerbe usus est; totam Aegyptum gravibus proscriptionibus caedibusque foedavit. Ea tamen occasione ordinavit provide multa et disposuit, quae ad nostram aetatem manent.

'During the same time Constantius Caesar was fighting well in Gaul. One day near Lingones he experienced adverse and successful luck. For when a sudden barbarian assault had compelled him to seek refuge in the city, he was forced by headlong necessity to be raised up the wall by a rope since the gates were barred. Scarcely five hours later he was relieved by the arrival of the army, and almost sixty thousand Alamanni were killed. Maximian Augustus defeated the Quingentiani in Africa and peace was restored. Diocletian conquered and killed Achilleus at Alexandria after an almost eight month siege. He behaved bitterly after his victory, defiling Egypt with serious proscriptions and slaughter. Nevertheless on that occasion he organized and disposed of affairs with foresight, making arrangements that have endured to our time.'

The other campaigns of the tetrarchs are now briefly summarized. Constantius was fighting with success in Gaul. Historical epitomes often provide brief summaries of noteworthy episodes, in this case how once Constantius experienced extremes of fortune on one and the same day: he was taken up the wall of Lingones by rope when he was besieged by barbarians, and five hours later the arrival of relief columns spelled doom for around sixty thousand Alamanni. Maximian meanwhile fought in Africa, and Diocletian in Egypt. Eutropius is critical of the latter: he is credited with being harsh in the wake of victory, with proscriptions and slaughter: *Victoria acerbe usus est* is strong Latin – literally, 'he used his victory bitterly.' Despite this, he is noted too for having set into motion arrangements in government that remain to the author's own time.

Galerius Maximianus primum adversus Narseum proelium insecundum habuit inter Callinicum Carrasque congressus, cum inconsulte magis quam ignave dimicasset; admodum enim parva manu cum copiosissimo hoste commisit. Pulsus igitur et ad Diocletianum profectus cum ei in itinere occurrisset, tanta insolentia a Diocletiano fertur exceptus, ut per aliquot passuum milia purpuratus tradatur ad vehiculum cucurrisse.

'Galerius Maximian at first had an unlucky encounter against Narseus between Callinicus and Carrhae, when he fought more with lack of preparation than with cowardice – for he had joined battle with a small force against a vast enemy host. Having been driven from the battlefield he made his way to Diocletian, and when he encountered him on the way he was treated with such insolence that for several miles it is said that he ran by his carriage in his purple.'

Galerius fought against the Persians in reckless fashion, engaging against a far stronger enemy host without sufficient planning. Compelled to withdraw, he was humiliated by Diocletian, who forced his colleague to run by his carriage. We see a hint here too of the personality trait cited by Eutropius in his brief mention of Diocletian in Egypt – *tanta insolentia* highlights the anger and impatience of the tetrarch. One has the image of the great Caesar Galerius compelled to chase after the furious Diocletian, with the Augustus refusing to deign to engage with his defeated, humiliated subordinate.

Mox tamen per Illyricum Moesiamque contractis copiis rursus cum Narseo, Hormisdae et Saporis avo, in Armenia maiore pugnavit successu ingenti nec minore consilio, simul fortitudine, quippe qui etiam speculatoris munus cum altero aut tertio equite susceperit. Pulso Narseo castra eius diripuit; uxores, sorores, liberos cepit, infinitam extrinsecus Persarum nobilitatem, gazam Persicam copiosissimam. Ipsum in ultimas regni solitudines egit. Quare a Diocletiano in Mesopotamia cum praesidiis tum morante ovans regressus ingenti honore susceptus est. Varia deinceps et simul et viritim bella gesserunt Carpis et Basternis subactis, Sarmatis victis, quarum nationum ingentes captivorum copias in Romanis finibus locaverunt.

'Nevertheless soon thereafter forces were collected through Illyricum and Moesia, and he fought again with Narseus, Homisdas, and the grandfather of Sapor in Greater Armenia, with great success and not less counsel and fortitude, for with one or two cavalrymen he undertook the duty of a reconnaissance mission. Narseus was driven to flight and his camp was destroyed; Galerius took his wives, sisters, children, and a huge amount of Persian wealth as well as a vast number of the Persian nobility besides. He drove the king into the last wastelands of his kingdom. Therefore in Mesopotamia he was received by Diocletian with great honour as he returned in ovation. Individually and in concert both men then waged wars and defeated the Carpi and the Basternae, as well as the Sarmatians – from which nations they relocated huge numbers of captives within the borders of Rome.'

Eutropius continues his laconic, bare recitation of the facts of weighty events. Reinforcements for renewed Persian campaigns were conscripted from units available through Illyricum and Moesia. In Greater Armenia, there was tremendous victory, including the capture of the Persian imperial wives, sisters, and children, together with immense wealth and plunder. Galerius' reputation had been restored, and he was received by Diocletian in Mesopotamia with honour and an ovation. Wars were then conducted against the Carpi and others, including the Sarmatians; huge numbers of captives from these peoples were relocated within Rome's borders (i.e. to respond to the agricultural needs occasioned by depopulation).

Diocletianus moratus callide fuit, sagax praeterea et admodum subtilis ingenii, et qui severitatem suam aliena invidia vellet explere. Diligentissimus tamen et sollertissimus princeps et qui imperio Romano primus regiae consuetudinis formam magis quam Romanae libertatis invexerit adorarique se iussit, cum ante eum cuncti salutarentur. Ornamenta gemmarum vestibus calciamentisque indidit. Nam prius imperii insigne in chlamyde purpurea tantum erat, reliqua communia.

'Diocletian by disposition was clever, also sagacious and of very subtle intelligence. He was the sort of man who wanted to satisfy his own cruelty at the expense of making others appear to bear the blame. Nevertheless he was most diligent and expert. He was the first who introduced to the Roman empire the form of regal habit rather than Roman liberty, and he ordered that he be adored, though before him all emperors were saluted. He added jewelled ornaments to his clothing and shoes. For before him the insignia of imperial power had been only a purple cloak, with everything else being in common with other men.'

This is the closest that Eutropius comes to something approximating what we might call a comprehensive psychological assessment of his subject, as he expands on earlier comments about the emperor's personality. Diocletian was clever and sagacious, with an extraordinarily subtle mind. He was a master of making other people seem responsible for the negative feelings occasioned by his own harshness.[37] The Latin word *severitas* gives us the English 'severity', which is an antonym for clemency. Diocletian is associated with a propensity for being severe in his judgments, but crafty enough to know how to deflect criticism. Eutropius at once comments on the emperor's wish to be adored as if he were a god on earth – in other words, not only did he wish to avoid blame for his cruel actions, but he wanted to be revered as if he were Jupiter. There is more than a hint of vanity in the detail about jewelled shoes and raiment adorned with gemstones. And yet he was most diligent and active in his duties, and more than competent. It is a mixed assessment, where the achievements are extraordinary, with certain disturbing features of personality complicating the picture of a man who had attained greatness, though not without ample space for criticism and censure. And even for the fourth century epitomist, there is a note about what we might call republican virtues – that is to say, Diocletian had nothing of the sort. His management style and his affectation of divine status were the antithesis of the traditions of the Roman Republic.

An expert in human personality studies could find much material for reflection in these brief comments of the late antique epitomizer. Diocletian had ascended from total obscurity to the heights of authority. As emperor, there was ample evidence that his roots had an effect on how he managed imperial affairs, and on how he interacted with his fellow tetrarchs.

Herculius autem propalam ferus et incivilis ingenii, asperitatem suam etiam vultus horrore significans. Hic naturae suae indulgens Diocletiano in omnibus est saevioribus consiliis obsecutus. Cum tamen ingravescente aevo parum se idoneum Diocletianus moderando imperio esse sentiret, auctor Herculio fuit, ut in vitam privatam concederent et stationem tuendae rei publicae viridioribus iunioribusque mandarent. Cui aegre collega obtemperavit. Tamen uterque uno die privato habitu imperii insigne mutavit, Nicomediae Diocletianus, Herculius Mediolani, post triumphum inclitum, quem Romae ex numerosis gentibus egerant, pompa ferculorum inlustri, qua Narsei coniuges sororesque et liberi ante currum ducti sunt. Concesserunt tamen Salonas unus, alter in Lucaniam.

'Herculius however was openly vicious and of uncouth manner, one who indicated his harshness by the terror of his visage. Indulging his own nature, he followed Diocletian in all that man's more savage plans. Nevertheless when Diocletian felt that because of advancing age he was no longer suitable for the task of administering the empire, he suggested the plan that they both should retire to private life and should hand over the responsibility of looking after the affairs of state to younger and more vigorous men. His colleague agreed to this with difficulty. All the same both men changed the insignia of imperial power for private dress, Diocletian at Nicomedia and Maximian at Mediolanum, after a notable triumph they conducted at Rome, with a glorious procession of images in which the wives, sisters, and children of Narseus were led before the chariot. Nevertheless the one man retired to Salona, the other to Lucania.'

'Herculius' – that is, Maximian – wore his uncouth, uncivilized and angry visage as a clear indicator of his nature. As Diocletian grew older and felt himself increasingly unequal to the task of ruling the empire, he was the author of the plan that Maximian and he should retire and hand over the burdens of rule to younger men. Maximian agreed, but he was persuaded only after great difficulty. On one and the same day, nevertheless, they renounced their power and returned to private life. There was one final great celebration of their honour, with the customary images of the gods and emblems of the conquered nations.

If Diocletian was indeed harsh or even savage, there was an element of dissimulation that he was able to display as well. Maximian was incapable of such subtleties, or at least unwilling to bother to employ them.

Diocletianus privatus in villa, quae haud procul a Salonis est, praeclaro otio consenuit, inusitata virtute usus, ut solus omnium post conditum Romanum imperium ex tanto fastigio sponte ad privatae vitae statum civilitatemque remearet. Contigit igitur ei, quod nulli post natos homines, ut cum privatus obisset, inter Divos tamen referretur.

'Diocletian grew old in outstanding leisure as a private citizen in his villa, which was not far from Salona. He exercised a novel virtue, being the only man out of everyone after the founding of the Roman empire who went back to the civilian state of private life after having held such high office. And therefore something befell him that had happened to no one else in history – though he died a private citizen, nevertheless he was enrolled among the gods.'

The close of Eutropius' account comes with a eulogistic note that emphasizes how Diocletian was unique in his status as an imperial retiree,[38] with the historian observing that the retired emperor was unique too in another way – he was a private citizen when he was enrolled among the gods. In the end, Diocletian obtained what he clearly wanted post mortem – confirmed status as a divinity.

Here is the characteristically laconic eulogy in Festus (again from the Budé text):

Sub Diocletiano principe pompa victoriae de Persis nota est. Maximianus Caesar, prima congressione, cum contra innumeram multitudinem cum paucis acriter dimicasset, pulsus recessit. Hic tanta indignatione a Diocletiano exceptus est, ut ante carpentum eius per aliquot millia passuum cucurrerit purpuratus: et cum vix impetrasset, ut reparato de limitaneis Daciae exercitu, eventum Martis repeteret, in Armenia maiore ipse imperator cura duobus equitibus exploravit hostes: et cum viginti quinque millibus militum superveniens castris hostilibus, subito innumera Persarum agmina adgressus est, et ad internecionem cecidit. Rex Persarum Narseus effugit; uxor eius, et filiae captae sunt; et cum maxima pudicitiae custodia reservatae. Pro qua admiratione Persae non modo armis, sed etiam moribus, superiores esse Romanos confessi sunt: Mesopotamiam cum Transtigritanis quinque regionibus dediderunt: paceque facta, usque ad nostram memoriam in fide perdurarunt.

'Under the emperor Diocletian a procession of victory over the Persians was noteworthy. Maximian Caesar, in his first engagement, when against an innumerable multitude he had fought fiercely with a few on his side, withdrew when he was driven back. He was received by Diocletian with such indignation, that he ran in his purple for some miles in front of Diocletian's carriage. And when scarcely he had obtained from him authorization that he might seek the outcome of war again, with his army having been rebuilt from the borderlands of Dacia, in Greater Armenia the commander himself with two cavalrymen carefully reconnoitred the enemy. With twenty-five thousand men then he fell suddenly on the innumerable battlelines of the Persians, and fell on them to the point of annihilation. The Persian king Narses fled; his wife and daughters were seized and were held with the greatest care for their chastity. On account of admiration the Persians confessed that the Romans were superior not only in arms, but in character. They surrendered Mesopotamia, with the five Transtigritanian regions. And with peace having been established, they preserved their loyalty until our memory.'

We can see here why Enmann's thesis has been attractive to some scholars. Festus seems to have been working from the same material as Eutropius, providing coverage in briefer scope of the same events.

The introduction of Diocletian in the *Liber de Caesaribus* of Aurelius Victor emphasizes certain venal aspects of the emperor's character that clouded his status as an otherwise great and respectable man (also in the Budé series):

Sed postquam odore tabescentium membrorum scelus proditum est, ducum consilio tribunorumque Valerius Diocletianus domesticos regens ob sapientiam deligitur, magnus vir, his moribus tamen: quippe qui primus ex auro veste quaesita serici ac purpurae gemmarumque vim plantis concupiverit. Quae quamquam plus quam civilia tumidique et affluentis animi, levia tamen prae ceteris. Namque se primus omnium Caligulam post Domitianumque dominum palam dici passus et adorari se appellarique uti deum. Quis rebus, quantum ingenium est, compertum habeo humillimos quosque, maxime ubi alta accesserint, superbia atque ambitione immodicos esse.

'But after the crime was betrayed by the odour of the decaying limbs, by the advice of the leaders and of the tribunes Valerius Diocletian (who was ruling the members of the imperial household) was chosen on account of his wisdom. He was a great man, nevertheless he had these habits: he was the first emperor, Aurelius Victor claims, to have used purple and silk robes, with gemstones even adorning his footwear. Which things – although they were more than of a civil nature, and though they were of a swollen and lavish mind, nevertheless they were trivial compared to other things. For first of all after Caligula and Domitian he allowed himself openly to be called "master" and to be adored and to be addressed as if he were a god. By which things, as much as there is natural capacity, I have discovered that the most humble men, they that have ascended to high things, are the most immoderate in their ambition.'

All of this business of gold and jewels, Aurelius Victor concedes freely, was less than republican in virtue, but it was not as serious as allowing people to worship you as a god, or to be referred to as a *dominus* or 'lord' and 'master'. The biographer's judgment is simple: even the most humble of men are rendered prideful and ambitious when they have been catapulted to the heights of power. Caligula and Domitian are cited as stereotypical examples of bad emperors; they however had been the scions of imperial families, one might argue, not men raised from the lowest classes to the highest office. If there is any implicit mitigation being offered here for Diocletian's actions, it is what might be termed a sort of insecurity about his status. And later Aurelius Victor will praise Diocletian for having an excellent enough nature to be able to resign from his high office, as well as for behaving in a manner like a parent to Rome.[39] He is praised for his rooting out of informants and those who would seek to profit from trumped up charges of conspiracy. Finally, while Victor notes that men have disputed the reasons for Diocletian's abdication (we shall see that some thought that he had been pressured into it), his conclusion is simple and laudatory: Diocletian had an excellent character, for all his succumbing earlier in his life to immoderate pride on account of his dramatic change of fortune. Victor also makes the interesting and wise observation that Diocletian saw the trouble that was coming for the empire, and therefore chose to exit power (despite being in good health) at exactly the right moment. No other ancient source credits him with this logic, and it may well hold a kernel of truth.[40]

The epitome of the Caesars attributed to Aurelius Victor may be cited next (the text again is in the Budé series):

Diocletianus Dalmata, Anulini senatoris libertinus, matre pariter atque oppido nomine Dioclea, quorum vocabulis, donec imperium sumeret, Diocles appellatus, ubi orbis Romani potentiam cepit, Graium nomen in Romanum morem convertit, imperavit annis viginti quinque. Is Maximianum Augustum effecit; Constantium et Galerium Maximianum, cognomento Armentarium, Caesares creavit, tradens Constantio Theodoram, Herculii Maximiani privignam, abiecta uxore priori. Hoc tempore Charausio in Galliis, Achilleus apud Aegyptum, Iulianus in Italia imperatores effecti diverso exitu periere. E quibus Iulianus acto per costas pugione in ignem se abiecit. Diocletianus vero apud Nicomediam sponte imperiales fasces relinquens in propriis agris consenuit. Qui dum ab Herculio atque Galerio ad recipiendum imperium rogaretur, tamquam pestem aliquam detestans in hunc modum respondit: "Utinam Salonae possetis visere olera nostris manibus instituta, profecto numquam istud temptandum iudicaretis". Vixit annos sexaginta octo, ex quis communi habitu prope novem egit. Morte consumptus est, ut satis patuit, per formidinem voluntaria. Quippe cum a Constantino atque Licinio vocatus ad festa nuptiarum per senectam, quo minus interesse valeret, excusavisset, rescriptis minacibus acceptis, quibus increpabatur Maxentio favisse ac Maximino favere, suspectans necem dedecorosam venenum dicitur hausisse.

'Diocletian was a Dalmatian, the freedman of the senator Anulinus, from a mother and town both named Dioclea, from which name he was called Diocles until he assumed command, when he took the power of the Roman world, having translated his Greek name into Latin. He ruled for twenty-five years. He made Maximian an Augustus, and made Constantius and Galerius Maximian (nicknamed "Armentarius") Caesars, handing over to Constantius Theodora, the stepdaughter of Herculius Maximian, with his first wife having been set aside. In this time Carausius in Gaul, Achilleus in Egypt, and Julian in Italy[41] became commanders, and perished in diverse manners. Among these Julian, with a dagger having been driven through his ribs, threw himself into a fire. Diocletian at Nicomedia voluntarily put aside the *fasces* and grew old in his own fields. When he was asked by Herculius and Galerius to recover his imperial position, he responded in this manner, as if he were cursing it as some pestilential thing: "If only at Salona you were able to see the vegetables that were planted by my own hands, then you would never judge that I should try to do that." He lived for sixty-eight years, of which he passed almost nine in a common state. He died, as is clear enough, a suicide on account of fear. Indeed when he was summoned to a nuptial celebration by Constantine and Licinius, he excused himself on account of his old age, by which the less was he healthy enough to be present. He received threatening letters in response, in which he was accused of hating Maxentius and of favouring Maximian. Suspecting a shameful death was near, he is said to have drunk poison.'

The vegetable story became legendary, even if not every ancient source alludes to it. The suicide narrative offers an interesting window into alleged internecine squabbling and disagreement within the first and second tetrarchies. The summary also paints a picture of an exhausted Diocletian: the emphasis on his age is coupled with the vegetable anecdote, as well as the image of a man who may, after all, have simply wanted to stay at home and to avoid a social engagement. Consumed with anxiety and prone to fear – after all, so many of his predecessors had died violently – Diocletian is said to have taken poison, in order to avoid the risk of a more ignominious death.[42] The reference to nine years *communi habitu* is to his retirement – nine years in the state and dress of a civilian – quite the voluntary change for the man who was fond of purple and gemstones.

Diocletian is cited also in the history of Paulus Orosius, who lived in the late fourth and early fifth centuries.[43] A Christian, his *Historiae adversus paganos* survives in seven books. In Orosius' brief account in Book 7, Carus was killed by a lightning bolt and Numerian by a plot of Aper. Diocletian assumes power and promptly slays Aper. Carinus is defeated with difficulty in battle – Orosius is one of our surviving sources for the conclusion that Margus was not an easy engagement. There is no mention in Orosius of any betrayal of Carinus by his own men – the only explanation for Diocletian's victory is the great labour he expended in winning his engagement.

The Bagaudae rebellion under Amanadus and Aelianus is referenced next, with the same notation we have seen elsewhere – Diocletian entrusted Maximian with the suppression of the tumult, giving him the name Herculius Caesar. Maximian's victory is achieved due to the superiority of Roman army discipline after rustic incompetence. Carausius is introduced, again with emphasis on his low birth but outstanding skill. The same details are reported about why and how the future rebel ran afoul of Maximian. Achilleus in Egypt and the Quinquegentiani in Africa,[44] as well as Narses in Persia round out the now familiar catalogue of imperial problems. There is no rebellious Julian cited, either in Italy or Africa. Diocletian completes the tetrarchy arrangement and solidifies it by marriage arrangements. Carausius holds out in Britain valiantly for seven years, only to be slain by the duplicity of Allectus; after three years he is defeated after being besieged by Asclepiodotus. Constantius wins his difficult victory at Lingones, and Maximian triumphs in Africa. Diocletian defeats Achilleus in Egypt, but again he is cited for his cruelty and excess in the wake of his victory. Galerius suffers his losses against the Persians, and is treated 'most arrogantly' (*arrogantissime*) by Diocletian. That very arrogance tempers and refines Galerius, who soon returns to the fray against the Persians, with very different outcome. Diocletian and Galerius fight the Carpi, the Basternae, and the Sarmatians, and they relocate many conquered peoples in Roman territory.

Thus is the sense acquired of déjà vu, as one sees another historian utilizing the brief narrative of similar 'global histories' that try to tell much in short compass, with only brief glimpses of authorial analysis to enliven the dry recitation of events. Orosius was a Christian, and it is not surprising that he proceeds in his account to give mention to the persecutions. Diocletian in the east and Maximian in the west oversee the worst assault on the faith ever recorded, in what is cited as the tenth persecution after Nero. The entire episode lasts for a decade; an earthquake in Syria causes devastation at Tyre and Sidon, with many thousands dead – Orosius clearly views the natural disaster as a divine verdict on the imperial persecution. In the second year of the persecution, Diocletian persuades an unwilling Maximian to retire, and the two men make their abdications respectively at Nicomedia and Mediolanum. Orosius does not return to the story of Diocletian: there is no account of his role in mediating later disputes in the tetrarchy, no account of his death. It is, one might think, the revenge of a Christian apologist against the grand persecutor – Diocletian is left in obscurity, without even a mention of his demise.

Orosius was a Christian writer of a universal history. Eusebius was a bishop of Caesarea who wrote a fourth century Greek language history of Christianity in ten books that survives (there is a convenient two-volume edition in the Loeb Classical Library). Book 6 carries the story through Decius, while Book 7 proceeds to the time of the Great Persecution, the account of which continues into Book 8. Eusebius also wrote separately on the martyrs of Palestine whose suffering came as part of acts of persecution to which he was an eyewitness; a shorter version seems to have been incorporated into the first edition of the church history.[45]

And, next, we may quote what survives of the account of Diocletian in the late historian Jordanes (the text from Mommsen's *Monumenta Germaniae Historica*):

Dioclitianus Delmata, scribe filius, imperator electus regnavit ann. xx. Hic etenim mox in regno levatus est, ilico Aprum in militum contione percussit, iurans sine suo scelere illum Numerianum interemisse. Et mox in consortio suo Maximianum Herculium ascivit. Qui Maximianus rusticorum multitudine oppressa, quos Bacaudas dicunt, pacem Galliis reddidit. Quo tempore Carausius sumpta purpura Brittanias occupaverat, Narseus rex Persarum Horienti bellum intulerat, Quinquegentiani Africam infestaverant, Achilleus Egyptum invaserat. Ob quae Constantius et Galerius Maximianus Caesares adsumuntur in regno. Quorum Constantius Claudii ex filia nepus fuit, Galerius in Dacia non longe a Serdica natus. Atque ut eos Dioclitianus etiam adfinitate coniungeret, Constantius prevignam Herculii Theodoram accepit, ex qua et sex liberos procreavit; Galerius autem Valeriam Dioclitiani filiam accepit, utrique pristino matrimonio repudiantes. Carporum si quidem gens tunc devicta et in Romanum solum translata est. Tunc etenim primus omnium imperatorum Dioclitianus adorari se ut deum praecepit et gemmas vestibus calciamentisque inseruit diademaque in capite, cum ante eum omnes clamidem tantum purpuream, ut a privatis discernerentur, habebant et ut ceteri iudices salutabantur. Adsumpta ergo unusquisque principum expeditione Dioclitianus Aegypti tyrannum octavo mense devictum provinciam cunctam subegit. Maximianus Herculius in Africa Quinquegentianos exsuperavit. Constantius iuxta Lingonas una die LX milia Alamannorum cecidit. Galerius Maximianus victus primo proelio a Narseo ante carpentum Dioclitiani purpuratus cucurrit. Qua verecundia conpunctus secundo viriliter dimicavit, superavit Narseum, uxores eius abegit ac liberos, et condigno honore a Dioclitiano susceptus est. Post quam victoriam mirabiliter Dioclitianus et Maximianus Romae triumphaverunt antecedentibus sibi liberis uxoribusque regis Persarum praedaque illa ingenti gentium diversarum. Sic quoque concitata persecutione in Christianos Dioclitianus

'Diocletian of Dalmatia, the son of a scribe, having been elected emperor reigned for twenty years. When he was elevated to power, right away he slew Aper in an assembly of the soldiers, swearing that Aper had killed Numerian, and that he himself was innocent of any involvement. Soon he welcomed Maximian into power with him. Maximian restored peace to the Gauls after the rebellion of the rustics they call the Bagaudae. In that time Carausius seized the Britains, having assumed purple. Narseus, the king of the Persians, brought war to the orient. The Quinquegentiani attacked Africa. Achilles invaded Egypt. On account of which things Constantius and Galerius Maximian were assumed into power as Caesars. Galerius was born not far from Serdica. And in order that Diocletian might join them by affinity as well, Constantius received Theodora the stepdaughter of Herculius, from whom he had six children; Galerius received Valeria, the daughter of Diocletian, both of them repudiating their earlier marriages. The nation of the Carpi was then conquered, and transferred to Roman soil. Then Diocletian first of all the emperors ordered himself to be adored as a god and inserted gems in his vesture and his shoes, and placed a diadem on his head. Before him the emperors only had a purple cloak to distinguish themselves from private citizens, and were saluted as were other judges. Each of the emperors took up an expedition. Diocletian conquered a tyrant in Egypt in the eighth month and subdued the entire province. Maximian Herculius in Africa conquered the Quinquegentiani. Constantius was at Lingones, where he slew sixty thousand Alamanni in one day. Galerius Maximian was conquered in his first encounter with Narseus, and he ran before the carriage of Diocletian clad in his purple. Chastened by shame on account of this, he performed heroically in his second battle, and conquered Narseus, taking away his wives and children. Diocletian received him with honour equal to his own. After which victory, wondrously did Diocletian and Maximian celebrate a triumph in Rome, with the children and wives of the king of the Persians walking before them, and with the great plunder of diverse lands. Thus also, with a persecution having been set into motion against the Christians, Diocletian.'

And so the narrative breaks off. Jordanes was a sixth century eastern Roman official, who wrote histories both of the Romans and the Goths.

The Latin cited above for the Diocletian/tetrarchy passage is a good example of his late, early medieval Latin. The Diocletian narrative is not complete, and so we lack Jordanes' account of the emperor's end. Overall his account is marked by a certain detachment from the material, though he is one of our sources (alongside Victor, from whom he clearly derived his knowledge) for the oft-repeated claim that it was Diocletian who introduced imperial divine worship, a topic to which we shall return. We may note that there is no rebel Julian in Jordanes' account.

Another source of some (though limited) relevance for students of Diocletian is the historian Zosimus, who authored a Greek language history of the Roman empire early in the sixth century (i.e. a few decades before Jordanes). Zosimus provides a rapid overview of Greek history from the war at Troy to Alexander the Great, before proceeding to look at Roman republican and imperial history, focusing with increasing attention on the reigns of Roman emperors. Book 1 reaches the reign of Probus; unfortunately there is a lacuna at the start of Book 2, such that the surviving text resumes after the abdications of Diocletian and Maximian. Zosimus is thus of extremely limited value for the history of the second tetrarchy and the aftermath of Diocletian's reign.

Lastly, we may note one of the most controversial of the surviving texts, the so-called *Anonymus Valesianus I: Origo Constantini Imperatoris*. A relatively brief work, it opens abruptly with the note that Diocletian ruled with Herculius Maximinus for twenty years, before proceeding to the life of Constantius. The text takes its name from its first modern editor, who printed it with Ammianus Marcellinus (and so the Loeb Classical Library, for example, prints it conveniently as part of its edition of Ammianus). The *Origo* does not offer any insight into Diocletian, and is of limited value with respect to the other members of the tetrarchy.

To begin, none of these sources can be compared in any way to the great histories of Livy and Tacitus. Indeed sometimes historians of Latin literature point to the surviving historical lore of the period as evidence for the great decline experienced by Rome. By their very nature the works cited above are more or less brief in scope, aiming to provide snippets of information about their subject, and almost nothing by way of analysis or interpretation of events. Unlike the experience of reading Tacitus, for example, one learns nothing appreciable about the personality of a Eutropius or a Festus. The epitome provides a handbook, not a historiographical treatment of complicated events. Chronology is rough and relative, and there is nothing in the way of detail about battles and military engagements.

To be sure, there was still a tradition of writing vast Roman histories in the fourth century – one need only note the celebrated *Res Gestae* of Ammianus Marcellinus (c. 330–c. 391–400), which aspired to cover the entire period from the reign of Nerva in 96 to the death of Valens in 378. For the student of 353–378, his value is incalculable, and our knowledge of earlier periods would be immeasurably stronger if we had his entire history. For most of Ammianus' work is lost (including all the Diocletian material). Ammianus is considered to be the last great historian of classical Rome, though few would consider him anywhere near the equal of his far more famous predecessors. However, unlike Livy and Tacitus, Ammianus served in the military and was able to invest his history with first hand familiarity and knowledge of army life. Still a student of the fall of the Roman Republic or of the first century CE can draw on numerous sources of high quality. The student of the third and fourth centuries faces significant challenges in this regard. Ammianus has sometimes been called the last of the classical Roman historians, and there is some justification for this appellation. Every study ever written of Diocletian would be significantly richer and appreciably different if we had access to the complete Ammianus.

Complicating the picture of our period is the existence of another set of imperial lives, the so-called *Historia Augusta* or 'Augustan History'. This work has sometimes been referred to as the 'Lives of the Later Caesars', containing as it does biographies of the emperors from 117 to 284 – tantalizingly ending, in other words, just before the reign of Diocletian. The collection is attributed to the *Scriptores Historiae Augustae*, a group of six men who allegedly wrote their works beginning in the reign of Diocletian. Scholars have struggled with the questions of authorship and date of the work; the general consensus is that it is the work of one man, probably in the late fourth or even early fifth century CE. We may be frustrated by several of the problems surrounding the *Augustan History*, but for better or worse there are stretches of the period it covers for which it provides the only surviving continuous record. It is thus priceless, notwithstanding all the difficulties it poses. And for Diocletian, it provides some of the meagre surviving details that we need to help to assemble his life. The biographies of these later emperors were clearly written in imitation of the similar work of Suetonius. Like all works of ancient history and biography, they must be used carefully, with great attention to the art of source criticism. The study of their origin and the history of the collection is a complex one, fraught with controversy. And in the case of our subject, there is not even a separate life for us to consider.

The Augustan history ranks Diocletian's predecessor Carus among the better emperors of Rome, noting that his principal negative quality was that his death led to the reign of Carinus. Diocletian and his fellow tetrarchs receive (unsurprisingly) unstinting praise in the brief allusions to them, with the note that each of them received a separate biography by one Claudius Eusthenius, who is cited as being a secretary to Diocletian. We know nothing of this individual, who is mentioned nowhere else.

In summary, all of this is to say that Diocletian has not been treated well by the ravages of time and circumstance. We possess relatively few extant literary sources for his reign. We know far more about certain events in Roman history from the first century BCE than we do of many from the fourth century CE, largely in consequence of the dearth of surviving evidence. Coupled with the less than noble origins of Diocletian, we find a recipe for mystery and enigma.

Diocletian was born into a chaotic empire, and at the time of his death things would seem to be poised on another precipice. Remarkably, not only did Diocletian advance from truly inauspicious beginnings to the pinnacle of power, but he acquitted himself well in his post, securing a lasting peace for Rome and enjoying his own voluntary retirement. He clearly entered military service, though we cannot be sure of any of the circumstances of his admission or early advancement. All that we can do is speculate based on our knowledge of the Roman army in his day.

First, a practical note is in order for those who wish to consult the aforementioned primary sources more closely. One may turn to the Loeb Classical Library for the *Historia Augusta*. This exists in that series complete in a three-volume edition that has been revised as of the summer of 2022, with the usual facing page Latin text with English translation.[46] The *Breviaria* of Eutropius and Festus, as well as all of the surviving works ascribed to Aurelius Victor, have appeared in the *Collection des universités de France* (i.e. the Budé series cited above), with Latin texts, facing French translations and extensive notes.[47] None of these works have appeared in the Loeb series, or in the Oxford World's Classics or Penguin Classics libraries. Arnobius has likewise been edited for the Budé collection, in a five-volume edition with exhaustive commentary, of particular use for appreciating the evidence he provides for Roman religion and mythology in the Diocletianic era, as well as early Christian theology. Lactantius' *De Mortibus Persecutorum* has been edited and translated by J.L. Creed (Oxford, 1984), as the first volume in their early Christian texts series.[48]

Our lack of extensive, reliable evidence for the life and reign of Diocletian is not entirely a bad thing for the study of his achievement. Often our knowledge of a particular period, event, or significant figure in Roman history is hampered by the difficulty of evaluating the surviving works of literature that offer attestation. Tiberius, for example, is notoriously savaged by the historian Tacitus, just as so much of our knowledge of Caesar is conditioned by sources as disparate as the correspondence of Cicero and the biography of Suetonius. For Diocletian we have so few extant sources (and what we have tends to offer a 'bare bones' summation of events rather than analysis) that we are able to appraise certain aspects of his reign with a more balanced eye, even if one of the prices we pay is uncertainty about such basics as chronology. To begin with, Diocletian clearly absorbed the practical lessons of soldiery and military training and army life. His accomplishments were eminently rooted in the realities of daily life in the empire, especially with respect to the maintenance and upkeep of the military. He was willing to come to terms with rivals and partners in the sharing of power. He was a master organizer and efficient administrator. He had firm views on how to preserve order throughout the imperial provinces. And, not least, he was expert in developing a rational system to solve what he clearly correctly identified as the major problem in imperial Roman history up to his day: the question of the succession. Diocletian would do what Augustus had failed in some aspects to achieve. He would leave behind a clearly defined process for how to guarantee that Rome always had orderly transfers of power.

To be sure, his system would not last long in practice, and so Diocletian has suffered criticism for the fact that what he proposed did not prove (again, in some regards at least) to be of enduring value. The position taken in these pages will be that Diocletian's proposed system of imperial succession was a logical one, of superior value to the efforts and practices of his predecessors, at least given the tenor of the times. To the extent that it did not work for very long in real world practice, it illustrated all too clearly and even poignantly the failure of logic to stand up to human vanity, ambition, and avarice. It may have been naïve of Diocletian to assume that anyone would be as willing as he was to step away from the height of power, willing and even eager to assume the life of a gentleman farmer. As we have noted, it was an image that harked back to the storied lore of Cincinnatus, the great Roman republican hero who exemplified the image of the citizen servant who was willing to assume total power for the benefit of the state, and to abdicate from such heights of achievement when his job was completed satisfactorily.

Let us begin by examining the basic outline of the Diocletian succession scheme, a scheme that was based on elements of earlier precedent and practice, now codified in a more official and organized manner. It was a scheme that may have developed piecemeal, as circumstances called for a refinement and modification of the original plan, as Diocletian proceeded from sole rule to dyarchy to a third and fourth colleague. It was based on the conclusion that the empire had become too vast and too unwieldy to be managed effectively and efficiently by one man. That one man would thus need colleagues to assist him in the ruling of Rome. In all there would be four co-rulers, in two grades of power. The top two colleagues would be the so-called *Augusti* or Augustuses. The two junior colleagues were the *Caesares* or the Caesars. Each of these men would be based in a different city of the empire, all the more efficiently to be able to respond to crises on this or that border or in this or that region. The Augustuses would eventually voluntarily resign from power, and the Caesars would thus be promoted, with the chance to select their own pair of new junior colleagues to continue to maintain the system in perpetuity. When we say with the chance to select, we must emphasize the word 'chance'. The retiring Augustuses would obviously be involved in the decision, to a greater or lesser extent. Indeed we shall see that this matter of the succession raised one element of irony. Diocletian was much given to the development of codified rules and regulations to help to regularize and to provide some legal framework for many elements of Roman life. But to the best of our knowledge, there was no codified system to determine the selection of the Caesars. There was, for example, no majority or unanimous vote requirement to help to determine the outcome of the selection process. Gentlemen's agreements are sometimes expected to result in gentlemanly, effective settlements.

Prior to the Diocletian reform, the imperial succession, as we have seen, was based on two possible outcomes: the promotion of one's son by blood, or the selection of a worthy man to be adopted into your imperial family to serve as an anointed successor. There are inherent problems with any of these three systems – in the case of Diocletian, principally with securing the timely agreement of the Augustuses to abdicate from power jointly so as to allow the Caesars to advance and to bring in a new pair of sharers in power. But arguably Diocletian's system was far superior to what had been practised in the past. Here monarchy gave way to shared rule (even if shared by the members of a very exclusive club). There was in theory a chance to promote one's son, or to maintain the hallowed tradition of seeking out the most qualified and skilful men for the task. There was greater efficiency in having men with administrative and military power and competence closer to crisis points. There was a chance for increased imperial bureaucracy to maintain not one but four imperial courts, with an increase in civil servant positions. In theory, those living in what had hitherto been the hinterlands of the empire now had a chance to feel more closely connected to the central authority, a central authority that was now diffused into four different imperial capitals.

Again, we must note that Diocletian was not the inventor of the basic principles of this succession scheme. Previous emperors had practised versions of the 'anointed successor' or 'best man' model, including the assignment of significant tasks and areas of responsibility for the heir apparent. Diocletian, we shall see, was responsible for the refinement and perfection of a system whose genesis could be traced all the way to various elements of the Augustan efforts at securing a stable imperial succession.[49]

The system that Diocletian put into place did not last long in practice, but it left an indelible mark on the later organization of cities and regions in Europe. It laid the groundwork for the organization of the dioceses into which Christianity would be divided in an increasingly official way in the wake of state recognition and adoption of the religion. It provided for the development of the political and economic power of several imperial cities other than Rome. And, in some sense, it set the stage for the later division of the empire that would ensure the continuation of Roman imperial identity in the east for almost a millennium after the fall of the western empire in 476 CE.

Chapter 2

Servile Origins, Imperial Destiny

B ut we may return to the obscure boy and his shadowy origins in what is today the modern nation-state of Croatia.[1] In the absence of any clear evidence concerning more than half his life, we are left with the chance to survey the history of the Roman world during Diocletian's formative years. Suffice to say, it was an age of unremitting chaos. A new administrative job seemed to have emerged: usurper. Usurpers were men who aspired to be emperor, usually because they had the benefits of an army command and an emperor who was distracted with problems elsewhere in the empire. Usurpers did not have long life expectancy in most instances, though this demographic reality does not seem to have lessened the attraction and popularity of the position. Far too many military leaders were willing to risk life and limb for the chance to be emperor, even in the face of the knowledge that so many had failed before them. Further, these internecine struggles were being carried out in the face of unprecedented external threats to the empire. Each would-be emperor seemed to be possessed of the idea that he was best positioned to solve a particular set of crises. Coupled with this rise of a virtual class of military adventurers was the fact that several of the emperors of the age had an array of sons that would have been the envy of an Augustus or a Marcus Aurelius. There was an uneasy mix of military veteran commanders and young imperial scions under the guardianship of this or that government official. It was a recipe for further chaos in an environment already riddled with problems. Diocletian's birthplace, too, was not one of the more peaceful or relaxed of imperial provinces, even if for the first part of his life, at least, the most serious troubles were taking place in relatively distant locales. The young Diocletian likely did not experience barbarian incursions in Salona, or the threat of civil war anywhere immediately in the vicinity of his hometown. But Dalmatia as a region was a frontier place thanks to the collapse of the Danube border regions.

The region of Roman Dalmatia had been one of the many territories conquered, at least in part, in Roman republican times. The future Augustus actually conducted military campaigns in the northern part of Dalmatia because of the persistent problem of raids on the commerce and livelihood of north-eastern Italy. Problems persisted in the area well into the tenure of Augustus. Diocletian was by no means the first emperor to hail from somewhere outside Italy. It would also be misleading and inaccurate to argue that Dalmatia was some rugged and uncivilized hinterland of the empire. In the days of Augustus, it would have been unthinkable for a leading Roman political figure to have his origins outside Italy, especially if it were not certain that he had Italian connections somewhere in his lineage. Diocletian was a product of the provincial system, a child, as it were, of the vast network that Rome had put into place across the Mediterranean and relatively far inland.

Diocletian's traditional birthplace was Salona – the modern Solin. Solin remains a town on the Adriatic Sea, of more than twenty thousand residents. In Roman times Salona was the provincial capital. The town has proudly endured straight through to the twentieth century and beyond, with its recent history of the difficulties attendant on the breakup of the former Yugoslavia and the emergence of the various Balkan countries that achieved independence thereby. Diocletian remains the proudest 'native son' of Solin, and his birthplace remains a tourist attraction in the region. Again we do well to remember that we have no definitive evidence of Salona as the future emperor's birthplace, though we may be reasonably certain that he hailed either from there or from relatively nearby. He would choose to end his life in fortified luxury not far from his natal place, in the palace now famous to tourists and scholars alike at Split, some ninety minutes away on foot.[2] While the exact year of his birth, as we have noted, is uncertain, we do know that the official celebrations in honour of it were held on 22 December, and so we may be confident of the date. His death would come in the same month.

Dalmatia was a cradle of salvific emperors: 'The men who were responsible for saving the Empire, Claudius II (Gothicus), Probus, and Aurelian were all of Illyrian origin, while the greatest of them, Diocletian, was born somewhere in the territory around Salona.'[3] The author of this study can attest to the pride of taxi drivers from airports in pointing out the glories of Illyria, and its place in preserving Rome.

There is evidence that Diocletian was 68 when he died, though his exact date of death is unknown. Working backwards from 312 (in our view the best candidate year for his death) would give us 244 for the year of birth. The range of 242–5 is possible. Our best guess would be to assign 244–312 as Diocletian's dates, though certainty, we cannot emphasize enough, is elusive.

Depending on the exact year of Diocletian's birth, he entered life during the reign of either Gordian III or Philip the Arab.[4] Philip was emperor from 244 to 249, and it was during his tenure that Rome celebrated its millennium in April 248 CE – one thousand years after the legendary founding of the city by Romulus in 753 BCE. Philip was like many a Roman emperor in the third century, beset with problems both at home and abroad. Philip was either killed in battle or assassinated in a civil conflict in northern Italy in September 249, with his rival Decius assuming the purple of Roman imperial power. Like Diocletian, Decius was a native of what is today the former Yugoslavia – he was born at Sirmium, the modern Sremska Mitrovica in central Serbia.[5]

Decius would die in battle fighting the Goths in June 251, after fewer than two years in power. He would prefigure Diocletian in another regard besides his Illyrian origins – he was also a notorious persecutor of Christians, with a conviction that at least one of the sources of trouble for the seemingly interminable, insurmountable problems that beset Rome was the disregard of the traditional religious observances of the pagan deities.[6] As we shall in the case of Diocletian, scholars have debated the actual intention of Decius' edicts of January 250. He certainly mandated sacrifices and other rites for the intention of the safety and preservation of the empire, an order that would have rankled devotees of a monotheistic religion like Christianity. One could argue that Christianity was not in and of itself a target of Decius, insofar as his stated goal was the preservation of Rome by prayer to her traditional, ancestral deities – but no faithful Christian was likely to be happy about (or willing to participate in) sacrifices to pagan gods. What is certain is that such leading Christians as the pope in Rome – Saint Fabian – refused the imperial edict and were killed.[7]

The Christians, in any case, would be able to argue that Decius was struck down for his impiety. King Kniva of the Goths led an invasion of Roman territory across the Danube and the Balkans turned into a battlefield as the Goths made their significant foray into the pages of surviving history.[8] Decius was destined to be the first Roman emperor to die in battle against a foreign adversary, killed on the soil of modern day Bulgaria along with his son. Diocletian was a boy when these dramatic events unfolded.

Decius was succeeded by Trebonianus Gallus, who thus advanced from being the governor of the province of Moesia Superior to being emperor. Moesia was located largely in what is today Serbia, and Gallus had been trusted with that difficult frontier position by his predecessor in apparent consideration of his skill and acumen. Gallus was able to secure an end to the immediate Gothic threat by trading land for gold – the Goths would vacate Roman territory in exchange for being allowed to keep their plunder and being paid an annuity (i.e. a subsidy to behave). It is a testament to the confused and confusing nature of the times that our surviving sources include the, perhaps unsurprising, story that Gallus had actually conspired with the Goths against Decius, all so that a governor could ascend to the purple. Decius had died with a son in battle, but he had another son – Hostilian – who was in Rome. In the aftermath of Decius' death, the army had proclaimed Gallus emperor, while Hostilian assumed power in Rome. Gallus quickly agreed to rule jointly with Hostilian, probably for the sake of avoiding a civil war in a time of crisis. Curiously, Hostilian's fate is ultimately uncertain. He seems to have died in late 251, perhaps from plague – but certainly his death simplified matters for Gallus, who had his own son – Volusian. Gallus may have been innocent of any conspiracy with the Goths to kill Decius, and may even have been on genuinely friendly and close terms with Decius' family. But Roman history had offered ample proof of the challenges of having two emperors, especially from two different families.

These domestic difficulties were, however, ultimately utterly insignificant in the face of what would have qualified as front-page news in foreign affairs. The Persians would invade the eastern Roman empire under their great ruler Shapur I. The Scythians would launch their own invasions of Roman territory. Gallus and his son Volusian soon faced a crisis far worse than that confronted by Decius and his son in the form of the Goths.

The Roman army had always held the keys to the safety and security of the empire, but now that fact was being illustrated on a near daily basis by catastrophic reports of invasion and largescale raids by hostile foreign tribes and powers. The army depended on the emperor for its payment and its benefits, as well as for successful leadership in the field against these numerous threats. It appears that Gallus soon lost the confidence of his men, or – perhaps it is better to say – another governor inspired greater confidence. The new governor of Moesia Superior, Aemilianus, was apparently among those who were disgusted by Gallus' payments to the Goths. Aemilianus was in charge of dealing with the continuing pacification of the Goths, who were not inclined to maintain a tranquil border existence with Rome. In 253 – only two years after the signing of their deal with Gallus – the Goths were claiming that they had not received all their tribute. They launched new invasions, thus adding to the weighty foreign threats that Rome faced. Aemilianus would be the man of the hour, defeating the Goths and invading their lands.

Aemilianus would become but the latest in a long line of usually ill-fated men to be proclaimed emperor by his troops. Civil war would once again go close in hand with foreign conflict. Aemilianus would soon enough proceed to enter Italy, ready to face Gallus and his son Volusian in battle. He would win, such that by the end of summer in 253 his imperial rivals were dead, killed by their own men in the hope of securing the new emperor's favour. Many Roman rulers of the age had to face the question of whether they were more likely to be slain by a barbarian or one of their own men.

Aemilianus – the latest ruler in Diocletian's boyhood – might seem to be one of the more interesting figures of the period. After his defeat of Gallus, he proceeded to Rome to consolidate his power. Needless to say, the senate was sceptical of this latest usurper. But Aemilianus posed an eminently reasonable suggestion: let the senate manage the domestic affairs of the empire, and let him – the victor over the Goths – proceed to handle the Persian threat in the east. The senate heartily acquiesced to this proposal, and Aemilianus quickly left to prepare for his campaign.

All of this would come to naught. In the end, Aemilianus would be murdered by his own men, no later than the middle of September of that fateful year of 253. The background of this latest assassination was the advance of another Roman governor, Publius Licinius Valerianus – the future emperor Valerian. It seems that Valerian had been summoned by Gallus for aid against Aemilianus, only to arrive too late to render any assistance to the doomed emperor. Or, perhaps, Valerian decided to bring his forces into Italy only after the news arrived of Gallus' death. Valerian, in any case, was able to consolidate his own power successfully, not least with the assistance of his son Publius Licinius Egnatius Gallienus, who was proclaimed his de facto co-ruler.[9] Valerian proposed to proceed east to face the Persian threat, while Gallienus would handle troubles in the west, namely the invasion of Germanic tribes across both the Rhine and the Danube.

It can be all too easy to look back on periods such as this with an air of incredulity, wondering how emperors could so readily be overthrown or engage in civil conflicts when multiple borders of the empire were being overrun by formidable foes. One key to understanding the age is to appreciate the relatively slow speed of communication. News could not possibly spread fast enough to allow for considered appraisal of crises and problems. The empire was simply too large to be managed efficiently, and emperors would understandably mistrust governors of border provinces who had large armies. Those forces were necessary to maintain border security, but they could also be used as tools of civil war and usurpation. Indeed, it is reasonable to question why anyone would want the job of being emperor in the mid-third century, given the mountain of crises on the imperial desk.

One of the tasks of any student of the reign of Diocletian is to examine the problem of whether or not he was simply luckier than his military predecessors. One by one the list of men who met violent deaths in an effort to rule the Roman empire had grown longer. Diocletian could profit from a long history of failed precursors, with lessons that had not always been absorbed by his predecessors, men who fell prey to perils not dissimilar to those that had ensnared their forebears. One cannot repeat enough times how dangerous it was to be an emperor in this century.

Decius had been the first emperor to die in battle against a foreign invader, and Valerian would be the first to be captured in battle. He would die a prisoner of Shapur I, having failed in his mission to put an end to the Persian threat in the Roman east. It is impossible to overestimate the consequences of the catastrophe. Rome faced peril on her eastern border, alongside the Germanic troubles that Valerian's son Gallienus was managing (with some success) in the west. Foreign affairs were more than complicated enough for two men to direct, but the very fact of imperial distraction seems to have encouraged yet another eruption of the problem of usurpation. Ingenuus was a Roman military commander in Pannonia who had been tasked by Gallienus with two weighty responsibilities, one public and one private.[10] The public task was responding to the invasion of Pannonia by Sarmatian tribesman. The private was the education of Gallienus' son, Valerian II. The boy died in 258 at about 8 years of age, a circumstance that seems to have aroused Gallienus' ire against Ingenuus. Fearful for his future, Ingenuus seems to have sensed that the capture of Valerian by the Persians in 260 afforded him a chance to secure his future.

One can almost predict the outcome of the story. Ingenuus was proclaimed emperor by his own troops in 260. Gallienus was forced to respond to the domestic threat. His advance against Ingenuus weakened the front against the Germanic tribes, since he had been compelled to take a significant portion of his forces with him to meet Ingenuus. Gallienus was successful in crushing the revolt, but major invasions ensued on the western front. By 'major' we mean no less than the penetration of barbarians all the way into southern Spain, and the first (at least noteworthy) invasion of Italy by foreign enemies in centuries. We do not know the exact chronology of these invasions given the quality or lack thereof of our sources. The Alamanni (or Alemanni) launched their assault against Rome sometime between 258 and 260.[11] The Alamanni were one of the three major divisions of the Germanic tribes, alongside the Saxons and the Franks.[12] To a certain degree, the problem Rome faced with her northern neighbours was that the Germans had become significantly more organized with the passage of time, and internal problems and decline in Rome served only to exacerbate the problem posed by the enhanced skills and improved civil administration of the increasingly united German tribes.

The harsh reality for Rome was that the Rhine border was already in a state of serious weakness, even before the Ingenuus revolt in Pannonia; invasion was possible if not likely even prior to Gallienus' removal of significant forces from the western frontier. The crisis was such that the senate was compelled to raise forces in haste to meet the threat to the heart of the empire. The Alamanni were defeated, and Gallienus was able to intercept and destroy some of the retreating forces – but the whole episode was an ominous foreshadowing of what could happen in the face of weakening borders and increased internal dissension and turmoil.

Indeed around this same time, another revolt erupted against imperial rule, this time in the Balkans. Troops along the Danube declared their commander Regalianus emperor sometime in 260, for reasons that are now more or less lost to history. We are not even certain how he died, though it may have been a combination of foreign and domestic opposition: the Roxolani were invading, and either they killed him by themselves, or with the assistance of some of his own men who had become dissatisfied with him.[13] Perhaps Gallienus managed to arrive on the scene and defeat him – again, our sources are conflicted on the point.

Certainly the border provinces in Pannonia and Moesia were often in a state of upheaval because of barbarian incursions, with concomitant conflict with Rome because of a perceived lack of immediate attention to local crises. In the chaos of the mid-third century, we cannot be sure if Regalianus was somehow involved in the Ingenuus revolt, or if his uprising was independent. We are not even certain if his death came in the fateful year of 260, or in 261. Regalianus is remembered today more for numismatics than anything – he reigned long enough to mint his own coins. In the hobbyist world of collecting Roman coins, Regalianus issues are prized because so few exist.

We should not be surprised that the capture of Valerian in the east led to the rise of further claimants to the purple. The fiscal officer Fulvius Macrianus apparently considered the fact that he had two sons (Macrianus the Younger and Quietus) was sufficient guarantee (admittedly alongside the support of one of Valerian's military commanders) that he could make a credible attempt to usurp power, at least on behalf of his offspring. Macrianus took his homonymous son with him to advance west, leaving Quietus with forces in the east. Gallienus' commander Aureolus met the Macriani in battle somewhere in Thrace in 261, defeating them. Aureolus had loyally served Gallienus in meeting the incipient threat to his reign, but his loyalty would prove to be of limited duration.

Gallienus faced a more serious usurper in the person of Marcus Cassianus Latinius Postumus. Postumus would prove successful in actually splitting off a part of the Roman Empire, establishing a miniature empire – usually referred to as the Gallic Empire – in Gaul, Germany, Britain and Spain. He would rule this empire from 260 to 269, years during which Diocletian would have come of age in the Balkans, the period during which he is likely to have commenced his military career.

How did Postumus emerge as yet another rival to the throne, let alone the founder of a breakaway empire that endured for several years (no small feat in these troubled times)? The root problem was one that Diocletian would later understand all too well. An emperor cannot be in more than one place at one time. Bilocation is impossible, and there were too many problems both internal and external to neglect sensitive regions. Postumus was a commander in the west who, simply put, came into conflict with Gallienus' officials in the emperor's absence. More specifically, he seems to have clashed with the prefect Silvanus, who was the guardian of Gallienus' son Saloninus. Postumus and his soldiers appear to have secured a significant amount of loot that Silvanus ordered to be handed over. Postumus and his men were offended at the notion of having to do the bidding of some underling of the distant emperor (who had, after all, his aforementioned eastern problems to deal with in the troubled year of 260). Postumus' army drove out Silvanus and Saloninus, who were compelled to flee with loyal troops to guard their escape. Postumus was proclaimed emperor, and he proceeded at once to chase Gallienus' son and prefect. Both men were doomed to be killed by Postumus' army. Gallienus had now lost two sons; it is no surprise that he never tried to involve his third (Egnatius Marinianus) in the management of government.

Postumus was emperor, at least locally. He seems to have been possessed of a desire to maintain a manageable realm that could be expanded carefully and with great forethought. We are not entirely certain where his capital was, but it was either at Colonia Claudia Ara Agrippinensium (the modern Köln or Cologne), or at Augusta Treverorum (the modern Trier). He did not bother to persuade the Roman senate that they should recognize his rule – he simply appointed his own senate. It was a miniature Roman Empire, a parallel empire that was clearly in a state of imitative secession. All of the usual trappings of Roman government were mimicked in Gaul. It was a novel concept, one might think: rather than immediately asserting authority over the entire empire, Postumus seems to have established an intentionally smaller state, one which had the chance to expand only when expansion seemed feasible and safe. The methods used – and, to be sure, the problems that confronted Gallienus elsewhere – meant that Postumus would be able to enjoy his reign for the better part of a decade. It was an extraordinary accomplishment in an age when many emperors measured their reigns in months rather than years. It would serve as something of a model for Carausius when he would try to set up his British realm within a realm.

We are quite uncertain as to what Postumus' ultimate vision was. He was a definite product of local, provincial concerns for the safety of Roman territory in the face of barbarian incursions (the same motivation would lie at the heart of the commencement of the similar breakaway region that would emerge soon enough in the east, in Palmyra). Postumus was smart enough to appreciate that there were any number of foreign foes who would immediately strike at his miniature empire if he travelled too far. He knew that there were always other military commanders who were ready to launch their own bid for supreme power. It is hard to argue against the conclusion that Postumus survived for as long as he did in large measure because he did not overplay his hand, at least not at this early stage. More difficult is the explication of why everything he did in his realm was a mirror of Roman government. In other words, there was not the slightest effort to make the Gallic Empire 'Gallic' except in territory. It was clearly a Roman Empire, simply one that was not centred on Rome. What exactly Postumus envisaged as the connection between his provinces and the rest of the empire is unclear.

Postumus had a few years to develop his nascent empire without interference from Gallienus, who was far too preoccupied with problems elsewhere on the empire's borders to respond in appreciable force to the new usurper. Some might argue that he should have recognized that Postumus posed a more serious threat to his reign than any of his previous rivals, though this is a conclusion all too easy to reach with the benefit of hindsight, and by downplaying the significance of the other threats that confronted Gallienus. Finally in 265, the emperor advanced against his rival. Diocletian was perhaps 20 at this point, still living in complete obscurity. Gallienus' campaign of 265 failed. A key factor in understanding the failure of his efforts is appreciating the role of his subordinate commander, the aforementioned Aureolus. Our sources here are as confused as ever. It is possible that Aureolus was deliberately seeking to undermine Gallienus. It is conceivable that he was simply careless and incompetent. We are not sure exactly how serious a setback

Gallienus suffered. There is some evidence that points to the recovery of some territory from Postumus as a result of this campaign. Aureolus would in the end follow the path of so many ill-fated military figures before him. He would become a usurper himself, first in an open effort to align himself with Postumus, and then in an attempt to secure power for himself.

Aureolus was far less significant than Postumus, and thus easier to dispense with relatively quickly. It is interesting to note that Postumus does not seem to have been particularly interested in allying himself with the newest usurper. Aureolus had no chance of survival, it no doubt seemed, without the backing of the Gallic Empire. He found himself trapped in the city of Mediolanum (the modern Milan), under siege by Gallienus.

Fortune, however, has a way of proving herself capricious. Gallienus was killed in 268 (probably in September) while conducting his assault on Mediolanum in pursuit of Aureolus. We are not entirely certain of the circumstances of his assassination. He was clearly unpopular at this point among at least some significant portion of his officer corps. We cannot with any definitive assurance say that Gallienus' successor Claudius II was responsible or culpable for his predecessor's death. We do know that he called for sparing the lives of Gallienus' surviving family members when the senate was ready to call for their heads, and that he asked for the deification of the slain emperor. Aureolus was slain in the same year as Gallienus, after failing to succeed in trying to surrender to his new besiegers.

Why was Gallienus suddenly deemed worthy of elimination? The truth of the matter is lost to history, but it may not have been particularly dramatic or noteworthy. Rather, Gallienus may simply have survived for too long, rushing from one crisis to another as part of some effort to maintain his realm. For whatever reason or reasons, a majority of his officers wanted him dead, and Claudius was the choice to succeed him. Gallienus would prove to be a significant cautionary example for Diocletian.

What is noteworthy is that the years between Postumus' victory in 265 and the death of Aureolus in 268 seem to have been calm and even prosperous years for the Gallic Empire. Why Postumus did not act quickly and decisively in support of his would-be ally Aureolus is one of the many mysteries of the period. Certainly it is easy to look back on 268 as an advantageous moment for Postumus in which to strike hard against Gallienus – but this he did not do, perhaps because he was unaware of the fortune of the moment (or maybe he was too timid). It is perhaps circumstantial evidence that he intended to maintain his relatively small empire, without wishing to engage in jockeying for wider power. He may have judged that the threats to his own realm were still sufficiently ominous so as to demand his presence. Here we can only speculate and surmise, in the absence of definitive evidence. By the autumn of 268 Postumus had already accomplished what some would have considered a miracle – mere survival for so long. He was not possessed of anything approximating rashness or hastiness. Even if he did have a plan for further conquest or expansion, it was clearly a plan that was intended to be executed with care and precision, and extreme patience.

It is possible that both Postumus and Gallienus were vanquished, ultimately, by men who grew weary of their slow progress. Postumus would live to inaugurate the new year of 269, but soon after he would face his own usurper in the person of his commander in Germany, Laelianus. Laelianus was defeated and slain, but Postumus was soon after also killed – by his own men. It was a virtual catalogue of deaths of usurpers. Postumus' soldiers had seized the rebel city of Moguntiacum (the modern Mainz), and they wished to vent their fury and satisfy their lust for plunder by sacking it. Characteristically, Postumus tried to restrain them from their bloodthirsty avarice, and was slain for his efforts. His men replaced him with one Marius, whose first act in power was to allow his soldiers leave to sack Moguntiacum. But after only two or three months at the helm of the Gallic Empire, Marius was also killed (this sort of history truly writes itself with bloody ink), at the behest of Postumus' onetime colleague Marcus Piavonius Victorinus.

Victorinus thus became the third emperor of this empire in miniature. The year 269 was already a 'Year of Three Emperors'. The instability had almost immediate consequences. Gaul, Germany, and Britain swore allegiance to Victorinus, but Spain rebelled and declared its loyalty to Claudius II – thus restoring part of the Roman Empire without the shedding of any blood. Victorinus was thus instantly deprived of a significant portion of his territory, and Claudius saw the opportunity to try to secure the defection of cities in Gaul. He would not be entirely successful in his efforts, but he also did not push the case too hard in the face of more pressing problems elsewhere.

Rome therefore remained split into two parts, and a third division was in the works. It is perhaps no surprise that the chaos on the Persian border led to a crisis there that would mushroom into another exceptionally difficult challenge for the empire – the formation of another breakaway region in the east. The centre of the new problem was the city of Palmyra, an ancient site located in the central part of what is today the republic of Syria. At the time of Shapur's aggression against Rome, Palmyra was an autonomous city in the Roman province of Syria Phoenice. Palmyra was one of the most prosperous and economically developed towns in the east; the invasion of the Persians was seen by Palmyra as a catastrophic threat to economic stability and the livelihood of the region. In consequence Palmyra was quite happy to remain allied to Rome and to help to expel the Persians from Roman territory.

In the end, Palmyra – under the leadership of the remarkable Odenathus – would prove to be highly successful in its campaign against Persia. Indeed, in some ways it would prove to be too successful. Odenathus declared his loyalty to Gallienus and was of immense help to the emperor in overseeing the Roman response to the threat from Shapur. By the end of 262 or the start of 263, Odenathus was so victorious in his military advances against Persia that he was even ready to contemplate an attack on the Persian capital at Ctesiphon. Increasingly he must have been of the unshakeable belief that Palmyra was able to handle its own problems, in the absence of the interventions of Rome.

Odenathus is the man most responsible for the recovery of the Roman territories that had been lost to Persia. It was a stunning reversal of the setbacks that had reached their lowest point in the capture of Valerian. Persia had overplayed her hand, and Palmyra was on site, as it were, ready to pounce. Palmyra at this point was officially still a part of the Roman empire – whatever autonomy it enjoyed in internal affairs – but in reality Odenathus was now the ruler of a Palmyran kingdom, a powerful realm that had scored significant victories over the dread Persian foe.

It would prove to be no surprise that Palmyra would decide that it could go its own way. In some regards, the breakaway of Palmyra in the east made more sense than the formation of the Gallic Empire in the west. Matters would prove complicated because of the fact that, like so many before him in the history of Rome in the third century, Odenathus would be assassinated – probably in 267, but perhaps as early as 266 or as late as 268. Scholars question who exactly was behind the conspiracy to kill the highly successful Palmyrene. Some have wondered if Gallienus had decided that his eastern ally was perhaps becoming too much of a potential threat to his own rule. Others have tried to cast blame on the Persians, who certainly hated Odenathus. There was also the wife of Odenathus to consider, the woman who would become more famous than her husband – Queen Zenobia.[14] And still other candidates can be amassed for either coming up with the conspiracy or at least acquiescing to it – again, Odenathus had acquired many enemies. Odenathus died with a son of 10 years of age, Vaballathus – he was officially the successor, though under the custody and regency of his mother Zenobia. It would be Zenobia who would decide to separate Palmyra from Rome and to be mistress of her own kingdom, a new Cleopatra, as it were, for a new age.

Postumus; Ingenuus; Regalianus; Aureolus; Macrianus; Macrianus the Younger; Quietus – these are but seven of a group of men who are referred to in the Augustan History as the 'Thirty Tyrants.' All of them were alleged rivals of Gallienus. Some of the thirty may well be fictitious names. There had been Thirty Tyrants at Athens after the loss of the Peloponnesian War, and so it was appropriate to have an equal number of upstarts during the crisis of the third century.

Diocletian, meanwhile, was approaching 30 years of age. Again we have no clear sense of what he was doing in this period, other than continuing his service in the Roman military. It is a source of significant speculation to wonder what his reaction was to the news that must have reached him of the dramatic events that were unfolding throughout the empire. Geographically he would have been relatively isolated from the worst of the problems with which Rome was afflicted.

What, meanwhile, of Claudius II? His list of problems was long. He would succeed in avoiding a violent end – he fell victim to a plague early in 270 and died at Sirmium while preparing to strike against the Vandals who were raiding Pannonia. Claudius II is more familiarly known by his epithet Claudius Gothicus, because he was so successful in his campaigns against them – most notably at the Battle of Naissus in 268 or 269 – that he managed to end their threat to Rome for a century. That victory occurred near Naissus in modern Serbia, the city that would become famous as the birthplace of Constantine the Great and other emperors. Today it is a locale that is ardently proud of its heritage as a so-called Imperial City, its airport named after Constantine, and its tourism industry largely geared toward the celebration of that great Roman ruler.

Claudius was thus one of the more successful of the soldier emperors, though his efforts were restricted largely to foreign affairs. He was probably wise in not become entangled in a long and risky campaign against Victorinus in the west while the Gothic and other foreign crises were still so pressing in the east. His work was cut short by the plague that is best known to us because a description of it is extant from the pen of the Christian bishop Cyprian of Carthage, who was slain in September 258 as part of the general persecution of Christians under Valerian.

Claudius was succeeded by his brother Quintillus, though it would be a short reign of probably some six months. Quintillus' accession is another matter of controversy. It is not clear if he was the choice of the army, or of the senate, or of both. His death is no less mysterious; he may have been a suicide. It was dangerous to be an emperor, and it was almost as equally perilous to be one of his relatives. Quintillus is another of those shadowy figures of Roman history whose life and death coincided with the rise of a far more famous man, one who in some ways can be considered a proto-Diocletian, certainly a precursor to our subject: Aurelian. If Claudius had been among the greater and more memorable men of his age, Aurelian would eclipse him.

Lucius Domitius Aurelianus was yet another 'soldier emperor', a man from the Danube frontier, of low birth, who found a home and successful career in the army.[15] He rose to be a highly successful cavalry commander under Gallienus. As with Diocletian, so with Aurelian we can work backwards to determine at least an approximate birth date – probably (September) 214, thus making him some thirty years older than his later successor. If we postulate an entrance into the army at around 20, then Aurelian joined the Roman military at exactly the time affairs were being to unravel in the wake of the assassination of Alexander Severus. But the date of one's recruitment into the army is difficult to pinpoint with certainty. Vegetius' military handbook (which may be dated to the late fourth/early fifth century) encourages the admission of men as they enter puberty, so that they can be trained in athletics and proper discipline.

Diocletian could have been as young as 14 when he entered the military, and so too Aurelian.

Our meagre sources for the life of Aurelian credit him with extraordinary prowess in battle and exceptional signs of future greatness. This is the sort of stock in trade comment of hagiographical literature that is approached cautiously by modern scholars, with reserve and suspicion. There is no question, however, that a man of humble origins who rose to become one of the most successful emperors of his age likely did display exceptional qualities in his younger years that made his ascent possible. Aurelian was there in 268 when Claudius won his victory over the Goths at Naissus, by which time he was a cavalry commander and had acquitted himself amply as a high-ranking member of the old guard from Gallienus' heyday. He was involved in the siege of Aureolus at Mediolanum, and it is unclear where he stood on the question of the killing of his onetime employer Gallienus – clearly he transitioned seamlessly from one regime to another, and it is likely that he was a partisan of Claudius, ready to see a change in imperial government.

Aurelian would have been in his mid-fifties when Claudius became emperor. He had risen fast during the reign of Gallienus, but his real progress in power came under the new regime. Claudius and his new top commander Aurelian had much work to do to secure the frontier against the invasion of the Alamanni; by early in 269 they were already on the march and in combat against both that enemy and the Juthungi. Victory was fleeting; news quickly arrived of still other massive barbarian incursions into the Balkans, and Aurelian was assigned the task of responding to the latest border crisis.

Aurelian proceeded with an advance force, and soon Claudius followed with the main body of his forces. The scene was what for the Romans was north-eastern Macedonia, that region that today is divided between Greece and the republic now known as North Macedonia. The Goths had penetrated as far as the Greek city of Thessalonica. This serious crisis was quickly enough resolved by Aurelian: the Goths were pushed out of the area and pursued far north, though in a typically costly campaign that was a harbinger of later problems of attrition and the maintenance of manpower – this was an exceedingly hazardous time to be a member of the juggernaut that was the Roman army.

War and plague continued without abatement through 270. The Romans were able to declare something of a victory by the end of summer that year, though plague took the life of Claudius. We have observed that the transition from Claudius to Aurelian was fraught with some controversy and turmoil, namely given the question of the emperor's brother Quintillus. Certainly the brother stood no practical chance against the distinguished military commander and victor over the Goths. Indeed most people with any knowledge of the campaigns of 269–270 would have given more credit to Aurelian than to his emperor for what had been achieved.

In 270, Aurelian inherited a mess, like so many of his recent predecessors. Diocletian would have been still in his twenties, certainly serving in the military, though we have no knowledge as to what exactly he was participating in or accomplishing in these busy years. Aurelian faced breakaway movements in both west and east, as well as extensive threats along the borders of empire. There was no time to rest or to relish the attainment of the purple; almost at once campaigns were resumed against Germanic invasions. The Alamanni were aggressive in moving against northern Italy in 271, and Aurelian was not always victorious in his efforts to check the advance of his foe. It was another age in which Rome herself feared of possible attack if the Germans were able to penetrate deep into the peninsula. When archaeologists study the so-called Aurelian Walls, they are investigating the defensive works that Aurelian commissioned as part of his response to the barbarian threat. The need for Rome to be fortified in this way is a silent testimony to the situation in the late third century CE. It was an implicit acknowledgement that the possibility of foreign invasion into Latium and central Italy was all too real. The days when Italy could expect to be spared direct assault were long gone. Many of the threats that confronted Italy and the empire in this age were a harbinger of what would come – the ultimate collapse of order in the western empire, a collapse that was delayed because of men like those featured in this study.

Aurelian was another example of eminent practicality in the management of army and empire. He was balanced in his appraisal of when one should fight and when one should set up a defensive position; he was also acutely aware of what could and could not be held in battle and after. After securing his position in northern Italy, Aurelian swept east and fought the Goths even beyond the Danube – but he followed up his victories with a decision not to try to hold Roman territory in the province of Dacia north of the Danube. This region has few if any appreciable natural defences, and Aurelian decided – no doubt wisely – that it was simply too expensive to defend against foreign assault. He reorganized the region, setting up a capital for a reconstituted province of Dacia Aureliana with Serdica as its capital – the modern Sofia, the capital of Bulgaria.

Aurelian was more focused on the east than on the west, at least for the moment. The breakaway movement in Palmyra was his next focus. When last we spoke of this latest threat to the stability of the Roman Empire, Queen Zenobia was attempting to expand Palmyran domination in the east. Her work in this regard can be considered a typical blend of acumen and skill while taking advantage of the conditions of time and place. In short, her achievements were appreciable and great, but she was also in a position to expand rapidly in the face of limited resistance. In these situations, conquerors always run the risk of taking too much, too fast, and that may have been the case with Zenobia. She was eventually, it seems, in control of territory even into Egypt, with its obvious threat to the Roman grain supply from that storied breadbasket of empire.[16] Matters had long been out of hand in the east, and Aurelian faced a problem that could no longer be ignored.

Our sources are not nearly as helpful as we might like here. We have no reliable account of how Zenobia might have managed to expand so far, so quickly. Some might even question whether she really was in control and possession of as much territory as the breakaway Palmyran Empire is said to have amassed. Zenobia could not afford to be focused only on Rome in the west; she also had the problem of defending against Persia. There is evidence of military victories against Roman forces and garrisons as Palmyra expanded, but clearly there was also a significant groundswell of support for the queen's regime, at least in some quarters. The greatest mystery and question surrounds the Egyptian expansion, which is not as well documented as the Palmyran advances in Judaea, for example. In reality, though, we may conclude that Zenobia surpassed – and surpassed by far – anything that Cleopatra had managed to accomplish.

For Zenobia has inevitably been the subject of comparisons with the Egyptian, Hellenistic monarch of the Augustan Age, the last of her

Ptolemaic line. It appears that the 'Palmyran Cleopatra' was far more formidable and successful in her endeavours than Egypt's last Ptolemaic ruler. Zenobia certainly controlled more territory in what would have to have been a lightning military advance. What remains less than clear is what the queen's overall intentions were, especially in such dramatic steps as the capture of Egypt and the taking control of Roman grain supplies in the east.

We do well to remember that the Palmyran situation was always somewhat ambiguous in nature. The Palmyrenes were masters of playing a delicate and arguably disingenuous game of recognizing Roman authority in principle, even as it was flouted in practice. The genesis of this diplomatic stratagem was the fact that the unwieldly, sprawling empire was so difficult to control from a central authority that in the face of legitimate crises – like the Persian threat under Shapur – local potentates were forced to take matters into their hands. What can and did develop in such a situation is the seeming incongruity of having an empire within an empire that acknowledges the authority of someone like Aurelian, even as it functions independently of him and does as it wishes. Zenobia was in the additionally complicated position of being the regent for her son Vaballathus, who was hailed by the Palmyrenes as *rex* and *imperator* – that is, as 'king' and 'commander' – even though he was ruling and commanding nothing.

Certainly the Palmyrenes believed that they were more competent in managing and responding to such threats as the Persian menace on their own, and without help or direction from authorities in Rome. In this view recent history had proven them to have a legitimate argument. But we cannot avoid the conclusion that we simply do not know enough about what Zenobia intended, which certainly may have changed over the course of the duration of her reign. We know, for example, some interesting details from the evidence of coinage. Numismatic records reveal such shifting paradigms as the recognition of Aurelian as emperor and Vaballathus as king, and eventually the detail that Aurelian began to reign in 270, but Vaballathus in 267 – which would be interpreted as asserting that Vaballathus was the senior partner in what was apparently conceived of as a joint system of rule.

Scholars can debate whether Aurelian agreed to any such ambiguity or pretence in the early days of his administration. Certainly his list of problems was extensive, and he had no realistic chance immediately on accession in 270 of launching some major campaign in the east. What follows is speculative analysis. Zenobia's Palmyra may have reached the conclusion that Persia, not Rome, was the most pressing threat to the stability of their economic empire. Aware as they were of the vast difficulties facing Rome in the west from the combined threat of barbarian incursions and the incessant civil conflicts that were most powerfully manifested in the existence of a Gallic Empire, which was still functioning years after its establishment, Palmyra may have decided – likely by a joint conclusion of Zenobia and her top officials – that the eastern part of the Palmyran Empire should be ruled separately, with peaceful co-existence with Rome that was, after all, able to be ensured by economic realities – that is, by the question of access to Egyptian grain. Zenobia may have felt that in essence she was ensuring the security of Roman interests in the east by agreeing to provide military security against Persia and the economic boon of grain and commerce, in exchange for the recognition that Palmyra was essentially an independent state, able to manage its own affairs and to control in territory (and attendant economic power) the entirety of the Roman East. A sarcastic Palmyrene might argue that the Romans did not have the manpower or the ability to maintain the east, and that the Palmyran vision was the best possible outcome for Rome in her hour of crisis.

We observed above that there can be a critical moment where too much is taken too quickly. Aurelian ultimately was not interested in a continuing confused situation, and was not remotely tolerant of what he no doubt considered the terrorism of holding back grain supplies from Rome. He mustered his forces for an invasion and reconquest of the east. The year 272 would be decisive for the fate of Palmyra.

At some point Zenobia started removing Aurelian from her coinage. As with many wars in human history, no doubt the Palmyrenes argued that Rome was being aggressive as the emperor proceeded to prepare for an eastern campaign. The Romans would have been of the opinion that they had tolerated one too many instances of affront and appreciable threat from the secessionist region. What is interesting is how easily Aurelian regained territory in the spring of 272. There were no hard-fought battles or attempts at defence against the Roman reconquest. There seems to have been a combination of local disinterest in war, coupled with Zenobia's withdrawal of forces into Syrian territory – that is, into the heart of Palmyra. It was a drawing in of the enemy, one might think, with no effort to maintain the far-flung regions that had been seized almost as quickly as they were now lost. It is possible that Zenobia realized that the grain seizure in Egypt had constituted a *casus belli*, and that now by essentially surrendering Egypt, Palmyra was acknowledging the Roman cause for complaint, beside cherishing the hope that Aurelian would make some peaceful accommodation with Zenobia. After all, the Romans still had significant problems elsewhere in the empire, and many a Roman conqueror had made the fateful decision to advance too far east, only to become embroiled in a seemingly endless war in the vast expanses of Syria and Judaea. Persia remained a threat too, and the Palmyrenes may have calculated that Aurelian would not want to weaken his forces (and theirs) in the east, with the risk that after peace had been achieved by force of arms, the Persians would take advantage of the drained state of the Roman military to launch renewed assaults.

Aurelian was not interested in negotiating with Zenobia, however. We cannot be certain of the extent of his education and knowledge of history, but he likely had the image of Cleopatra in his mind as he proceeded to Antioch. The Battle of Immae was fought some twenty-five miles north of the city, and the Romans defeated the Palmyran defenders. It was a disaster of immense proportions for Zenobia. She could not defend even the home territory of the Palmyrenes, notwithstanding how she had essentially surrendered so much land without a fight. Aurelian was able to take Antioch without much in the way of additional trouble, and he was able to proceed south into what is today the territory of the Syrian republic, to the city of ancient Emesa – the modern Homs.

In some ways the Battle of Emesa was a microcosm of the Palmyran mistakes against Rome. The Palmyrenes had the main body of their military with Zenobia at Emesa, an estimated seventy thousand troops. The Romans had a significantly larger army, largely because after his takeover of Antioch, Aurelian was able to tend to administrative affairs and the levying of additional troops. The Palmyrenes performed brilliantly in the early stages of the battle, even to the point of seemingly driving the Romans back in a full scale retreat. In such situations, disciplined armies are careful to maintain formation and not to become disorganized and overly eager in the pursuit of the enemy. The Palmyrenes were not so cautious in the heat of battle, no doubt under the conclusion that they had won a major victory. Their lines broke, and the Roman infantry was able to regroup and envelop the Palmyran cavalry, cutting them to pieces. Aurelian had taken the decisive step in the recovery of the Roman East, and Zenobia had followed in something of the footsteps of Cleopatra.

For it was a massive disaster for Zenobia, who apparently lost the bulk of her cavalry force in what became a massacre. Zenobia was forced to flee with the survivors to Palmyra, where she had no choice but to prepare for a siege. Her forces had tried to do too much, too fast at the Battle of Emesa, just as they had probably taken far too much too quickly in their westward advance to Egypt that had so provoked the Romans. The Gallic Empire, in contrast, had never tried to achieve such vast territorial land grabs. Cleopatra had made her gamble on the sea at Actium, and Zenobia on land in the deserts of modern Syria. Both queens would lose everything.

Zenobia was now in something of the position with which she had threatened Rome. She had seized the grain supply of Egypt and had menaced Rome with the image of starvation and food shortages. Now it was all too easy for Aurelian to cut off the queen's access to supplies as he surrounded Palmyra. What is certain from what transpired is that no help would be on the way for Zenobia. She had been a clear enemy to Persia, and there seems to have been no effort on the part of that empire to take advantage of the current crisis in any way. There are stories in the surviving evidence that the queen considered the possibility of seeking a Palmyran-Persian alliance against Aurelian's Rome, but if she ever thought that such a plan was feasible, it failed to materialize.

Ancient sieges were often protracted affairs. In the present case, it seems that Zenobia had not prepared for a lengthy stay in her city – and certainly Aurelian was willing to expend time in the effort of entrapping her. Devoid of readily available military operations, the queen seems to have decided to flee the city. It is difficult to determine exactly what to make of our evidence here. There is the romantic description of the adventure of a queen on camelback, racing off to the east in hope of perhaps finding those aforementioned Persian allies. The effort to escape is reminiscent of the report that Cleopatra considered a similar flight east, perhaps sailing away towards India even, in the wake of her defeat. What is certain is that the attempt was desperate and had only the most remote chance of success. Zenobia was captured, and Palmyra surrendered in August 272 – the city could not hold out, and with the queen in chains there was no point in continued resistance. Dromedarian flight would not save Palmyra's princess.

The Palmyran breakaway empire was finished. Zenobia's fate has been the subject of speculation; she and her son were taken to Emesa, along with her leading officers and counsellors. Most of the prisoners were killed, though likely Zenobia and her son were spared – we are told even that she ended up living in a villa in Latium, married even to a Roman senator or nobleman. There was a less than happy ending for the queen in the report that she was decapitated – but again, we cannot be certain of her end. Here too there is room for consideration of the parallel life of Cleopatra. Egypt's queen notoriously committed suicide by snakebite before she could be captured and paraded in a Roman triumph. That suicide allowed Octavian to avoid the spectacle of ordering the death of a woman, even a woman who had waged war against Rome.[17] Zenobia may well have been exhibited with her son in Rome in Aurelian's triumphal procession of 274, and then quietly killed. The story of the villa – complete with the report that the house in which she lived became a tourist attraction – may have arisen precisely because the queen's death was discreetly managed. Certainly we hear nothing more of Zenobia in the record, and histories usually record her death as occurring c. 274. To this day, arguably Aurelian's reign is most remembered for his successful handling of the Palmyran problem, with the romantic lore of the Zenobia story lending a certain glamour and memorable flair to the sometimes monotonous and tedious record of recurrent barbarian incursions and seemingly incessant eruptions of civil conflict.

There are some interesting, poorly documented episodes that are cited from after the defeat of Palmyra. We hear of a possible usurper – one Firmus – in Egypt. There were apparently some relatively minor clashes with the Persians. Palmyra seems to have rebelled a second time, requiring Aurelian to return to the city in 273 – this time to sack and destroy it. The ancient Palmyra had largely been spared in 272, and it was a common enough mistake in the annals of Roman history for an enemy of the empire to think that rebellious behaviour could ensue again after the invading army had departed. One has the sense that Aurelian lost all patience with Palmyra in 273, such that he was willing to ensure that whatever the usefulness of having a bulwark against Persia, Palmyra was too much of a bother – and so his men were allowed to do as they wished in plundering the rich capital.

The mopping up operations now over, Aurelian was not able to relax long in Rome with his triumph in the east. Rome had recaptured much territory, but the Gallic Empire remained an independent, breakaway realm. The story of what happened in the west is less dramatic than the Palmyran adventure, but it is a testament to the acumen and ability of Aurelian. When last we focused on events in the Gallic Empire, Victorinus had taken power, and the Spanish territory he controlled in theory almost immediately declared its return to Roman rule – Claudius' victory without having fired a shot. Victorinus was ultimately fated to be murdered in 271 by one of his own military officers. This was apparently one of those instances where assassination did not come because of some would-be usurper or rival for power, but because a jealous husband was upset that Victorinus had seduced his wife. Victorinus had a devoted mother, who saw to the deification of her son, and to the appointment of Gaius Pius Esuvius Tetricus as his successor – Tetricus I.

Tetricus inherited a difficult situation. The Gallic Empire always faced the same problems as its Roman parent: external and internal threats. Tetricus would be the last emperor of the Gallic breakaway region. He did name his son Tetricus II as his Caesar and possibly his co-Augustus – but his short reign was distinguished by the incursions of Germanic tribes into his territory, and by the fact that Aurelian was now ready to regain Rome's lost western lands. The clock was ticking, and Aurelian was adding success to success.

By late winter and early spring of 274, Aurelian was ready for his campaign against the weakened Tetricus. What happened is not entirely clear – the Battle of Châlons is not one of the better documented Roman military engagements. The outcome of the encounter is not, however, in dispute – Aurelian won, and the Gallic Empire died on the battlefield. Tetricus was spared, and he lived on to die of natural causes in 274. There are stories that Tetricus did not wish to fight, and that everything was in fact arranged in advance by him via negotiations with Aurelian – he would agree to desert, in effect, at the commencement of the battle, so as to betray his cause to his adversary.

In instances like this, scholars tend to wonder if the reports we have reflect the propaganda of the victor. Aurelian might have looked better if the story could be told that the Gallic emperor had been treacherous, rather than that there had been some hard-fought battle against a worthy foe. Others might argue that Aurelian's reputation would have been greater if he had not been handed the victory by some prearranged subterfuge. The truth is lost in the absence of further evidence. But Aurelian could rest secure in the fact that in the space of some four years, he had reunited the Roman Empire. He had fought against foreign enemies as diverse as the Goths and the Persians, and he had ended the challenging circumstance of Rome facing secessionist empires in both west and east.

We have noted that Aurelian was in some ways a proto-Diocletian (so too was Probus), not least in the matter of reuniting Rome. The two emperors were similar in background, and both manifested great competence in military affairs. Diocletian would face secessionist realms, and he would see them defeated (even if he had more help than Aurelian). Arguably Aurelian entered office with a more difficult task, given the existence of rebellions on both sides of the empire. It is difficult to assess how Aurelian would have managed domestic affairs, given that the bulk of his reign was occupied with the resolution of foreign crises. For Diocletian, Aurelian provided a cautionary tale of what could happen even to an extraordinarily successful man. There may have been something of a similar temperament, too, in both military men: a tendency toward severity and harsh discipline. This quality could serve an army commander very well, especially in trying circumstances. But Aurelian served as a reminder that it could also cost a ruler his life.

For an ambitious man, Aurelian also posed an irresistible challenge. He had more than earned the title of restorer of the Roman world that was accorded to him. And yet even in the wake of his great deeds, the Roman world was in chaos and at risk of renewed trouble. Those who would dare to succeed Aurelian would be faced with the challenge of exceeding his accomplishments, and of providing a more stable future – even if personal survival needed to be one's immediate priority. Diocletian's most important, formative education may have been received during the reign of the ill-fated man whose life witnessed both pinnacle and precipice. The man who had not received much in the way of formal education learned his lessons from the *exempla* of his ill-fated predecessors.[18]

Chapter 3

The Advent of Diocletian

Diocletian was in his twenties, then, when Rome was restored to an integral, vast empire. Aurelian had proven to be the most successful emperor of his age, capable of battle prowess as well as diplomatic success. We are told that Aurelian received the title *Restitutor Orbis* – 'Restorer of the World'. It was a justified honorific, one that had precedent to be sure – both Valerian and Gallienus had also been granted it. Most would agree that in the case of Aurelian, it was more than well deserved. If he had not met an untimely end, there is every reason to believe that Aurelian would have been a strong candidate for the ranks of the greatest emperors of Rome, at least in the arena of foreign affairs.

Aurelian had solved many of the crises on his problem list, and certainly had restored Rome's internal security to a large degree. The Persian menace still remained, and it seems that it was first on the emperor's mind after his settlement of the Gallic Empire question. Aurelian was in a fortunate position: Persia had suffered some troubles of its own, and was internally weakened. The emperor prepared to return east for a great campaign, but he was to die before he could cross the Hellespont to Asia.

Aurelian's death was ignominious compared to his life.[1] He was assassinated in Thrace after a strange set of unfortunate circumstances. We are told that a secretary had told a lie and was afraid of the punishment he might face from the notoriously disciplined Aurelian. And so the secretary exercised his secretarial craft and added to his sins by forging a list of men the emperor allegedly wished to have eliminated. He showed the document to the right people, and Aurelian was slain in September 275.

What happened in the wake of Aurelian's assassination was extraordinary. Aurelian had been, on the whole, a popular emperor. He was successful, and had accomplished much in a relatively brief span of years. He was not overthrown because some talented, ambitious military official wanted to challenge him for power. Indeed, he was on the verge of another campaign that might well have changed the future course of Roman history for the better – if anyone in the age was able to challenge Persia, it was Aurelian. The previous decades had seen a seemingly unending parade of disasters, and now the great emperor was dead because a secretary was afraid of being punished for mendacity. That secretary had changed the course of history with a forged list of names. Such are the vicissitudes of fate by which great men sometimes fall prey to unworthy ends.

The Roman military now, it seems, gave the senate the freedom to choose a new emperor. It was in some ways the end of the period of the Barracks Emperors, with something of a rebirth of the traditional republican system of Roman government. In one of the supreme ironies of Roman imperial history, the man chosen to serve as emperor was one Marcus Claudius Tacitus – a man who could claim (plausibly if not accurately) that he was descended from the famous second century CE Roman historian Tacitus.[2] That historian had railed against the tyranny of Tiberius, and now his namesake emperor was assuming power in an atmosphere of renewed republicanism and rebirth. Even if for nothing else, we can thank the emperor Tacitus for being responsible in some way at least for the preservation of the histories of Tacitus – the new regime saw to it that copies of the historian's work were preserved. The hour of restored senatorial liberty would be all too fleeting, but it was a moment that was laden with the memory of the impassioned prose of the historian of yore. Apparently it was the case that by the time of Aurelian, Tacitus was not widely read. His Latin can be difficult, and no doubt the sentiments expressed in his pages were not in high favour in the days of more or less autocratic emperors from the army camp.

Not surprisingly, perhaps, the story of the army's return of imperial selection prerogatives to the senate was debated even in ancient times, with some claiming that the military had actually chosen Tacitus. A conspiracy theorist might think that the whole story of the restored senatorial privilege was occasioned by the coincidence of the new emperor's name. We know almost nothing of Tacitus' early life (again, nobody could have expected that he would be famous), and we have no clear sense of his age at the time he assumed power – he was said by some to have been an older man. But it is significant that no military commander was given the job, and there may be something to be said for the tradition that the army was embarrassed by the death of Aurelian.

Tacitus is recorded as having focused on two priorities in the twin areas of domestic and foreign affairs. The credit he receives for restoring senatorial privileges and prerogatives is no surprise given his own political, non-military background. His response to external threats focused on the usual twin perils in west and east. In the east, the assassination of Aurelian had resulted in a crisis among the forces that the emperor had mustered for his planned assault on Persia. Significant numbers of mercenary auxiliary troops had been assembled from the barbarians, and now they had no job in the wake of Aurelian's death. They turned to the plunder and rapine of towns in the east, thus forcing military operations to subdue them. In the west, the Alamanni and the Franks were on the move, ready to invade Roman Gaul.

It is probable that Tacitus died of illness in Cappadocia in June or July 276, after just about half a year in power. Not surprisingly, there are reports that he may have been assassinated in a military plot. It may be argued that the brief reign of Tacitus marks a noteworthy turning point in imperial history. Something clearly happened between the immediate aftermath of Aurelian's assassination, and the death of his successor. It was either a supreme instance of bad luck – the older Tacitus perhaps worn out and felled by fever amid the rigours of campaigns – or it was a reversion to the bad history of frequent military coups and upheavals. Tacitus was succeeded immediately by his maternal half-brother Marcus Annius Florianus, who had been appointed as praetorian prefect and assigned responsibility for responding to renewed Gothic incursions into Pannonia. It seems that as soon as he received word of the death of his brother, Florian declared himself emperor, with the backing of the senate. But despite the perils posed by foreign enemies, the domestic scene was once again to be plunged into chaos.

While we are uncertain as to the circumstances of Tacitus' demise, we are all too well aware that his brother was doomed almost from the start. At the time his reign commenced, he was engaged in campaigns against the Goths that continued with impressive success. But soon enough he received word that one of Aurelian's military commanders (who had also served with distinction under Tacitus) had decided to make his own play for supreme power. Whatever embarrassment the army may have felt in the wake of Aurelian's untimely violent death had passed.

Marcus Aurelius Probus was another Balkan native, born in Sirmium sometime between 230 and 235 – in other words, something like a decade to a dozen or so years older than Diocletian. He had a distinguished early career in the army, with swift advancement and notable successes in such campaigns as the reconquest of Egypt from the Palmyran Empire. Tacitus appointed Probus as the chief military commander in the Roman East, with the obvious task of keeping a careful eye on Persian encroachment. Probus may have been earmarked by Aurelian for possible succession, but this is impossible to prove.[3]

As usual in this period, exact chronology and circumstances are wanting. Certainly Probus emerged as a credible rival to Florian. Probus was better positioned to launch an effort to seize power – in some ways he was like a new Palmyra, able to control Egyptian grain supplies and thereby affect life and morale in the west. Florian concluded that he had no choice but to advance against Probus, and he led his army into Asia Minor. We know that in September 276, after fewer than three months in power Florian was assassinated by his own men. They had been taken from the Gothic frontier into an unfamiliar and quite different climate, and there are reports that the summer heat had taken a significant toll on their fighting ability and their patience. Civil war was not the most palatable of activities in the heat of what is today central Turkey. Probus was thus able to consolidate his power and to move quickly to the cooler climate of the west to face the Gothic threat that Florian had left unresolved.

It was in a sense as if history were again repeating itself – a new reign meant that the new emperor had to respond immediately to the latest crisis. In 277 Probus won significant victories against the Goths, who sued for peace. He then proceeded to deal with the Alamanni in Gaul, as well as with the Frankish threat. Probus was able to cross the river Rhine and to engage the barbarians on their own soil. Some of those scholars who seek reasons for the decline and fall of the western empire consider the response that Probus took to the problem of depopulation after near constant warfare.[4] He organized the settlement of barbarians on Roman lands, where they were supposed to provide border defence and agricultural work in exchange for a peaceful livelihood. It was an immediate help in restoring some sense of normal life in the long-troubled regions, but it would come with its own consequences and problems.

Probus is said to have fought the Vandals, and also the Blemmyes in Egypt as he continued military campaigns in 279 and 280. There were the usual usurpers and domestic threats, even as far as in distant Britain. It was only in 281 that the exceedingly busy emperor seems to have been able to pause long enough to enjoy a Roman triumph. Persia and the east remained an unresolved problem, and eerily Probus would here follow in something of the footsteps of his equally competent recent predecessor Aurelian. In 282 he proceeded on his way to the east, proceeding first toward his hometown of Sirmium.

Here he would be assassinated in the autumn of 282, under the mysterious circumstances that accompany so many of the imperial deaths of this dark century. There was another usurper, it seems – one Marcus Numerius Carus, a praetorian commander. Some reports say that Probus sent forces to engage Carus, but that when they switched their allegiance to the usurper (another not unique incident in this age), Probus was soon slain by his own men. Others claim that Probus annoyed his soldiers by expecting them to perform menial tasks to keep them busy when they were not engaged in fighting – men who were expected to fight against barbarian foes were not usually inclined to drain marshes and to engage in manual labour when they were not in combat. Indeed, some evidence indicates that Carus was not actually a usurper, but that he was merely selected by the army to replace Probus after his men mutinied.

Carus was another of those figures who came to power with sons, in this case a convenient pair. Carinus and Numerian provided support for the neophyte emperor. Carus had been born around 222, and so he was about twenty years older than Diocletian, and a decade older than his predecessor Probus. Carus is one of the more shadowy figures in a shadowy age. Little is known for certain about his early life, let alone his brief reign. He left his son Carinus in charge of managing the west, and he proceeded with Numerian to tend to Probus' planned expedition against the Persians. For all the mystery and unanswered questions about Carus' brief reign, one thing stands out: he accomplished an impressive array of military victories against foreign foes in a strikingly brief span of time. On his way east he engaged the Quadi and the Sarmatians on the Danube, securing significant victories. He crossed over into Asia, and was able to strike hard against Persia. King Vahram (or Bahram) II was distracted by rebellions and campaigns in what is today Afghanistan, and he failed to mount a credible defence against Carus and Numerian. The Romans may have succeeded even in capturing Ctesiphon, just over twenty miles from contemporary Baghdad. This was a smashing blow against Persian might, revenge, one might say, for the humiliation of Valerian. It was the fulfilment of the dream of Aurelian and so many other Roman military men.

And then, sometime in the summer of 283, Carus seems to have been killed by a lightning bolt.

The story is laden with religious and superstitious undertones. Jupiter was the god of lightning, and there was a readily accepted version of events in which Carus was the victim of divine wrath at his advance across the River Tigris, beyond what the gods had granted by destiny, it was argued, to Roman rule. Carus was cast down as if by some rebellious giant from ancient mythology, a challenger of the gods who was silenced by a divine bolt from the blue, as it were. There is no definitive evidence to compel us to believe that the emperor was slain in some conspiracy, or by the enemy. He was, in all likelihood, dead of natural causes – he was, after all, over 60 years of age and engaged in exceptionally busy and hazardous activities for the entirety of his year in power.[5] Still, assassination cannot be ruled out. Whatever the cause, Carus' death was another of those imperial losses that had particular significance. While he had two sons, one has the impression that they were not prepared or ready to assume imperial power. The lightning bolt would be of lasting consequence.

The reign of the emperor Carus is the first in which we have certainty about the career of Diocles, the future Diocletian. In 282, Diocles was named commander of the *Protectores domestici*, a cavalry unit of the imperial household. If one thinks of a mounted emperor with his closest companions arrayed on horseback around him, that is the exact image of Diocles' elite position. The future emperor would have been in his late thirties at this point, at the youngest – perhaps he was already 40. In 283 he would receive a consulship – his first. He was involved in the expedition to Persia and would have been in the emperor's entourage when the fateful lightning bolt struck. Now he would be in the service of the successor.

Carus' son Numerian was no Alexander the Great with visions of eastern conquest. Numerian had no intention of prosecuting any further campaigns against Persia, and in fact he had no interest in maintaining Roman rule across the Tigris. It was a case of surrendering real estate that had just been won, with the hopeful wish that the Persians had been sufficiently bloodied so as to secure a lasting eastern peace. There was, to be sure, the obvious problem: Numerian was now co-emperor with his brother Carinus, who was on the other side of the Roman world in Gaul.

We know that Numerian did not leave the east in a hurried or disorganized fashion. This was no rout that demanded a hasty exit. The Romans had won enormous victories, and the Persians were in no position to strike back (at least not in the immediate). We know that by the spring of 284, Numerian was in Emesa in Syria. By the autumn he was in Asia Minor, again slowly making his way west and clearly seeing to the administration and settlement of the territories through which he crossed.

But like his father, Numerian was doomed to die in the east. The tale is strange, like that of the paternal lightning bolt. At some point there had been a report circulated by his entourage that the emperor needed to travel by curtained coach, given that he was suffering from an eye disorder that the sun was irritating. Soon enough there was a stench of decay, and the revelation of the dead body of the emperor in his carriage. Now two members of the imperial family were dead.

Needless to say, the death of Numerian was suspicious.[6] At the very least, there was likely some subterfuge afoot to keep the news of his death secret for some time. There is the usual suspicion that he was assassinated. Diocles was on the scene, now witness to a second imperial death. This time, there was no son to succeed to the purple – there was a brother in the west, Carinus.

From the evidence we have, Diocles appears in our narrative as if some mirage – though he was a trusted and certainly respected member of the imperial entourage, and certainly known to the army. He was not unique in being a military man of high rank close to the emperor whose origins and earlier career are obscure. Indeed, at the time of Numerian's death there was another such man in the imperial entourage who enters the pages of history seemingly out of nowhere, the praetorian prefect Aper. We know precious little about the man whose name is the Latin for 'wild boar.' His full name may have been Lucius Flavius Aper. We cannot even say where or when he was born. We know that he owed his high rank to Carus, and he was likely the father-in-law of Numerian. Some have speculated that he had designs on the purple and have indulged in the dramatic vision of a man responsible for the death of one and then a second emperor. Aper was certainly accused of being responsible for the death of Numerian – suspicion was unsurprisingly aroused by his attempts to conceal the death of the emperor.

This is the juncture of history where Diocles made his fateful, forceful advance. We are told that Aper was struck and killed by Diocles on the charge of having conspired to kill Numerian, the assassination coming as the climax of a momentous army assembly in the wake of the latest imperial death. Aper was put on trial at Nicomedia (the modern Izmit in Turkey), and his guilt was swiftly pronounced, the penalty the sword of Diocles.[7] Aper, apparently, was given little if any chance to acquit himself, and there was the usual suspicion afoot that Diocles may have been responsible in some way for the elimination of Numerian. 'The detail that it was Diocletian himself who cut down Aper in front of the army could not be excised from the tradition, a reminder of the martial nature of Roman society.'[8]

Can we untangle the truth of what happened in the Roman East? The death of Carus is less suspicious than that of Numerian. The sexagenarian on campaign could easily have fallen prey to natural causes, and lightning strikes – while relatively uncommon – do happen. The story of the lightning may even have been an embellishment of some storm that occurred around the time of Carus' death.

The lightning bolt tale is not as suspicious as the macabre report of the imperial carriage with its curtain concealing a decomposing body. The dead Numerian was young, and presumably in full vigour. Williams wonders if he had conjunctivitis on account of long exposure to desert conditions.[9] Ocular troubles or not, his death would naturally be more out of the ordinary than that of his father. Why, too, would Aper seek to conceal the death? Was he innocent of any involvement in what was simply a death by natural causes, and now fearful that he would be blamed? Such a suspicion would not be unwarranted. Was he worried that there would be a potential power struggle, and that his position was in jeopardy – especially if he were in some way viewed with suspicion for Numerian's untimely demise? Was he in league with Diocles to eliminate the young emperor, with a ruthless Diocles then deciding that one conspirator was better than two? Was Aper always intended as a so-called patsy who would be blamed for the death of Numerian?

While we must underscore that there can be no certainty in light of the available evidence, it seems plausible at least to consider that after the death of Carus – either by natural causes then turned into dramatic fancy about fateful bolts of divine retribution – there was considerable debate and thought in the imperial military entourage about the future.[10] There was much work to do to make an orderly move westward, and Numerian was slow and methodical – perhaps because he was not entirely certain what should be done in the wake of his father's sudden death. Somewhere along the way toward the Hellespont, Numerian's top officers decided that the young emperor needed to be replaced. This was of course always a difficult plan to countenance and to conceive – here made more complicated by the existence of Carinus in the west.

Let us imagine that Aper and Diocles were complicit in the plot to eliminate Numerian. Aper had the position of closer access to the emperor, and the family connection by marriage. Diocles would have been a likely first choice of potential partner in executing the conspiracy, if indeed Aper were interested in seeing his son-in-law dead. Regicides have typically fared poorly, with new rulers not always inclined to reward the man who made their position possible. If you are a regicide and then you assume the crown yourself, you condemn yourself to labouring always under the shadow of having committed murder for your throne.

Aper had the easier opportunity to assassinate Numerian. Diocles was in the better position to blame the whole affair on Aper, with his precipitous execution of the regicide the best chance to ensure that he would remain unstained by any charge of culpability for the assassination, with the only man who could accuse him of conspiracy conveniently and quickly dead – the assassin punished by right revenge and the exercise of justice for the dead emperor.

Aper, then, would be the imperial assassin. He would instantly be in a dangerous and delicate position. How would the death be reported? If Numerian were poisoned in a manner that resulted in any lividity or other bodily sign, decomposition was of course a gruesome way to avoid any chance of suspicion of murder. On the other hand, the premature death of the emperor was guaranteed to arouse some concern and question. Edward Gibbon famously asked the rhetorical question of whether there were no aromatics in the imperial camp to conceal the stench of decay.

We are left, then, with the problem of construing what exactly the plan of Aper and Diocles would have been in the wake of Aper's murdering of the emperor. What did the conspirators envision doing? When did Diocles break with Aper? How was the death of Numerian supposed to be announced, and why was there so long a delay?

Still another factor to be considered is that after the whole episode of Numerian's death and Aper's slaying at the hand of Diocles, there would be no effort on the part of the soon to be new emperor to come to any accommodation with Numerian's brother Carinus. Numerian could be avenged, in other words, by the blood of the accused assassin Aper – but the imperial brother was not to be honoured either as emperor or as co-emperor.

The easiest solution to the mystery is to argue that Numerian did indeed die of natural causes, and that Aper was immediately terrified because of the obvious suspicion of murder. In this scenario, Aper tries to decide what to do and attempts to keep the death a secret for as long as possible. The presence of unguents in camp aside, at some point the soldiers would have demanded to see the emperor, and no imperial demise could be kept secret indefinitely. Numerian's death would have been suspicious even if Carus had not died so soon before – now it was simply too much for most people easily to believe.

This solution also explains why Diocles did not immediately acclaim Carinus as emperor – something the men in Numerian's camp clearly did not press to see happen. On the contrary, they called for Diocles to be emperor, and the cavalry commander from Salona did not object. It was 20 November 284, and Diocles had commenced his reign at something close to the age of 40 – perhaps 42. He is said to have made a dramatic gesture with his sword, swearing before the gods of Olympus that he was not responsible for the death of his predecessor – a claim that could well be true or false, with his statement and action appropriate in either instance. There was a report that soon circulated, too, that a female mystic – a Druid – had once made a prediction of Diocles' future greatness when he was serving with the military in Gaul – at least if we can believe the *Augustan History*. She had said that he would become emperor when he had slain a boar – which of course he did in the killing of 'Aper'. Williams gives a dramatic, florid account of the drama of the day – but his purple prose is justified.[11] The onetime slave or – at best – son of a freedman was now proclaimed Augustus by the army, and there had been a practically stage-managed assassination of the man who was possibly a scapegoat more than a wild boar.[12] The man who had been born as Diocles would soon assume the name of Gaius Aurelius Valerius Diocletianus, and he would reign for over two decades.[13]

This story about the Druid and the boar from the *Historia Augusta* is one of those tales that is not taken seriously by most scholars. It does make allusion to a time when a younger Diocletian was serving in Gaul, an assignment that is also not considered to have been likely. The same author of the *Augustan History*'s Life of Carus relates that when Diocletian killed Aper, he quoted a passage from Virgil's epic *Aeneid*, where the hero made a vaunting boast about how his enemy was being slain by the hand of great Aeneas. Diocletian may have known his Virgil – quotes from the poet can be cited from graffiti at Pompeii, and he was renowned as the most celebrated of Roman verse authors – but his comment about Aeneas also reflects his association of himself with the long line of Caesars and indeed members of the Julian *gens* that traced its lineage back to Trojan Aeneas.[14] Allegedly Diocletian always made sure to slay boars at hunts after the prediction of the Druid. He is said to have commented sarcastically that he killed all the boars, and others enjoyed the meat – a reference to the power won by Aurelian and his successors. According to the author of the Augustan life of Carus, Carinus, and Numerian, Diocletian could not pass up the chance to kill a man named 'Aper' and even claimed that he did so only to fulfil the prophecy, with regret that he could not temper justice with mercy. Of all the statements about the emperor in the life, this may be the most risible.

The boar had been slain, but Diocletian had other pressing problems, such that there would be no immediate chance to enjoy his ascent to the purple. Carinus had been left in the west by his father Carus, with responsibility for handling the problems in Gaul. Our evidence seems to point to an efficient administration of affairs, especially in operations against the Quadi. At some point Carinus returned from Gaul to Rome, where the surviving sources – some would say under the influence of Diocletian's inevitable, eventual propaganda machine – paint a picture of decadence and debauchery. Carinus is said to have indulged his passions, especially for women. Reports of the luxurious living of the son apparently reached the father, who considered deposing him in favour of a distinguished military man by the name of Constantius Chlorus – someone who will soon enough come to play a significant part in our story. In some ways the story that would emerge would present an interesting balance between Diocletian and Constantius, with both men serving as military men of exceptional records in the orbits of the two sons of Carus. Both men were destined to serve as tetrarchs in the soon to be inaugurated new system of management.

We have no knowledge of what Constantius was thinking on receipt of the news about the death of Numerian. But for certain Carinus was in an exceedingly perilous position after the death of his brother. There was every indication that Diocletian had no interest in coming to any sort of accommodation with him, and that a civil war was inevitable should Carinus wish to maintain any hold on power. Carinus' military reputation – whatever it was – was apparently eclipsed by the personal detestation in which he was held by many of those close to him. Diocletian has been called the man of the hour for good reason – the dynasty that Carus had sought to inaugurate was doomed.

We have noted the significance of Diocletian's unwillingness to negotiate with Numerian's older brother. This does not necessarily point to his complicity in the death of Numerian on the part of the new emperor. The bad reputation of Carinus may have been a legitimately earned black mark on his record, one that made it easy for Diocletian to amass support in the latest efforts to simplify the chessboard. There are reports from this same period that there was trouble elsewhere in the empire from the usual problem of would-be usurpers. We hear of Carinus having to advance against one Marcus Aurelius Sabinus Julianus, who seems to have raised a revolt in Pannonia when the word arrived of the deaths of Carus and Numerian. 'Julian of Pannonia' was probably slain in battle by Carinus' forces, perhaps in northern Italy, perhaps in Illyricum – we have seen how the name 'Julian' is used confusedly of rebels in this age. Usurpers were an all too common feature of third century Roman life, but one could argue that Carinus was held in no particular esteem in the wake of his brother's death – Diocletian was not the only man willing to make a move to eliminate him. Again, the tradition that survives points to the idea that Carinus was in the habit of behaving badly with women, thus arousing the hostility of a few too many enemies in the military and the senate. Diocletian could have embellished such stories, or Carinus could have been all too guilty of the charges.

Whatever the truth of the matter in terms of the emperor's private life, what is certain is that Carinus was defeated with relative ease by Diocletian. He was killed in battle, perhaps, if not probably, by one of his officers. The place was not far from present day Belgrade in Serbia, the date sometime in July 285. The battle – known to military historians as the Battle of Margus – is one of the countless army engagements from Roman antiquity about which we know next to nothing, save the key detail – Diocletian won.

If we are looking for evidence at Margus of Diocletian's skill as a strategist or tactician, the dearth of details makes analysis and conclusion impossible.[15] The only possibly impressive detail that is recorded is that Carinus controlled an appreciably larger army than his foe, but there is also no question that many if not most of Carinus' men had no interest in fighting hard and dying for him on a hot summer day in ancient Serbia, at least not against fellow Romans. Civil wars are always difficult to prosecute from a morale point of view, and Diocletian was held in greater esteem, it would seem, than Carinus. There is every reason to accept the truth of the tradition that Carinus was slain by one of his own officers. The identity of such an assassin is unknown – we may recall that regicides tend to fare poorly, at least when their action is widely known.

In this case, one candidate for any suspicion is the consul and praetorian prefect Titus Claudius Aurelius Aristobulus. The suspicion arises from the fact that he was kept in office by Diocletian, which does not qualify in itself as evidence of his betrayal of Carinus. The story goes that Carinus had forced Aristobulus' wife into an affair, and that the consul and prefect was merely exercising his prerogative of vengeance. There are some reports that say that the Battle of Margus turned on the force of Aristobulus' killing of Carinus on the field, given that before the assassination Carinus was actually faring well against his rival.

What we find, then, is an interesting pair of mysteries involving Diocletian and the sons of Carus. The mysteries regarding what happened to the two men – clear obstacles to Diocletian assuming power – are enhanced by the additional element we have noted of the way in which

Diocletian seems to have appeared seemingly out of nowhere, catapulted suddenly to the highest rank of Roman power. Was Numerian killed by Aper, or by a conspiracy of Aper and the future emperor? Was Carinus betrayed by his prefect, angry over the harassment and assault of his wife? Was Diocletian the beneficiary of luck and fortune in both instances?

Certainly Diocletian was willing to stake his life and liberty on making an attempt at rule in the aftermath of Numerian's death. The Battle of Margus was no sham fight, especially given the size of Carinus' force relative to what Diocletian had with him. But what is clear is that Diocletian had a better reputation among the soldiery than Carinus, and that for the military, at least, he was the man of the hour. Even if Diocletian had no part whatsoever in any conspiracy against Carus or Numerian, he was certainly a usurper when it came to the rule of Carinus. In this he was aided by the great unpopularity of Carinus, such that no one seems to have been greatly troubled by his elimination.

Diocletian had made a stunning bid for power, and whatever the genesis of his advance, he had performed successfully enough to be able to proceed to consolidate his power. Like all of his recent predecessors, numerous problems at home and abroad offered a negative note to his elation at achieving his position. The most serious of the domestic concerns was Diocletian's relationship to the senate. Here he may have made his peace in part by the appointment as Roman *praefectus urbi* or 'Prefect of the City' of Lucius Caesonius Ovinius Manlius Rufinianus Bassus. Rufinianus Bassus was older than Diocletian, having been born around 227 – and he was of noble, indeed patrician rank. In short, by birth alone he was the opposite of Diocletian, and the new emperor's embrace of Rufinianus Bassus as a colleague was a deliberate mark of respect for the old senatorial order and aristocracy, for the republican tradition and Roman institutions. It was one of Diocletian's first appointments, and one of his finest in terms of quelling any immediate objections or resentment occasioned by his takeover.

It may be a testament to the efficiency and durability of Diocletian's propaganda that so many intractable mysteries surround his accession. Margus may have been one of the most significant Roman civil war battles for which we know next to nothing, either with respect to details about the progress of the battle – or battles, if Diocletian and Carinus clashed more than once – or how Diocletian won. David Potter comments, 'Any further speculation about his earlier career and deeds would be pointless. It is the man who emerges in the next few years who matters.'[16] These sentiments would be appreciated, no doubt, by the new emperor himself. His military *virtus* and record had secured for him the support of the army, which respected their new commander above all for being one of them.[17]

One thing seems clear: there would be no hunting down of those who were associated closely with Carinus. No reign of terror seems to have followed Diocletian's victory. The new emperor was willing to begin with a clean slate.[18] The army was firmly behind Diocletian, and at this point in Roman history nothing mattered more.[19] The lack of proscriptions or reprisals may be taken to be circumstantial evidence for how in the end the army was not willing to die for Carinus and might have been willing even to kill him to secure peace under Diocletian.

There is some debate as to what Diocletian did immediately in the aftermath of the Battle of Margus. It is possible that he tended at once to campaigns against the Quadi and the Marcomanni. At some point he entered Italy, at least northern Italy – but Rome does not seem to have been an early destination of concern of the emperor. The avoidance of Rome could be attributed in part to the desire to deal expeditiously with the many problems confronting the empire – or, perhaps, Rome was not so important anymore. Some have raised the idea that Diocletian – for all his deference to the senate – may have intended to send a message to the senators that the capital was not, after all, the only focal point in the world. It seems more likely that there was simply too much to do in a short time, and that Diocletian was already well aware that one of the problems faced by the empire was to have multiple centres of power – not that Rome was no longer the most important of those centres, but that there were serious crises on numerous fronts. There was little reason to go to Rome right now, given that the senate had acquiesced to his accession.

We shall return to this point in our story. In some ways Diocletian's relationship with Rome became one of the sources of weakness for his system. He was correct in his assessment that in terms of frontier management, Rome was of next to no importance. There was logic in the idea that a huge realm needed to have ready centres of power in the different regions of the empire, especially close to problem points. For a man of military background and mindset, this attitude of ambivalence toward Rome was not so much some philosophical opposition to the traditions of republican government, as a manifestation of practicality. This is not to say that Diocletian was not anti-republican – the charge levelled against him by Aurelius Victor, for example, is likely to be a legitimate one. Rather, it is to argue that for Diocletian the immediate reality confronting Rome paradoxically had little room for concern about Rome. Cities like Mediolanum were more important. The unintended consequence of this analysis was that Rome herself would become a centre of disaffection, of a feeling of being ignored despite being the ancient capital of the empire and the most important of its cities in its own estimation – a verdict not shared by the emperor. And we do well to remember that Diocletian would manage to visit Rome but once in his career – albeit for a major anniversary. The neglect was studied and deliberate, whatever the rationale.

Diocletian was not worried overmuch about Rome and the senate, but he seems to have realized that he was sitting on something of a time bomb. Even exceptionally competent emperors from his lifetime like Aurelian and Probus had died violently. To become emperor in this age was to invite assassination and to court conspiracy. Even if Diocletian had not been involved in any such chicanery of his own to attain power, he knew that he was in a precarious position in which time was not on his side. He had absorbed lessons in the formative and middle years of his life, and now whatever he had learned would be put into practice as he commenced his reign.

This seems to be the most compelling reason for his swift decision to find an imperial colleague. Another justification for the decision was the sprawling nature of the empire. There was precedent, as we have seen, for having a colleague. Diocletian was in an interesting position in that he had no sons. This precluded the establishment of some instant dynasty – but then again, Carus had failed in his dynastic scheme with his sons Numerian and Carinus, and the hour may not have seemed opportune for another such familial power arrangement. Diocletian was able to turn to the 'other' old method of finding colleagues to aid in rule – the selection of the best man for the job. Diocletian would turn monarchy into dyarchy, and soon into tetrarchy. But first he needed a partner in his labours, a man who would come from a similar background of practicality and military experience.

Chapter 4

The Tetrarchy Takes Shape

The man destined to be the emperor Maximian was born around 250, and was thus just a few years younger than Diocletian – but even a few years allowed Diocletian to argue that he was the senior partner in view of age. Sirmium once again was the home of an emperor – this would be a 'Yugoslav' partnership, to give an anachronistic appellation to the arrangement.[1] Maximian seems to have had a career almost identical to Diocletian's. He was another veteran soldier, raised with the virtues and values of the Roman army in almost the same part of the world. The two men likely had known each for some time, at least during the recent troubles. They would have diverse fates.

Here we may pause to digress over how, for example, we know information like Maximian's birthplace. We know he built a palace near Sirmium, and we know that his parents were said to have been offering hireling labour there. Scholars therefore make the deduction that Maximian hailed from there. At some point he met Diocletian – an introduction and meeting about which we know next to nothing.

Certainly the two men were able to cooperate and had amicable relations as the fateful events of 284 unfolded. There are those who think that Maximian was always aware of the Diocletian plan to take power and to share it with him in some way. There has also been speculative analysis that Diocletian had in mind something like the arrangement between Augustus and Marcus Vipsanius Agrippa, his most trusted associate in military and government matters (with Maximian eventually being more of an equal to Diocletian than Agrippa ever was to Augustus).[2] Diocletian, so this theory would argue, was the organizational genius, while Maximian was the superlative general.[3] Some evidence for the soundness of this theory comes from Margus, where Diocletian seems to have had appreciable difficulty in securing a victory. But Maximian would have his share of significant problems in the field as well.

There is some controversy as to the exact nature of the initial relationship between Diocletian and Maximian, and to its unfolding over the next year or so, as the two men responded to various military crises. When was Maximian an Augustus with Diocletian? When was he the *filius Augusti* or 'son of Augustus'? When was he a Caesar?[4] Even by virtue of the fact that Diocletian was the one who chose Maximian and not vice versa, there was a clear hierarchy at play here, with Diocletian as the senior partner, even if only a little more senior, as we might say.[5] The elevation of Maximian took place in Mediolanum and not Rome – another detail that has been interpreted by some as evidence of the fact that Rome was not, after all, any longer the centre of the empire. The date was probably July 285 (perhaps the twenty-first) – and as so often in recent history, there was little time to celebrate, and much work to be done for the colleagues in empire. It was about eight or so months since the acclamation of Diocletian at Nicomedia. Much had already been accomplished, but the list of problems and crises was extensive. There is some evidence that the proclamation of Maximian as a fellow Augustus with Diocletian came as early as the Kalends of April 286.[6] Doublets in government had existed since the days of the foundation of the Roman Republic and the plan for two consuls; Diocletian had been the one to invite Maximian to share power and not vice versa, and so even if both men were Augustuses, Diocletian would always retain a certain higher authority, even if not by force of law.

What problems faced the empire of 285 that required a military response? It is in this period that we begin to hear of a threat that would recur until the collapse of the western empire – the so-called 'Bagaudae' or 'bagaudae.' The etymology of the name is not certainly known; it has been linked to a Gaulish word for fighter or brigand. Who they were is also a matter of some speculation. They may have been mere peasants, frustrated and economically depressed raiders who took advantage of what relaxation in security there was to launch raids on property and goods. They may have represented a more stable and organized group, an entity seeking nothing less than an independent polity. Certainly whoever they were and whatever they were seeking to achieve, Diocletian concluded that it required an emperor to see to their suppression – and this does indicate a problem of some severity, and likely one that was about more than mere policing duties.

On the other hand, the Bagaudae seem to have had something of a ragtag quality to them, with poor equipment and regular problems with supply maintenance. One gets the impression that they may have become adept at guerrilla warfare, proving to be an increasingly annoying irritant in an area that was already bordered by numerous hostile German tribes. The Bagaudae, in any case, were the first item on the imperial docket. It is noteworthy that by the end of 285, there would also be barbarian incursions across the Rhine into Gaul – the Burgundians in one force, the Chaibones and Heruli in another. Did they take advantage of depredations in Gaul at the hands of the increasingly infamous Bagaudae? Were they hoping to catch Roman armies by surprise, distracted as they might be with the pursuit of the latest foe? Whatever the exact motivations, the barbarians would strike in force, turning 285 into a year of yet more war and upheaval in Gaul.

One of the military units that Maximian is said to have recruited for his campaigns against rebels in Gaul would become famous in the history of Christianity. On 22 September, Christians to the present day celebrate the feast of Saint Mauritius (Maurice) and his companions, martyrs of the Theban Legion. In Christian lore, they were a Roman legion stationed in Egypt, which converted to Christianity. Recruited to assist in the Gallic campaigns, the legion suffered decimation at Acaunum – the modern Saint-Maurice in Switzerland. The cause of the dire sentence was that the Christian legionaries refused to engage in sacrifices to the emperor. After the decimation failed to convince the remaining soldiers to betray their Christian faith, the sentence of decimation was pronounced again and a third time, before finally the entire legion was slaughtered.

This account will not be found in any extant pagan sources. It dates to about the middle of the fifth century, and in the course of time there were other versions – including one in which the episode occurred at present day Cologne and not Saint-Maurice. Needless to say, the historicity of the story has been questioned. In the calendar reforms in the Roman liturgy after the Second Vatican Council, the feast of the Theban martyrs was relegated to local calendars – but the existence of the martyrs was not questioned. Certainly the tradition of the saints of the Theban Legion spread far and wide at a relatively early date, and was of great popularity throughout the Christian world. One of the most common of the objections to the story is disbelief that Maximian would order the massacre of an entire legion, especially at such a difficult moment for manpower. That said, there is also a tendency in some scholarship to downplay the persecution of Christians during various periods of Roman imperial history, with the argument that most of our evidence for the persecution comes from prejudiced and biased sources – early Christian tracts and treatises. We have mentioned Arnobius. He speaks only in general terms of religious persecution, with no details about individual martyrs or episodes such as that of Mauritius and his fellow legionaries.

The years 285–6 saw other western problems, one of which would become exceptionally serious. Already for some years now there had been another challenge from the barbarians: they were increasingly competent at engaging in coastal piracy. Maximian fatefully assigned one Mausaeus Carausius to the task of overseeing naval operations in what today we call the English Channel, with an eye to suppressing the pirate problem. He would become nothing less than 'Lord of Britain'.[7] The once highly vaunted *classis Britannica* or Britannic fleet had encountered significant challenges in responding to the pirate threat. The late twentieth century provided a reminder off the Horn of Africa that piracy can be difficult to combat even for highly competent and supplied navies – pirates can often strike hard and fast, with improvisation, and they can prove to be a bane even for the most sophisticated navies. Carausius learned something from his pirate foes – he would become known for his own lightning-fast response to threats.

Carausius was a foreigner, a Menapian from Gallia Belgica. Essentially, what Carausius did to arouse imperial displeasure and a death sentence was to profit a bit too much from his anti-piracy commission. He was in the habit, Maximian soon learned, of allowing the pirates to engage in significant plundering and looting before he would intercept and destroy them. Then, he would keep most of the wealth if not all for himself – thus benefiting significantly and illegally from his military commission.

Maximian and Diocletian were army men noted for their discipline and sense of order. Carausius was doing something that was absolutely *verboten* in the world of Roman military practice, and it is no surprise that Maximian ordered him to be arrested, with a clear intention of executing him. Carausius for his part took advantage of his naval abilities by proceeding to sail for Britain, where he became something far more significant and ambitious than a mere profiteering pirate hunter – he decided that there was every good reason why he should try to seek to survive by establishing his own breakaway empire in Roman Britain.

Often it can be useful in the study of third century Roman history to step back and to ponder the seemingly incredible happenings of the age. How many usurpers were there, and how many secessionist movements? How many military engagements and barbarian incursions? What was the death toll or the count of the wounded among the army and the civilian population? What were economic conditions like in the face of such regular upheaval and devastation? On a purely psychological level, what motivated anyone to want to risk seizing power?

Carausius was simply the latest in a long line of daring adventurers, one who decided that he had nothing to lose and everything to gain by his British gambit. He factored that he had several advantages. For one, he was in possession of a navy thanks to his commission to confront the pirates, and Maximian and Diocletian did not. Carausius' imperial pursuers had no way to transport forces to Britain to deal with the newest usurper. Further, Carausius had support and friends in Britain, enough so that any loyalists to Maximian and Diocletian would easily be eliminated. Britain had military forces, and in addition to the island base, Carausius had the backing of Gesoriacum on the continent – the modern Boulogne-sur-mer. Gesoriacum was the location of a Roman naval base, and had been Carausius' home of operation. Gesoriacum had military forces, and at least some of them were willing to side with the former commander of the Roman naval fleet.

Perhaps most importantly, Carausius had money – his profit from plundering had been significant. He was able to pay his own men handsomely, and to convince – not to say bribe – other men to join his cause. No doubt Carausius also benefited from the relative novelty of the new Roman regime. There may have been loyalty to Maximian and Diocletian in principle, as the newly recognized imperial authority – but Carausius had far greater local connections, and the advantage of a strong and wealthy position. Indeed in the Carausian revolt we see one of the clearest manifestations of the power of the island that would later be called Fortress Britain. Britain was in a distant corner of the empire – it was no Mediterranean base that could relatively easily be assaulted from all directions. It was a place where Carausius could expect only to become stronger as time passed.

It was something reminiscent of the Gallic Empire, except with the advantage of strong position. Some have questioned how seemingly easily Carausius was able to persuade legions to swear loyalty to him, given that we have no definitive evidence that he ever had involvement in land-based combat. There has been some speculation that in fact he must have participated in some campaigns, either in Britain or in Gaul – but there is no certain evidence of this. Money may have mattered more than military prowess or experience. Britain had silver mines, and so not only was Carausius able to mint coins, but he was able to produce higher quality and more valuable coins than Diocletian and Maximian – a major economic factor to explain how he was so successful for so long.[8]

Indeed, Carausius was destined to maintain his hold on power for the next seven years, thus proving to be one of the more resilient would-be claimants to at least some imperial authority. Thus from 286 to 293, the spectre of civil war and secessionist threats would remain for Rome. Maximian had achieved a position of high power, indeed what some would call virtual parity with Diocletian – but he had what must have seemed to be an insurmountable host of problems to manage in Gaul, Britain, and along the Rhine.

One of the few advantages that comes from having your enemy firmly ensconced on some island redoubt is that you can in some way ignore them. Those who choose to launch a defensive war may at some point pose an offensive threat, but with careful enough vigilance they may also safely be neglected for the moment. Maximian did just this, if only in view of necessity. The situation on the Rhine remained as unstable as usual, and if anything, the whole region was a potential, if not actual, hotbed of support for Carausius.

The western campaigns that Maximian waged in 286 and 287 are not well documented. Were we to lack the tenth panegyric to which we shall soon turn, we would know even less. The Burgundians, and Chaibones, and the Heruli do not seem to have had particularly good years, however. Maximian became another Roman conqueror who could boast that he had crossed the Rhine and cleared the opposite shore of barbarians. Maximian seems to have practised the art of scorched earth tactics, depriving the enemy of land and sustenance so as to drive him out. Diocletian would later follow his example when he joined his colleague in combined operations. Migration and the settlement of barbarians in border areas was a pressing topic of Roman social and military history in the age, and depriving the enemy of land was a strategy that was a double-edged sword.

The task along the German border never seemed to be finished, and there were always fresh reinforcements of barbarian forces to renew incursions and threats more or less serious. But Maximian and Diocletian were destined to be among the more successful and stabilizing of Roman commanders in this arena. For the moment, the focus would be on land combat, with the idea of preparing a naval force to assault Britain and to end the Carausius threat the secondary concern for the dual emperors.

Maximian seems to have spent most of 286–287 on his own, a reunion with Diocletian probably coming at some point early in 288. The two men were prepared to coordinate military attacks along Rome's northern border, with significant attention also to the restoration, renewal, and rehabilitative expansion of Roman infrastructure in the area. Various points in what today are the nations of Germany, France, Belgium, and the Netherlands were joined by an impressive network of roads and forts designed for military use.

At some point perhaps around 287, Diocletian and his colleague adopted interesting mythological titles. Diocletian would be known as *Iovius*, and Maximian as *Herculius* – that is, as the Jovian and Herculian ones.[9] For all we know it may have started as an affectionate bit of humour: Jupiter, or Jove, was the supreme god, and Hercules was his famous son, noteworthy for his great labours and conquests of disorder.

As often in Roman imperial history, we cannot be certain what vision Diocletian and his partner had for the borders and question of expansion of the empire. Was the Rhine to be the frontier, as others before them had decided? Certainly the Rhine was now to be fortified, adding a network of military defences to the natural protection afforded by the river. The year 288 was an exceptionally busy one both in terms of fighting and building, as well as in the question of the settlement of pacified barbarians in border regions – the omnipresent issue being the problem of sufficient manpower for the army that provided for the empire's very existence.

At this juncture we may make mention of a fortuitous consequence of the extended warfare and imperial attention to Gaul. The region was a leading area of the study and art of rhetoric, and one of the sources for the reigns of Diocletian and Maximian that we possess are the so-called *panegyrici* or 'panegyrics' that survive in celebration and honour of their achievements.[10]

The tradition of writing such encomia and laudatory speeches was an old one. We have such a speech of Pliny the Younger for the emperor Trajan that dates to January 100 CE – the first of what are known today as the 'Twelve Latin Panegyrics', an interesting and valuable corpus that can (with caution) be used to reconstruct some of the history of otherwise poorly attested reigns.[11]

The tenth panegyric in the collection dates to 289 and was delivered at Augusta Treverorum in celebration of Rome's birthday that April. The author is said to be one Mamertinus.[12] It was delivered in honour of Maximian, and thus looks both to past and future to celebrate his glory. The eleventh speech is also from Augusta Treverorum, and was written perhaps, if not probably, for the occasion of the emperor's birthday in 291, thus affording the chance for ready comparison between the two addresses (the eleventh panegyric is also said to be the work of Mamertinus). Notably, the speech of 289 anticipates an expedition against Carausius, while that of 291 discreetly makes no mention of what seems to have been a failed effort.

The tenth panegyric opens unsurprisingly with fulsome references to Hercules, the god with whom Maximian was associated. One problem posed by panegyrics is that they assume that their audiences know information that is lost or obscure to us, and so they can speak often of how the author will not delve into detail on some topic he cites only *en passant*. Exaggeration adds to the difficulties of extricating historical information. And so Maximian is credited with having traversed the Danube and the Euphrates borders, along with the Rhine and Atlantic frontiers. Indeed his origins are said to have been divine – a common conceit in this sort of literature – and that his remote origins in war-torn locales meant that his infant cries were concealed by the sound of clashing weapons. The panegyrist notes that this was part of the mythology surrounding Jupiter, who was hidden from his cannibalistic father Saturn on Crete, with noise from weapons employed to hide his wailing. In Maximian's case, mythology was history.

More specificity comes with the references to the campaigns against the Bagaudae and other marauders. The author apologizes for the note about the Bagaudae, commenting on how the victory deserves to be obscured rather than to be glorified, since it was over a people who were not really soldiers or formidable foes, but rather peasants who were mimicking fighters. More serious were the struggles against the Burgundians and the Alamanni, the Chaibones and the Heruli, campaigns waged in 285 and/ or 286. Commentaries and other secondary works of scholarship dispute some questions of chronology in this and other matters precisely because panegyrics are not given to providing orderly calendrical information – only sometimes do references such as to this or that consulship provide solid data for constructing a specific timeline. Williams accepts the date of 'late 285 or early 286' for the campaigns against the Heruli, with operations over the Rhine in 287; and a treaty with the Frankish monarch Gennobaudes in 288.[13]

What do we learn from a panegyric about tactics and strategy in military campaigns? Regarding the Chaibones and the Heruli, we hear that they were defeated in open warfare and at one blow – two pieces of information that reveal nothing of the battle or battles, or of the course thereof. Maximian was said to have used a few cohorts and not his entire army for the campaigns, so that his own courage might be highlighted. Panegyrics are always quick to praise their subject, and less likely to give even a number for the cohorts employed. Maximian is credited with dominating the battlefield by personal intervention, as if he were a river flowing over a plain – hyperbole again at the expense of detail. Lastly, the slaughter of the Chaibones and Heruli was so great, we are told, that the word of the victory came to the enemy not from survivors, but from the renown of Maximian's achievement – a final bit of boast to crown a typical description of imperial success.

The panegyrist mentions victories in Gaul, with not even a specific name of an enemy to cite in Maximian's credit. Maximian was soon crossing the Rhine – in other words, fighting not against invaders, but in enemy territory. Hercules is credited with the crossing of the Rhine that shelters the Germans, just as Jupiter (i.e. Diocletian) is praised for his own work before the Persian Euphrates.

Diocletian's own campaigns in Germany are mentioned next, localized to the area opposite Raetia. The author highlights how the two emperors were now able to meet (in 288) and to share stories of their mutual victories, their clasped hands underscoring the commonality of their fraternal endeavours. The two men are compared to the Heracleidae, the mythical sons of Hercules – complete harmony and shared vision is the watchword. And of course, Maximian and Diocletian are praised as surpassing their mythological comparands, for that is what panegyrics are wont to do. They ruled one undivided empire – indeed the emphasis was on the indivisibility of the Roman patrimony.[14]

Maximian is compared too to Alexander the Great for the restoration of kingdoms to client monarchs – we have mentioned Gennobaudes, who was probably a Frankish king. We learn about how impressed Gennobaudes was with the merciful and clement, generous and impressive Roman emperor – but details about the episode are elusive, for all the purple prose of panegyric. Again, it was probably late 288, if we wanted to try to deduce a date from the evidence.

Carausius is alluded to periphrastically – he is simply 'that pirate' – Latin literature of the empire enjoys depriving enemies of Rome of their names (Cleopatra suffers the same ignominious fate in Augustan Age writings). Maximian oversaw the construction of a channel fleet, though on the relative safety of rivers – a detail that has been taken to mean that Carausius controlled the English Channel. Weather could also have been a consideration; again we are left to speculate in the absence of detail.

The eleventh panegyric, as we have noted, is a *genethliacus* or birthday address. We mentioned the common panegyric rhetorical artifice of allusion. The *genethliacus* too is full of the customary tantalizing references to campaigns and political/military achievements, often cast in the frustrating language of a *praeteritio* – literally a 'passing over' whereby the author says that he will not talk about, for example, the expansion of the border region of Raetia that was accomplished by the sudden defeat of the enemy. This technique is a classic trick of rhetorical art, but it can stymie efforts to secure historical information for those sifting through the text.

Once again there is emphasis on the typology of Diocletian as Jupiter and Maximian as Hercules, with no embarrassment about mentioning the rebellion of the Titans with reference to the former, and the storied labours of the latter hero. Campaigns of Diocletian in Syria and then Pannonia are vaguely referenced, followed by mention of Maximian at the summit of Hercules Monoeceus. This seemingly strange, specific identification is deliberate: Hercules was connected to the legends of the founding of what is today the Principality of Monaco. Maximian was thought to have been occupied in the west, and Diocletian in the east; for the panegyrist, suddenly they were reunited in Italy to the surprise of all. Emphasis throughout is on restless devotion to the duty of defending the borders of the empire.

The *praeteritio* of the eleventh panegyric takes one through the early history of Diocletian's reign. Rome is said to have been liberated from despotism – a reference to Carinus, the seemingly deeply unpopular predecessor. Provinces were restored to obedience, with a clear note that their rebellion had been the fault of Carinus. Besides German victories and the aforementioned sudden slaughter of the enemy in Raetia, we learn that there were victories in Sarmatia against the noted fierce cavalry experts and against the Saracens.[15] The Franks came with their king to make obeisance – a detail connected by scholars to the report about the Roman client ruler Gennobaudes from the tenth panegyric. Vahram II in Persia is credited with the same eagerness for peace. Rivers dominate the geographical account of dyarchic victory: the Rhine, the Danube, the Nile, the Tigris and the Euphrates, not to mention the mighty River Ocean of ancient geographical conception – all of these bodies of water are said to have been as common to Maximian and Diocletian as if they were daylight striking the eyes. Victories in Syria; Raetia; over the Chaibones and the Heruli; across the Rhine and against pirates (i.e. Carausius) and the Franks have glorified the early years of the new regime.

Panegyrics by their very nature cast their subjects in the best possible light. This is the principal reason for the special care that must be taken in interpreting them. They are precious historical sources, but of problematic value. Incidental historical and biographical information can be obtained: Maximian's service on the Danube as well as the Euphrates early in his career, for example – the latter detail allowing us to conclude that he participated in the operations against Zenobia's Palmyran Empire. But panegyrics are less helpful in providing chronologies and details of campaigns, such as for the complicated events of 286–288. The tenth panegyric is one of our most important sources of information for the early years of the tetrarchy, especially for what was happening in the border regions of Gaul and Germany. For as frustrating as it can be to work through the bombastic language and the swift sketching of events, we would be significantly more ignorant of the period without this text. The 'birthday' panegyric is far less important for historians, given that it focuses more on the character of Maximian than on his deeds. Even leaving aside the question of how panegyrics necessarily indulge in lavish praise of their subjects, some scholars have tried to see if these two texts provide any indication of what was actually happening in the relationship between Maximian and Diocletian at the outset of the tetrarchy. In other words, is the fulsome praise and florid laudatory language merely the consequence of the genre, or is the author trying to obfuscate with respect to all too real tensions between the Augustuses?

Sometimes in the absence of extensive sources (especially of narrative histories and biographies), there is a tendency to read too much into the sources that we have. Such is the temptation when approaching these two panegyrics. Any theories or conclusions about amity or lack thereof between Maximian and Diocletian must remain speculative (even highly so). The eleventh panegyric is a text that devotes considerable attention simply to the account of the emperors convening at Mediolanum, with their advent to the city recalling the impressive feats of Rome's inveterate Carthaginian enemy Hannibal in surmounting the Alps – not because of any hint that Maximian and Diocletian were invaders, but on account of the exaggerated difficulties of their journey.

In an interesting twist on the genre, Maximian's birthday panegyric makes mention of civil wars among the barbarians, noting that they imitate Maximian's victories over them in their own struggles among themselves. In Sarmatia, Raetia, and across the Rhine, Maximian is honoured, so to speak, by this sanguinary emulation. Civil war was always one of the characteristic evils of Rome, a curse and bane that Roman authors complained about as the seeming lot of destiny for the city and empire. Now, the panegyrist observes, Maximian has done a great thing precisely because he has transferred civil war from Rome to her enemies – again, with emphasis on the fruits of unity and fraternity from the new regime's Jovian-Herculean protective arrangement.

The extended reference to these barbarian civil wars contains fascinating citation of the Tervingi, the Taifali, and the Gepids. The Tervingi are identified as a group of Goths, who with the help of the Taifali joined battle with the Vandals and the Gepids. While details are nowhere to be found, the names of the peoples are cited nowhere else earlier in surviving sources. Further, on the other side of the Roman world the Blemmyes do battle against the Ethiopians, though they are said to have used only light arrows – a note about weaponry, even in the absence of other clarifying information. All that matters to the author is that, thanks to Maximian, the army of the enemy is designed for civil war and not for attacking Roman interests.

A third member of what would come to be the first tetrarchy may now be introduced. We have mentioned already in passing Constantius Chlorus, who at one point had been considered for high appointment by Carinus. Constantius was born around 250, another Illyrian. He was another military man, who had risen to high rank during the reign of Carus – he was appointed governor of Dalmatia. Constantius was thus in a position to make his fateful choice once Diocletian had cast his die for war against Carinus. By 288, Constantius would be serving under Maximian as a praetorian prefect, with increasingly significant responsibilities in the western theatre. Such were the tasks that brought a man to the notice of higher officials, especially in times of transition.

We should note from the start that 'Chlorus' as a nickname for Constantius does not occur before the sixth century. He was Marcus Flavius Constantius, known to later history as Constantius I.[16] We may note too that Constantius may well have been appointed to join the tetrarchy ahead of his Caesarian colleague Galerius (whom we shall turn to below), such that although Galerius was Caesar to the senior Augustus, Maximian's Caesar, Constantius, technically outranked him. The evidence for this disputed point comes from such information as how Constantius' name is always listed before Galerius' in official citations – but it is one of the many areas of scholarly debate for this period.[17]

Constantius is best known today as the father of the man who would be known to history as Constantine the Great. Constantine was the son of Constantius' union with one Helena, a woman who would be better known to history as Saint Helen. We have no idea how they met, or even what the exact legal status of their union was. We do know that at some point after the assumption of his duties for Maximian, Constantius would repudiate her and marry Theodora, the daughter of the emperor. It was a significant alignment of the interests of the two men, and a clear mark of favour for the successful prefect – a man who would prove himself by assisting Maximian with operations on shores of both the Rhine and Danube, in particular against the Alamanni.

Helena is one of the more extraordinary women of antiquity. She began life perhaps as what we would label the common law wife of Constantius; she may have been a mere concubine. She ended her life famous in early Christian lore as the mother of the first Christian emperor, a woman who would travel to Judaea to recover the relics of the 'True Cross' on which Christ had been crucified, one of the most precious relics of her faith. We do not know for certain where Helena was born; the tradition which developed that she was actually a British princess has no basis in historical fact, but became an enduringly popular legend. We have no idea what Helena's life was like in the wake of Constantius' divorce of her in favour of a dynastic connection to Maximian; it was a low point in her fortunes that would be dramatically reversed in the subsequent career of her son. She is venerated highly by Catholics and the Orthodox church as a Christian saint, a woman responsible for much of what would become the toleration and eventual legalization of Christianity, the religion that would be embraced by her son.

Maximian's promotion of Constantius to his second-in-command paved the way for his ultimate advancement to be Caesar to Maximian's Augustus. It was a natural progression from having a dyarchy to having a tetrarchy: if an emperor could choose a colleague who could aspire to be an equal, then it made sense for each of those colleagues to be able to take on an underling, a junior colleague who would one day replace his benefactor. It allowed for a network of alliances that was designed, ultimately, to lessen the chance for the eruption of that familiar spectre from Roman history: civil war. Tetrarchies were in some ways sounder than triumvirates – there was always the risk of two turning against one by the simple process of outvoting and exclusion. One thinks of how easily Lepidus was dispensed with in his 'second triumvirate' arrangement with Octavian and Antony. Indeed there were inherent risks to any shared power system, but Diocletian's tetrarchy worked well at least during the years of his active participation in satisfying men ambitious for higher office.

Civil war had been deeply engrained in the Roman psyche: Romulus according to some traditions had slain his brother Remus. Fratricide was a defining quality of Rome, an ever-present fear that had manifested itself in countless internecine struggles throughout the history of both the Republic and the empire. The arrangements of Diocletian and Maximian were meant both to safeguard the emperor so that there would not be one target, as it were, for ambitious rivals – and to provide for sufficient outlets for ambition such that powerful men could find both significant positions and hope for ultimate advancement.

The system, we shall see, would not work – even if in theory it was at least as good if not better than any previous arrangement that had been tried. At various moments in Roman history, the threat of foreign attack had been sufficient to quell any civil disturbance. Conversely, there were times when one is left to wonder how capable and intelligent men could have engaged in hazardous and ongoing domestic squabbles in the face of significant peril from external enemies.

Constantius would prove to be instrumental in helping to prepare for the eventual defeat of Carausius. He would advance against the Franks even to the shores of the North Sea, cutting off support for Britain from her continental allies. Rome was able to re-establish the deposed king Gennobaudes, who was to serve as a client of Rome, responsible for securing the Franks as allies of Rome. Such buffer arrangements had a long history in Roman military and political practice, and in the present instance Constantius' advance was a means of choking off external support for Carausius' breakaway empire.

What was not being ignored in all of this was the east. The fact that both emperors eventually became engaged in joint military affairs in the west is a testament to the severity of the current crises there, and also likely to the fact that there may have been an element of distrust, as we have noted, between Diocletian and Maximian. While they knew each other and enjoyed mutual confidence and respect, their arrangement was being tested in the crucible of war. We do well not to speculate overmuch about tension between the two men – but later events would prove Maximian to be capable of daring, reckless and self-centred behaviour. Further, there seems to have been a conscious effort throughout the Diocletianic era to maintain in theory and practice the idea that there was one united empire. Even if there would be spheres of operation and multiple imperial courts located in strategic capitals, there was always careful preservation of the idea that these men cooperated in the rule of a single empire – even if reality on the ground required the emperors to tend to diverse problems.

Indeed, even early on in the dyarchy there was a clear intention for Maximian to manage western problems, and Diocletian eastern. We have observed that after he was declared Diocletian's colleague, Maximian proceeded at once to deal with the Bagaudae in Gaul, only to become embroiled in the complex and extensive troubles in the west. Diocletian proceeded east in 285, becoming involved in military operations against the Sarmatians before arriving in Nicomedia in Asia Minor for the winter of 285–286. Persia was of course the principal problem in the region, and a new regime brought with it the possibility that an inveterate enemy would test its new neighbour. We are not in possession of much information as to the state of the Persian Empire at this juncture, but we do know that there was little appetite for renewed warfare. Indeed Diocletian enjoyed something of a warming period in relations: King Vahram II sent presents and gifts to his neighbour, with an invitation for Diocletian to visit Persia. It was a stunning improvement in ties between Rome and Persia since the low point reached not so far in the past when Valerian was taken captive.

The likely explanation for the friendliness (at least on the surface) of Persia and Rome probably lies in exhaustion. Neither side was prepared or eager for a renewal of military operations. Rome was not alone in having troubles internal and external; the east had been riven by conflict and devastating strife for years. The breathing period that we learn of in 285–287 is no surprise.

The friendliness, too, was not limited to words, presents, and generous invitations. One of the constant sources of tension between Rome and Persia was the status of the kingdom of Armenia, which served as a de facto buffer zone between the two sprawling empires. Both Rome and Persia considered Armenia to be within their sphere of influence, and Armenia had been the powder keg for many an explosion of violence between the realms. Persia at this juncture appears officially to have given up any claims on Armenia, and in consequence Roman propaganda was able to make a reasonable boast that Diocletian was the bringer of peace to the east. One reason why Diocletian was able to journey west to help Maximian in the west was that the problems with Persia had been resolved by a combination of diplomacy and luck. A lesser man might have decided to relax and to remain in luxury in his eastern realm, content to enjoy his victories. Diocletian was concerned about the unity of the empire and the success of Maximian. He would have been well aware that a collapse of his colleague's position would have spelled eventual disaster for his own status.

There is considerable speculation and scholarly debate about the shifting elements of the relationship between the imperial colleagues. We have seen how at the start there was a clear balancing act between Diocletian being the senior partner and Maximian also being given such an extraordinary amount of independence that even ab initio he was a de facto co-emperor. We have seen that there is confusion about his exact honorific title at various points in the early history of the arrangement – Caesar, Son of Augustus, Augustus. Eventually there would be no doubt or confusion (deliberate or otherwise) – Maximian would be a full colleague and Augustus with Diocletian. Likely that was always the intention, even if the training period, as it were, was cut short by realities in the west. Diocletian may have been worried that his colleague would make some sort of accommodation with Carausius, thus posing the spectre of a west united against Diocletian's east.

As often it is impossible to be certain, but a likely scenario would be this. Diocletian was well aware that he needed a comrade in rule. Maximian would need to prove himself, just as would Diocletian. The fact that the eastern problems were for the moment easier to manage than the west was coincidence and fortune; the reverse could just as easily have been the case. Carausius' rebellion introduced a wild card into the game, but it was a wild card that had appeared more than once before in Roman history. Certainly there was a risk of Maximian and Carausius deciding that they would be better partners in rule than Maximian and Diocletian – but it was also highly unlikely that Maximian would betray his fellow Illyrian Diocletian for a Menapian. Diocletian came west because Maximian needed help, and there were no present crises that required imperial oversight in the east. The fact that his presence was a way to ensure that the two colleagues had a chance to work together in close concert was an added boon. Rome would have a vivid example of the cooperation of her joint rulers, and both Diocletian and Maximian would have a chance to assure each other merely by proximity and shared labours that they were indeed colleagues and not rivals. Carausius was comparatively unimportant in all this, shut off as he was on his island – an annoyance to be sure, and one that would need to be dealt with sooner or later – but an annoyance on the far side of the Roman world, of limited consequence for the rest of the empire.

Some have asserted that Diocletian was the political master, and Maximian the military. This is an interesting argument in view of the fact that Diocletian did indeed carry off a diplomatic coup with Persia early in his reign, while Maximian struggled in the west militarily. But in point of fact circumstances were such that Diocletian had an easier task than his colleague, and they could both claim to be capable military men. Especially after the Carausius episode, Maximian had more than enough to occupy any commander, and his difficulties in managing the west in and of themselves do not provide evidence to charge him fairly with any lack of ability. Both men were of similar background and training, even if Diocletian may have been more polished by this point (relatively speaking) in terms of education and learning.

We have mentioned that Maximian tried to engage Carausius sometime in 289, only to meet with setback. The only surviving noteworthy detail about the effort speaks of stormy weather that destroyed Maximian's navy as it sought to cross the English Channel. Storms at sea were a significant danger for ancient navigation and naval warfare, and many a Roman commander had seen his fleet destroyed or seriously discomfited by the peril. Meteorological prognostication could not hope to prevent such occurrences, and the waters in question are noteworthy for their difficult conditions. Certainly the story may have been invented to conceal some other reason for Maximian's failure, but there is no good reason to doubt its veracity. For a Roman commander in 289 to have to assault a fortified enemy in Britain was more difficult than what Caesar and Claudius had faced against Britain in far different times.

Diocletian returned to the west in time to meet with Maximian at Mediolanum in the winter of 290–291. Much has been speculated about the nature of the meetings and indeed of Diocletian's return to the west. The general consensus has been that Diocletian wanted to show in person that he still had absolute confidence in Maximian, despite the difficulties in the west. Probably overmuch has been made of the image of Maximian as weak and ineffectual. Again, his task was appreciably more difficult than the trouble confronted by Diocletian in the east. Communication issues were always a concern as well. We do well to note that the two emperors did not meet regularly; indeed after the 290–291 encounter, they would not see each other in person for over a decade. Letters by courier constituted the mode of discourse.

There was also something of a celebratory air to the meeting. Much had been accomplished, and overall there was far more stability to boast of than when Diocletian had made his fateful step forward to accept power in Nicomedia in November 284. The most extensive evidence that survives of the trip of the rulers to northern Italy in the winter of 290–1 is the eleventh panegyric, in which Mamertinus is at pains to use every rhetorical artifice to persuade his listeners and readers that all was well. Panegyric pablum aside, the event that winter was a commemoration of five years of more success than failure.

Mediolanum was once again the city of power, the meeting place of emperors. We learn of a delegation from the senate – but Rome was a sideshow for the moment, its status a consequence of the pressing problems in other theatres. The meeting in northern Italy would have been the expected combination of confirmation of reports by letter and planning for the future, most especially finally resolving the breakaway realm in Britain. The decision that was eventually reached in this regard would have significance for the future of the dyarchy.

It would always have been a source of potential weakness for Rome simply to have abandoned Carausius and his holdings to his own wishes. All our evidence points to Carausius as being a man who had no designs on any territory beyond what he held already. But to allow a usurper to hold illegally acquired land was to invite some future rebel commander to imitate the British pirate king. The fact that the rebellion was by now peaceful, and that Carausius seems to have been quite a competent leader – especially in economic affairs – was irrelevant. There is numismatic evidence that Carausius tried to emphasize that he was not so much a breakaway, independent ruler as one of three brothers, three Augustuses – Carausius as equal of Diocletian and Maximian. No coin minted by Diocletian ever acknowledged the fond propaganda.

Constantius Chlorus was to be given responsibility for the attack on Carausius. Once again we can but speculate on what may have happened here. Maximian had failed in his efforts, even if the reason for his defeat was due to weather and not his own ineptitude or incompetence. Still, the failure made it all too easy for Diocletian to reach the conclusion that Maximian should not be accorded a second command opportunity against Britain. Constantius was Maximian's son-in-law, and so his appointment to the new command made the Carausius War still clearly a family affair for Maximian. Further, the command was assigned as part of the birth of what history knows as a tetrarchy – a rule by four men. The year 293 would be the year that would see the establishment of the system we have described as the pairing of Augusti with Caesares: Diocletian and Maximian would have a pair of junior colleagues, in the present instance their sons-in-law.

We have no certain knowledge of when the plan for the tetrarchy was reached. Announced on the Kalends of March 293, it had been in the works, we can be sure, at least for some months.[18] Diocletian and Maximian had exercised what was, arguably, the most important of their prerogatives: the power to name their Caesars: 'only Diocletian and Maximian had the right and power to grant imperial status. No one could demand or negotiate for this and hope to succeed.'[19]

Diocletian's daughter Valeria was married to one Gaius Galerius, another military man who had served under such great emperors as Aurelian and Probus.[20] He was another Balkan native, probably born around 258 at Romulianum. Roman tradition had long sanctioned the practice of adoption to join families, and Maximian and Diocletian adopted Constantius and Galerius in 293 as part of the new government arrangement: the Caesars were now sons as well as sons-in-law of the Augustuses. Increasingly the imperial image of 'brothers' prevailed – Diocletian and Maximian were *fratres*. The Caesars were now adopted into the Valerian family. There is controversy as to when the two men were joined by marriage alliances to the imperial households. The tradition is a convenient one – the marriages were part of the promotion to status as Caesars – but they may have occurred earlier. Galerius had one disadvantage compared to Constantius – he had no son at the time of his promotion, let alone a mature son of 20 like the future Constantine the Great.

In immediate consequence, there could now be four spheres of operation instead of two.[21] This bureaucratic expansion probably seemed more than justified in light of both the ongoing crises in the west, and the realization that history had amply demonstrated how the east was likely to re-emerge as a problem area at any time.[22] Officially, Constantius would manage affairs in Britain and Gaul, while on the other side of the Roman world,

Galerius would see to the problems and administration of Egypt, Judaea, and Syria. It would be a sharing of administrative responsibilities that was more than called for by the crises of the hour. Almost immediately in the wake of the setting up of the tetrarchy, there would be conflicts in every corner of the empire that needed to be resolved, both reactively and proactively. The two Augustuses and the two Caesares would manage the huge empire, finally – in theory – setting up a framework that was at least in principle to last indefinitely.

There was, needless to say, no place for Carausius in any of this, and the clock was finally striking the zero hour for his secessionist empire. Constantius had a straightforward if arduous task, like Maximian before him: he would need to cut off completely all remaining continental support for Carausius, before seeing to the construction of a navy with which to assault Britain.

Gesoriacum remained a stronghold for Carausius, and Constantius proceeded to besiege it. The news that reached Britain was alarming: there was a clear renewal of imperial efforts to put an end to the breakaway island empire, and Carausius' position was weaker than ever both at home and abroad. He was assassinated by his treasury official Allectus, who made the same decision that had been made in so many other times and places – he thought that he could do better than his master. Allectus would be the second and last emperor of the British breakaway empire.

We know tantalizingly little about the subsequent events in the campaign of Constantius against Allectus. At some point the rebels seem to have recaptured lost territory on the continent, thus dealing a major setback to Constantius and proving that no matter who was in charge of the operation, the job of finally ending the Carausius adventure was exceedingly difficult. Indeed, Allectus was destined to hold on to power and life until 296 – such was the enormous task that confronted Constantius.

Allectus, for all his significance to the moment, is another of history's shadowy enigmas. We do not know, for example, exactly what triggered his killing of Carausius – though history is replete with parallel instances of assassination. The best case scenario that Constantius could have hoped for was that someone would seek to eliminate Allectus and to restore Roman rule over Britain – or that Allectus would do the same. The alternative was the nightmare proposition: to prepare a fleet that would have to sail over a difficult stretch of water to make a landing before launching ground operations. This is what Julius Caesar had been the first Roman to try to do, only to meet with less than stunningly successful results. It is what was finally attempted more auspiciously in the reign of Claudius. Maximian had apparently failed in his efforts in 289, perhaps only due to the fault of weather, though we cannot exclude the possibility that he moved too hastily. In the end Constantius would launch an invasion, but it would not be until September 296. The delay would have been occasioned in large part by the need to construct a fleet, itself no easy task. Allectus was not without ships – he had his own naval base located at what we know today as the Isle of Wight – the Roman Vectis or Vecta. Constantius decided wisely that he would need sufficient ships to launch a multi-pronged invasion, rather than to risk everything on one naval force. Overwhelming numbers were the order of the day: there would be a massive invasion fleet, one that would ensure a relatively quick victory and end to the Carausian, now Allectan rebellion. It probably occurred to Constantius that his new foe had a name that was reminiscent to that of the mythological Fury Allecto.

Allectus may have planned to try to sue for peace, but if so, we have no evidence that he was in any particular hurry, numismatic evidence of pacific overtones aside. He was also working on the time-honoured British tradition of preparing more warships to defend his island, and, no doubt, trying to shore up his own tenuous hold on power.[23]

But Constantius did not spend years solely occupied with the preparation of an invasion fleet. He was focused on extensive operations against those barbarians who had sided with Carausius, in particular the Franks – and he battled against the Alamanni, like so many before him. Maximian was able to cover his rear by overseeing the defence of northern Gaul and the mouth of the Rhine while his Caesar would be occupied with the great naval expedition. It would be the daring climax of the whole operation to subdue the breakaway British empire – one that had been living on borrowed time since it lost its continental foothold.[24]

Bad weather hampered the invasion that fateful autumn. Constantius seems to have been delayed in departing from Gesoriacum because of sea conditions. His deputy commander Julius Asclepiodotus was assigned the second naval force. Asclepiodotus was yet another distinguished veteran from the days of Aurelian and Probus. He was praetorian prefect under Constantius, and played the role in the current campaign of a classic Roman naval officer (we may note that few Roman military men had any special training, knowledge, or experience of naval warfare – Asclepiodotus seems to have been an especially skilled, or at least supremely lucky commander). He arrived in Britain before Constantius, sailing through fog to avoid Allectus' ships – a daring and bold move. On arrival in Britain, we are told that he ordered the burning of the ships. The gesture was a standard (at least occasionally) feature of ancient naval warfare – if you burn your ships, you encourage both yourself and your men to fight with renewed and exceptional vigour, since they have no easy means of returning home. The morale incentive was seen as so important that it outweighed the obvious financial loss of destroying expensive and valuable vessels. The burning was supposedly in dedication to the war god Mars.[25]

Allectus probably had an expectation that there would be an attempted invasion, but the limitations of communications would have worked against him at least as much if not more than against his foes. He could not have hoped to have defended the entire coastline opposite Gaul, and his best chance for success rested in having his own ships detect the enemy approach. Fortifications and land-based enterprises would have been a necessary expedient. The fact that we are told that Allectus retreated from the coast when he realized that Asclepiodotus had made a successful landing is interesting. The first line of defence for the island was weather. The second was the navy. The third was the land force. Did Allectus lose his nerve, or did he plan to draw in Asclepiodotus, hoping to assault him by ambush or otherwise unawares deeper inland? The latter seems the more likely possibility – but in this case, Constantius may have been able to make his own landing and cut off Allectus' retreat.

There is some evidence that what might have happened in actuality is that some of Asclepiodotus' vessels were separated from their main body by the foggy conditions, thus allowing them to secure their own landing zone and a new front – there may have been as many as three separate Roman landing sites, which would have added to the confusion of Allectus' defences. Or, possibly, Asclepiodotus' force was fortuitously separated by the fog, thus allowing his 'second' units to cut off Allectus – with Constantius arriving only after the action was finished. Allectus' fate, in any case, was to be chased down as far as Londinium, where he and his remaining loyalists were massacred.[26] The end of the episode revealed what had long been known: the problem had always been in crossing the channel, with the ground campaign a certain victory as soon as Constantius was able to secure a foothold.

Certainly the Constantius operation was a rousing and impressive success, one that could easily have been done in by bad weather. Luck was a factor in the victory, but the Caesar and his prefect had proven their ample abilities. After seven years, Britain had been restored to the empire, and the tetrarchy could boast of a major achievement and another significant restoration. Constantius spent time in Britain focused on administrative tasks and the organization of defences and fortifications, including the restoration of Hadrian's Wall. Throughout the history of the tetrarchy, there was significant attention paid to the problems of management and seemingly mundane bureaucratic tasks. Constantius was more than earning his reputation in his settlement of affairs in Britannia.

The eighth panegyric in the aforementioned collection of laudatory speeches in honour of emperors is devoted to the praise of Constantius on the occasion of the recovery of Britain. As with the other panegyrics, chronology is elusive. It may have been delivered in 297, though 298 is also a possible date. As with the tenth panegyric in honour of Maximian, the eighth for Constantius is a major source of information about the events surrounding the suppression of the Carausius/Allectus rebellion. Indeed, much of our knowledge of the episode derives from surviving panegyrics.

Once again *praeteritio* is a characteristic of the address. Matters are frustratingly passed over, with tantalizing references for contemporary students of the period. There is mention of the capture of a barbarian king who was occupied with preparing an ambush; of the burning and destruction of the land of the Alamanni from the bridge over the Rhine to the crossing of the Danube at Guntia – episodes that either were connected to campaigns attested elsewhere, or were independent actions of which nothing else is known. The Persians were conquered across the Tigris; Dacia restored to the empire; German and Raetian borders extended toward the Danube's headwaters; campaigns planned in Batavia and Britain. The Sarmatians were so utterly vanquished in 289 that only the name survived. Trophies were earned for victories in Egypt – we cannot be sure over whom exactly. The Carpi and the Moors are attested as other demonstrations of the glories of the tetrarchy. Constantine is said to have made Gaul his merely by virtue of his arrival – again the typical blandishing, fawning praise of the genre.

Constantine is credited with having trapped some of Carausius' forces within Gesoriacum. Finally we are given some practical details of what exactly was done: piles were driven at the entrance of the bay, and boulders were sunk so as to make the waterway impassable to the pirate's vessels. Britain, we are told, could no longer remain a rebellious affront to Rome. In the days of Gallienus, Rome had been so shorn of her provincial limbs, as it were, that Britain's defection was not felt as seriously as now. For today the Alamanni; the Sarmatians; the Persians; the Quadi; the Carpi – all of them have been in some way or another subjugated or rendered impotent.

Peace had been elusive for ages now in the Roman Empire. One of the hallmarks of the Augustan regime had been its justifiable boast about the establishment of peace throughout the empire. One problem after another continued to rear its violent head, and while Constantius was occupied with Britain and Maximian with minding the shop in Gaul, there was a renewed outbreak of trouble with Persia, not to mention significant problems along the Danube frontier and in Egypt. Of these three areas, the most serious challenges would come in Persia, and we shall address that series of engagements and renewed warfare before dealing with the conflicts in the Balkans and Africa.

This time the conflict arose because the Persian monarch Vahram II died in 293. He was replaced by Vahram III, a young and weak ruler whose weakness was exacerbated by the fact that one of the sons of the legendary Shapur I – a prince by the name of Narses – was eager to seize power for himself, as if to reclaim his father's crown. In 294 Narses did just that, and Rome had a new Persian ruler with whom to deal. Vahram III seems to have been spared; the son of Shapur does not seem to have wished to have his predecessor killed. The start of the reign of Narses seemed to portend continued peace and good relations. Narses sent the customary friendly diplomatic messages of amity and pacific intention.

But it seems that at home, Narses was busy making the argument that recent Persian monarchs had betrayed the great heritage of their predecessors. He engaged in a campaign to argue in favour of a more aggressive, expansionist Persian empire. Perhaps as early as 295, and certainly by the autumn of 296 – the date is not certain – Narses made his move against Armenia, and he had no intention of stopping at the Roman border. King Tiridates of Armenia could not resist a massed invasion by Persian cavalry and infantry without help, and whatever resistance to Narses he could muster independently was soon swept aside by the Persian juggernaut. We do well to remember that Persia was the only true rival of Rome as a nation state in this period. Persia was no loose confederation of allied tribes, but a counterbalance of an empire that evokes political science comparisons to other great imperial rivalries in world history. Narses had begun his reign confirming the peace treaty with Rome that had endured for some years. Now he was launching an act of aggression that he hoped, perhaps, would go unchecked – we have no idea what his exact plans were, but he was able surely to realize that war with Rome would be inevitable given the course he was pursuing.

Chapter 5

Border Control and the Maintenance of Empire

Galerius was the Constantius of the east, the understudy, as it were, to Diocletian. In the west, Constantius had won success in his apprenticeship by successfully managing the invasion of Britain and the suppression of the Carausius/Allectus rebellion. In the east, Galerius was expected to do the same in the face of Narses' invasion. There is no question that Galerius had a difficult task, arguably more challenging than that faced by Constantius. In the west there was mostly a logistical difficulty – how to transport forces successfully to Britain. In the east there was less of a problem in arriving at the battlefield – but considerably more difficulty once one engaged with the enemy.

Galerius, needless to say, did not do well in his first encounters with the Persians. There may have been clashes of indeterminate or mixed outcome, but soon enough there was an engagement that went exceedingly well for Persia's bold new king. Somewhere between what is today Harran in Turkey and Raqqa in Syria in what was probably the spring of 297, Narses defeated Galerius and struck a huge blow to Roman pride and morale. Scholars debate the question of whether Diocletian was present for the battle. We simply do not have the evidence to be sure, though we do know that in the aftermath of the engagement, Diocletian pinned all the blame for the loss on his son-in-law. We are told that Diocletian forced Galerius to walk before his own imperial carriage for the length of a mile, as if to show that the Caesar had disgraced his Augustus.[1] Here too there is controversy about how to interpret the story; some have asserted that the procession was simply observing the normal order of precedence and deference for the senior commander. But there can be no question that for the moment, at least, Galerius found himself in something worse than the position Maximian had once occupied in the west. Maximian had never suffered a defeat quite like Galerius', and the situation in the east was now once again critical in the face of an aggressive enemy – not a foe content to hide on a fortified island base.

Galerius, to be sure, faced a disciplined and frightful enemy. The Persians typically employed heavy cavalry, including elephant units. Their frontline units were heavily armoured and designed to repel legionary attacks. The strength of a Persian force was in horse and archer units. Persian infantry in comparison was weak and essentially little more than cannon fodder, comprised largely of drafted men with light arms, their main threat being their incredible numbers. If a Roman force could not check the Persian cavalry massed against it, the engagement was usually finished quickly. It would be wonderful to have details about how Galerius managed to lose his first test against the Persians. The most we know for sure is that he rushed in without much planning, which probably means that he did not realize just how significant a force Narses had, and of what composition.

We have noted that we lack definitive knowledge of Narses' intentions. Certainly he wished to retain Armenia as a permanent part of the Persian imperial sphere. Roman Mesopotamia was also on his wish list of territories. But in the wake of his defeat of Galerius, Narses did not make further offensive moves of any significance. It is possible that he was delaying to see if the Romans would make peace terms. He may have felt that he risked falling prey to previous Persian errors of overextension. He would have needed time to consolidate the vast swaths of land he had already seized by conquest.

There would not be renewed military activity on any large scale until the commencement of the spring campaigning season of 298. By then, Galerius and Diocletian were ready to launch their own attacks, going on the offensive against Narses. It is possible that the Persian king delayed too long in making any new aggressive moves; it is also conceivable that he intended to hold Armenia and Mesopotamia, and had no designs on other Roman territories. In any case, the Romans would now seek to recapture their lost land. Williams notes that Rome was able to capitalize now on how the Danube frontier had been secured – we are told in our sources that Galerius brought troops from those eastern regions to supplement his lost forces.[2]

What ensued is one of the more dramatic episodes of the military history of the tetrarchy. Galerius may have been shamed by Diocletian, but if so, the shaming had good and great effect. Galerius would soon make a name for himself as one of the great Roman conquerors against Persia, indeed an imperial figure who could claim some vengeance for the humiliation of Valerian decades before. Persia would once again receive more than a bloody nose, as she faced invasion and conquest in the face of the Roman juggernaut. Whatever preparations had been made – most notably the necessary recruitment of new legionaries and auxiliaries to replace losses and to supplement available manpower – Galerius would use his time to great advantage, methodically and patiently planning a massive strike against Rome's old enemy.

History knows of the Battle of Satala, though there are more questions than answers about the details of the clash. We do not, for example, know for sure the size of the opposing forces. The location of the battle is also in doubt; it was probably near the modern city of Erzurum in the eastern Anatolian (ancient Phasiane) region of Turkey. The strategy and plan of the Persians in the prelude to the engagement, however, is a bit easier to explicate.

It seems that once Narses was certain that Galerius planned to launch an offensive, he decided to withdraw the main body of his force from Mesopotamia into Armenia. The logic of this was mainly so that Galerius could not think of launching a strike against Ctesiphon, since any such move would expose Roman territories to invasion from Armenia. Armenia was also probably thought to be a more defensive position to hold than Mesopotamia, at least from the vantage point of geography and terrain. Here the problem was that the Persians were traditionally particularly strong in cavalry, and cavalry do not work so well in the mountainous rugged landscape of Armenia.

Galerius entered Armenia, likely aware that it was more than worth the gamble of demonstrating how the Roman infantry would fare better than the Persian cavalry. There were two clashes, it seems, the second of which is known traditionally as the Battle of Satala. Here it was destined that the Romans would capture not a king, but a king's wife and many of his relatives and entourage. We may recall how Galerius was said to have lost his first engagement with the Persians on account of lack of foresight. It seems that Satala was a win rooted in an astonishingly successful surprise attack, the fruit of excellent reconnaissance in which the emperor took the risk of heading out with a few horsemen to do much of the espionage work himself. Galerius had learned from his previous mistakes, and he had absorbed the lesson of his disgrace in the presence of Diocletian. The Romans and their Armenian allies were able to strike hard by surprise against the Persian main body, adding Satala to the ranks of such memorable engagements of ancient military history. It was probably over very quickly, with Narses becoming another storied Persian monarch in headlong flight, as if he were Darius running from Alexander.

The *Cambridge Ancient History* summarizes: 'Galerius marched into Armenia Maior and established a base at Satala, Narses came from his camp at Oskha to confront him and was defeated. Galerius pursued the retreating Persians to their camp and captured the king's harem and treasury while the king made good his escape.'[3]

Whatever the exact details and logistics, the Romans won a great victory, inflicting a serious disgrace on Narses and avenging the loss they had suffered the previous year. Galerius surely recalled how Alexander the Great had won a similar victory over another Persian king, capturing the women of Darius' household. He also remembered how Alexander had won a name for himself for decency and honour by treating the family with respect. Narses himself barely escaped the battle, having been wounded and was able to flee only with difficulty. There was tremendous loot and wealth to be collected, and the aftermath of the battle is the subject of a famous anecdote related in Ammianus Marcellinus. One of Galerius' men is said to have found a bag that was full of exquisite pearls. He threw away the pearls, ignorant of their value. He kept the bag. The story is redolent of the practical toughness of the Roman military, and the traditional Roman moral aversion to luxury and 'eastern' decadence.

We have observed that Narses may have planned to hold only Armenia and Mesopotamia. Conversely, the Romans wanted to do more in the immediate than merely recover lost territory. Galerius proceeded to waste no time in planning an invasion of Persia. This sort of adventure had been done before, and usually with the object of inflicting so serious a defeat and humiliation on the Persians that they would think twice before launching another strike on Roman territory. There would be no realization of the Alexandrian dream here of conquering the entire vast empire. Indeed in the past, Roman victories on Persian soil had often been followed almost at once by the relinquishing of the newly won lands. Galerius would win victory after victory, able even to visit the fabled ruins

The coastline of Vis, Croatia.

Korcula, Croatia.

An aerial view of Vis, Croatia.

Bust of Diocletian in Diocletian's Palace,
Split, Croatia.

Thermae complex of Ancient Issa on Vis, Croatia.

Port of Split, Croatia.

Mljet, Croatia.

Ruins of Salona, outside of Solin in Croatia.

Ancient Greek Necropolis of Issa, located right behind the tennis courts in the neighborhood of Gradina, Vis, Croatia.

Thermae complex of Ancient Issa on Vis, Croatia.

The Roman arena in Pula, Croatia.

Cathedral of Saint Domnius in Split.

Catedral de la Santa Creu i Santa Eulàlia, Barcelona. Eulalia was a prominent victim of the Diocletianic persecution.

of Babylon. 'It was the greatest single victory of the Tetrarchy.'[4] We need not be surprised at such exaggerations as the report that Galerius reached the fabled Indus River – but there was no need to gild the lily. Galerius had followed in the footsteps of Alexander, even if in the end there would be no complete subjugation and conquering of Persia. He had more than illustrated to Rome's ancient enemy that the tetrarchy was superior, and Rome had the upper hand – not least by virtue of the fact that she held Narses' family in custody, honourable custody though it was.

The invasion of Persia under Carus had been followed almost at once by the death of that emperor by lightning bolt. There had been no treaty, no official end to the war that delineated much beyond the idea that the Romans would retreat back across the Tigris. This time there would be a settlement that would eclipse Constantius' achievements in the west. There, Rome had succeeded in reclaiming lost territory. In the east, Rome would secure new lands and define a new border between the two empires. Persia was clearly the loser, and would make significant concessions in the face of her loss. The settlement achieved by Galerius and Diocletian would be lasting – three decades was a lifetime in these troubled times. The tetrarchy had proven itself capable of impressive successes on both sides of the empire, and with justice a triumphal arch was erected in Thessalonica in northern Greece in commemoration of Galerius' outstanding accomplishments. Again, we may note that the walk in front of Diocletian's carriage in disgrace had been good training for the Caesar, who now had a place in the roster of the great conquerors of Roman military history.[5]

The treaty that was signed between Rome and Persia is usually known as the Treaty of Nisibis, sometimes as the First Peace of Nisibis. It dates to 299, and was of territorial as well as economic significance. Diocletian was concerned always with practical arrangements of administration and management, and the signing of the treaty was followed immediately by the commencement of plans to fortify the border – he was determined to ensure that there would be no surprise breach of the agreement by a resurgent Persian empire. The Persians divided their realm into so-called satrapies; five of these were now given to Rome. There was no question that the Persians could not cross the Tigris – the river was a true border between the empires. In the Caucasus, the small kingdom of Iberia was definitively assigned to the Roman sphere of influence, with the Persians no longer able to appoint monarchs there. Nisibis would be the locus for trade between the empires – an economic decision of great significance and advantage for Rome. The Romans were now able to centralize and to control the exchange of goods across the border more effectively. The Persians had fewer markets at which to raise funds that could be of possible use in raising future armies to confront Rome. The Treaty of Nisibis, in short, made it clear that Rome was the senior partner in the peaceful coexistence of the neighbouring empires.

What Diocletian and Galerius accomplished in Persia would bring peace for forty years. In terms of the history of the third century, that was an impressive accomplishment. Today the Arch of Galerius in Thessalonica (the ancient Salonica) remains as an archaeological monument to his achievement, despite its imperfect and damaged state.[6] 'Special celebrations were held for the victorious eastern emperors as they entered Antioch in the late spring of 299.'[7]

Diocletian had now been in power for some fifteen years. The situation had been stabilized in both west and east. There were still significant problems along Rome's long northern border, but the immediate crises had been resolved. There were four men working together, in what had so far been a harmonious tetrarchy. Lost Roman territories had been restored, and new lands had been acquired. Now in his fifties, Diocletian had already achieved much, and had brought a measure of calm to much of the empire. It comes as little surprise that we have heard of no protest or word of criticism from the senate in Rome in our story thus far – the emperor was, after all, doing his job in responding to the myriad crises that he faced on accession to the purple. And, too, Diocletian was more or less ignoring Rome as a matter of principle, a principle that would someday have its negative consequences.

The four members of the tetrarchy did divide the empire between them, with an eye to organizational efficiency and areas of special concern and domain. Constantius had proven himself in Britain and Gaul, and this would be his particular realm. Galerius was the lord of the east. Diocletian was something of a homebody, we might say, taking the Balkans for his base of operations. Maximian had Spain, Africa, and Italy.

Again, the system was marked by a marvellous specificity that was blended with a certain studied ambiguity. In their own districts, the four men operated essentially as independent emperors, with sovereignty that was marked by their own imperial courts and retinues. It was a family affair, by marriage alliance and adoption if not by blood. It was a military affair, with all four men tested and proven by the blood of arms. There was an emphasis on unity. Even though there were four districts, it was one empire, and Diocletian was lord in Britain as much as he was lord in Thrace. Where the theoretical met the practical was in response to the usual exigencies of practicality and distance. And the four men had proven more than once that they could cooperate in addressing foreign threats. They were possessed of the realization that weakness or loss in one region could soon spread like a cancer.

For convenience's sake we may thus schematize the arrangement as it changed over time. From 284–286, Diocletian was Augustus. His arrangement with Maximian dates to 285, and would last until 305. From 293–305, Constantius and Galerius were the Caesars serving under the Augustuses. The initial arrangement between Diocletian and Maximian eludes definitive characterization given the state of the extant evidence (and may have been deliberately somewhat ambiguous) – the question we have considered of whether Maximian was initially a Caesar, a son of Augustus, or an Augustus. Starting in 293 the fraternal relationship of the Augustuses was given special emphasis.[8]

It is possible that 299 marks the high point of recent Roman history, and the zenith of the tetrarchy's achievements. The foreign crises that confronted Rome demanded a strong military, and the army was clearly in command of the empire. Rome was a highly militarized state, with an elaborate system of fortifications from northern England to the so-called *limes Arabicus* that Diocletian tended to the defence of in the wake of the Treaty of Nisibis. The spectre of civil war seemed to have receded from view, with the tetrarchs in a state of amity, content with the arrangement that had secured so much peace and prosperity for Rome.

And there were other victories and achievements. We have not spoken much of the situation on the river Danube, one of the more seemingly perpetual sources of border trouble for Rome. This region would also require pacification and attention, and it would be a focus both for Diocletian and Galerius – the tetrarchs responsible for the eastern half of the empire. The year 293, we have seen, was the key year in terms of the formation of the tetrarchy, and Diocletian had travelled that year to Asia Minor in order to accompany Galerius to his eastern area of responsibility.

Diocletian had two reasons for not remaining with his junior colleague. One was to tend to concerns elsewhere – namely, in the Balkans – and the other was to allow Galerius some time to develop a reputation and to secure his authority in the east in the absence of the shadow of his storied superior. Diocletian struck against the Sarmatians along the Danube front in c. 293–4, winning appreciable victories. This was another region where the emperor showed a concern for developing a network of defensive forts. Throughout what is today Serbia, Hungary, and Bulgaria, Diocletian established fortifications and a permanent military presence. This was likely a novel defensive line, one where previously the Romans had relied on the Danube for natural defence, with little devotion to strong defences north of the river. The Sarmatians were noted for exceptional mastery of cavalry arts, and the Romans would soon begin to employ them as auxiliaries in their own armed forces.

Rivers were a prominent feature of Roman boundary demarcation, whether the Rhine, the Danube, or the Tigris and Euphrates. In the case of the Danube the Romans had had experience with trying to make permanent settlements north of the river, only often to retreat back and to consider the holding of such territory to be impractical. Diocletian does not seem to have had a definitive limit in mind for expansion, but he certainly wanted a strongly defensible position on both sides of the river.

This was the border region closest to Diocletian's place of birth, and one has the sense that this was an area of particular concern to him. It was a challenging landscape to protect, but Diocletian was likely inspired both by love of a challenge and by an awareness that Rome could not afford to have a soft, weak spot on her frontier. What is known from literary and archaeological sources is that Diocletian succeeded impressively in his difficult task. The Danube would be defended by an awesome system of men and machines, buildings and towns with walls and towers.

The only real criticism that could be made against the efforts of Diocletian on the Danube would be the economic toll – all of the aforementioned construction and military endeavours were enormously expensive. Diocletian would have argued that the cost was necessary, and in this he was no doubt correct. In some ways the Danube had been the most neglected of the frontiers of the empire (largely on account of the immense challenge of holding it), and at last there was an appreciable, successful effort to make the defence of that region adequate and permanent. It would not be without setbacks; we shall see how Galerius would eventually have to deal with a major incursion of the Carpi and Bastarnae that managed to penetrate the defences of Tropaeum Traiani, the modern Adamclisi in modern south-eastern Romania, not far from the Bulgarian border. Again, much of our knowledge of tetrarchal activities in this region comes from what we might term a familiar evidentiary triad: panegyrics, inscriptions, and (not least) the titles that the emperors began to assume to commemorate victories.

The Danube was not the only eastern border region that posed a challenge. There had been uprisings and disturbances in Egypt.[9] There were in fact two outbreaks of trouble in the region, the second of which was the more serious. The first would be addressed by Galerius alone, the second by Diocletian. The problems in Egypt demonstrate yet again the unwieldy, sprawling nature of the empire and the difficulty of its governance. Most of the border corners of the empire required military intervention, and the imperial job description was a combination of military and civil administration.

It seems that the initial uprising in Egypt took place in (at the latest) 293, only to be followed in 297 by another more challenging crisis that occurred at the same time as the situation was increasingly problematic with Persia.[10] The chronology of these crucial eastern events is notoriously vexed.[11] The easiest way to explain what evidence we have is to conclude that there were two episodes of trouble in Egypt, the second of which was by far the more serious. Galerius handled the first crisis, and Diocletian the second. It is possible that Diocletian was concerned that there were elements in Egypt who were working in concert with Persia, though Persia need not be a factor in explaining discontent in Roman Egypt.

Egypt was a critical realm in the Roman Empire. Its own history was storied and ancient, and its economic significance to Rome was unparalleled. Galerius responded to the initial troubles there, and Diocletian to the more serious outbreak of revolt.[12] We know more about these latter problems than the former, in part because Diocletian was forced to respond to another threat of usurpation. The protests of 297 were economic in nature, a result of the imposition of a new tax system that had recently been implemented by the prefect Aristius Optatus – indeed, Diocletian's Egyptian war is often considered to be a classic example of a 'tax war'.[13] 'After the reforms of Diocletian, Egypt lost much of the idiosyncratic character that it had retained since Augustus.'[14] Egypt had long enjoyed special prerogatives and status in consequence of Cleopatra's machinations with Antony and the (temporary) end of the Roman civil wars; like Italy, Egypt under Diocletian was simply one of many territories of the empire.

Lucius Domitius Domitianus enters history here as yet another in the long line of failed would-be Roman potentates, a man immortalized in coinage, papyri, and in brief mention in modern pages of record.[15] Said record preserves absolutely no memory of his early life or his origins. Some have wondered if he was a prefect in Egypt, but this is supposition. He certainly revolted against the tetrarchy, and he was dead by the end of the year 297, leaving behind coinage as clues.[16] He was succeeded, as it were, as usurper by Aurelius Achilleus, who continued the doomed rebellion into 298. He seems to have served as an official under Domitianus, consigned by fate to be another death in Alexandria, besieged and finally put to death under Diocletian. It is interesting that while Achilleus is attested in literary records, numismatic evidence confirms that Domitianus was the leader of the rebellion, at least until his death – the key to the problem, in other words, being to imagine that the situation was akin to that of Carausius and Allectus in Britain, with a brief succession.[17] Coinage once again attests to the way in which Domitianus was like Carausius in that he styled himself as another imperial partner, a sharer in the power arrangement that Diocletian and his associates were enjoying.

The exact relationship between Domitianus and Achilleus is uncertain. In our quotations of surviving literary evidence, we have seen repeated references to Achilleus as the rebel in Egypt, with no mention of Domitianus. This has led some to speculate that Domitianus was the puppet figurehead, and Achilleus the power behind the throne, as it were.[18] Certainty is, as often, impossible.

What was the cause of this so-called 'tax war' in Egypt? We have mentioned both Diocletian's bureaucratic interests and his desire for increased efficiency in the empire, and the unique character of Egypt. Simply put, Egypt had been doing things in its own way, and Diocletian wanted to standardize such processes as taxation throughout the empire.[19] Egypt's capital Alexandria had a number of privileges, not least the right to mint coins. There had clearly already been discontent in the region, and as often when the imperial authority departed, trouble slowly but surely began to encroach on order: Galerius' leaving Egypt for the east saw a steady march towards renewed and more serious rebellion. We may conclude that tensions had been brewing in Egypt for some time, and the tax situation served as the catalyst for outright secessionist actions. But as often in the history of the age, we do not know what the exact intentions of men like Domitianus and Achilleus were. It is possible that they themselves had no clear vision of what was to happen – men are sometimes swept along by the tide of events.[20]

Discontent spread, and both countryside and city were in uprising and protest. The details of Diocletian's response are few and obscure. The siege of Alexandria may have lasted as long as eight months, and Achilleus may have held out in the city until as late as March 298 before he met his own doom like his superior before him.[21] Diocletian would be able to impose his economic and administrative reforms on Egypt, such that his desire for standardization be implemented in Alexandria as in all the other cities and towns of the empire. He would be able to travel the Nile, and to engage in another of his favourite activities: definitively settling border issues.

We have seen the figure 'eight months' quoted in our ancient sources. Alexandria was a well-defended city, and Diocletian had a laborious task ahead of him in besieging it, notwithstanding his significantly larger force. There is a legend associated with Diocletian's victory, namely that he vowed that he would not hold his men back from the slaughter of the recalcitrant Alexandrians until his horse had bathed its knees in their blood. The horse collapsed, such that the slaughter was called off earlier than expected. The Alexandrians were said to have erected a statue of the fateful steed in thanksgiving for their deliverance.[22]

The southern border region had not been one of the more troubled and problematic lines of demarcation, but here too the master of organization and efficiency exercised his usual will and practice. Philae was marked as the southern border of the Roman Empire in Egypt. It was one of the most sacred sites in the region, venerated as one of the burial places of the god Osiris.[23] An island near the First Cataract of the Nile, Philae is cited in many surviving Roman geographical and technical writings, including in the works of Seneca the Younger and Pliny the Elder. Rome here bordered the great region of Nubia, and Diocletian made official treaties with the Nobatae and the Blemmyes, which included the payment of gold stipends to secure a lasting agreement about the line of Roman control.

The Blemmyes are cited often and curiously in extant sources. For such Roman writers as Pomponius Mela and Pliny the Elder, they were quasi-fantastic beings, with no heads and faces on their chests. The Blemmyes were a desert people, capable of incursion into Roman territory – but never a threat to the extent familiar to anyone who was stationed along the Rhine or the Danube, let alone the Tigris and the Euphrates. Still, it is yet another indication of Diocletian's thorough nature and comprehensive view of the empire that no Roman corner was to be neglected. The tax uprising of 297–298 afforded him the chance to tend to the Nubian problem, and to settle definitively yet another Roman 'edge of the world'.

Diocletian seems to have remained in Egypt for most of 298, no doubt to ensure that history would not repeat itself and trouble would not resume as soon as he departed. He was needed by Galerius in the east, as we have seen, to face the far more serious Persian threat. Diocletian needed to guarantee that the Roman rear was secure before Persia was confronted again. Once again we are reminded of the indefatigable efforts of these men. When we consider that Diocletian had thus far spent almost the entirety of his fifteen years of rule on various military expeditions and campaigns, work that he commenced when he was already in his forties and after a lifetime of service in an army career, it becomes far easier to see why he would eventually seek both to retire from his imperial position and to remain retired. Augustus had had an exceptionally busy young manhood and early career, and had engaged in military campaigns both foreign and domestic, but he had then been able to focus largely on internal administration, enjoying the fruits of his successful efforts to bring peace to Rome. He was not a man destined to spend years of his reign on campaign. Diocletian, in contrast, had rarely had a moment to rest.

The problems in Egypt resulted in the settlement of yet another of Rome's border areas.[24] If we were to gaze at a map of the Roman world, there is a frontier region that we have not yet considered, and yet another zone of Roman influence that demanded attention from the tetrarchy: the more westerly areas of north Africa. Like most of the empire, this region too had fallen prey to the realities of decline and chaos in the third century. There were tribes here too, notably the Berbers who learned quickly that the absence of organized local authority in Roman areas was an invitation to capitalize on the neglect and to raid settlements for supplies and plunder. This was, like the Egyptian border, not an area that faced the sort of sustained invasions and threats that confronted Rome on the Rhine or the Danube. It was a comparatively minor theatre, but a real threat all the same to stability. Maximian would be the tetrarch to address the problem, in another example of the tetrarchy system in action – one of the group of four would rush to a troubled front. The timing was after Constantius had settled the Carausius/Allectus revolt in Britain. There was always the risk that Maximian would need to remain close to his Caesar to render aid if the problem proved intractable. Now Maximian had a chance to address the African problem. Local Roman authorities – the governor of Mauritania Caesariensis and his staff – had tried to fight the Berber raiders as early as 289. In 296, Maximian would prepare his own armed force to come to the aid of the governor. His journey would take him through Spain, eventually to the Pillars of Hercules and what we know today as the Strait of Gibraltar. Here he crossed into Mauretania Tingitana, into what is today Moroccan territory.[25]

The journey to Africa was not a peaceful march. For one thing, the Franks – incredibly, we might think – practised piracy even as far south as north Africa. Naval operations were always challenging, mostly because of what we have already discussed in terms of the hazards of storms and the great expense of maintaining a standing navy.[26] Maximian had to deal with pirates as well as with bandits and raiders in Spain. He would not be able to commence any operations against the Berbers until the spring of 297 – again, it was a work of pacification and restoration of order along vast swaths of territory, in this case an area that had been neglected for some time in the face of more pressing crises. The Berbers were a desert people, and they were adept at guerrilla warfare in the harsh climate. This was a difficult war for a commander who might have been inclined to impatience and distaste for the tedious prosecution of a war that was not among the more glorious of conflicts.

So long was the process of quelling the Berber threat that Maximian spent the winter of 297–298 in Carthage before commencing renewed operations. The border between Rome and such nomadic tribes as the Berbers had never been scrupulously defined. It was, after all, an inhospitable wasteland for most of its length. Maximian realized that this was a problem that would continue to plague Roman Mauritania unless he pursued the enemy deep into territory that had never been claimed by Rome. This is exactly what he did, forcing the Berbers into the Sahara Desert and aiming for a policy of slaughtering as many of them as he could to break their strength.[27] The whole operation was concluded that spring, and Maximian was able to claim a victory.

We have noted that Maximian had difficulties when he was fighting in Gaul and against Carausius. Some have been tempted to see the same sort of pattern in north Africa, based on the idea that it took so long for him to solve the Berber problem. Both crises posed significant difficulties, and it is likely that no commander could have solved the north African one much faster than Maximian. If anything, this was an easier operation to execute, if one had extreme patience – and in this instance, the emperor did. Maximian celebrated his victory in Carthage on 10 March 298, and the tetrarchy could claim yet another settlement along the vast borderlands of the empire. Even in these different theatres of conflict, Roman order was being restored.

It would be a tremendous boon to our knowledge of the age to have access to the imperial correspondence that must have poured forth from the four offices of the tetrarchs during this period, as reports followed on reports outlining the activities underway in different, distant corners of the empire. It was an age of near constant warfare in some region or another, but it was above all the hour of restoration and renewal. There was already a palpable sense of stability in the long tenure of Diocletian, and in the establishment of the tetrarchy he had secured, it no doubt seemed, the preservation of his reign from the sort of violent end that had befallen an Aurelian or a Probus. Economic security followed in the wake of pacification of war-torn fronts and the orderly coexistence of the cooperative tetrarchs. It was not exactly a Golden Age like that of Augustus or the reign of the Good Emperors, but it was a dramatic and vast improvement over what had prevailed for most of the third century.

Maximian returned from Africa to Europe early in the highly successful year 299, sailing for Italy. Italy was no border battleground of course, and it had been comparatively neglected thus far in the history of the tetrarchy. The frontiers were what had been collapsing, and it made sense that Diocletian and his colleagues did not pay much attention to life at the heart of the empire. Italy was in the zone of responsibility that had been allotted to Maximian, and it made sense for him to spend time there now given that once again it was a question of items on a list. None of the four tetrarchs had devoted much time to the sacred peninsula, and Rome was the home of the senate but not of much in the way of imperial interest.

That of course changed once an emperor was on Italian soil. Mediolanum and not Rome was Maximian's capital, but he was close enough to the city to be able to have far more in the way of interaction with the senate than had been the case before. The reports we have of this period are not entirely complimentary to the emperor. We must be careful of Christian sources that had good reason to be hostile to Maximian. The claim that he began to live a dissolute life of luxury and decadence is a stereotypical charge, but there is every reason to believe it to be true. Maximian had spent his entire life in the harsh conditions of the army, and he had just completed years of difficult campaigns in western Europe and northern Africa. To imagine that he decided now to live like an emperor in luxury is not difficult. To imagine that he had conflicts with the senate is also entirely believable. He had no experience of republican government, and years of tenure in positions where his every word was law. To imagine that the Bengal tiger, as it were, would suddenly behave nicely among the sheep is foolhardy. Did he order the deaths of senators around 301–302? Quite possibly: even a 'good emperor' like Hadrian had the same charge against him. If Maximian's behaviour was bad, it was a predictable consequence of the trajectory of his life, coupled with whatever natural propensity he may have had for autocracy and impatience with those he considered subordinates.

Early in the year 301, Diocletian saw the release of one of his most famous edicts, the *De Pretiis Rerum Venalium* or edict on maximum prices. Thanks to the fact that it was set up as an inscription in cities, the text has survived at least fragmentarily in both Greek and Latin. Like the *Laterculus* or the *Notitia*, the *Edictum* allows a window into a world, in this case an incredibly detailed array of goods and how much one could charge for them. 'It shows only a limited economic wisdom, but it bears all the marks of thoroughness and system, of leaving as little as possible to chance, which is characteristic of an essentially military approach to the state's problems.'[28] While we do not possess a complete text of the lengthy edict, we are able to know what was now fixed as the maximum costs for certain commodities, from shoes to lions for use in the amphitheatres. Beer and wine, meats and fish are all listed. At the very least, it serves as a testament to Diocletian's perhaps obsessive concern with micromanagement, and, it seems, as a reminder of how such efforts often come to naught. By all accounts the edict did not exactly revolutionize the Roman economy, or any efforts to control inflation. Edicts like the *de pretiis* would have been very difficult to enforce with anything approaching uniformity and consistency throughout the empire.

The edict on prices is not the only economic document from the period of which we have some fragmentary evidence. There was also a currency edict, which called for a doubling of the face value of imperial coinage and a determination that while old debts would use the old system, new debts would use the new, again for the sake of reducing inflation.[29]

Diocletian was always most at home in foreign policy and the direction of plans for safeguarding Rome's borders. He was interested in administration in general, but it is interesting that in economics and in the management of the Christian situation to which we shall soon turn our focus, he was far less successful than in his military and foreign policy initiatives. Similarly, in his conduct of the process for the development of the second tetrarchy, he met with results more disappointing than reassuring. While his hands were busy in every area of imperial government, like most men he had certain areas of special talent, and his achievements in other areas were less appreciable.[30]

Constantius – Maximian's most important subordinate – was occupied in the period from 300–302 with the continuing efforts to stabilize the west. There is every indication that he was able to do this without Maximian's help, and it is possible that both men preferred to allow Constantius to do the work alone. Maximian may have wanted rest and relaxation more than anything, and Constantius may have enjoyed the chance for solo glory. The Franks were still a threat, as well as Germanic tribes on the Rhine – in other words, the same headline as so often before in Roman press releases. On the domestic front, Constantius is credited with positive relations with the Roman senate, in contrast to his Augustus. This may be the result of Christian favour towards Constantius over Maximian in the writing of history, but there is no reason why one should disbelieve what could, after all, have been nothing less than the truth.

Constantius spent the period from 298–305 immersed in the maintenance of his Gallic portion of the empire, complete with the usual challenges on the Rhine. Much has been written about the Roman strategy over time with respect to Germanic tribes. There were dreams of crossing the Rhine and establishing secure Roman dominion deep into German territory, and on occasion there was some success (even impressively so) in endeavours of this sort. Any sort of retreat to the Rhine meant that there would be a constant need to engage in negotiation, diplomacy, and occasional warfare against the many tribes across the river, tribes that were sometimes in league with each other. One episode of uncertain date is emblematic of the problems that constantly beset the frontier. Constantius was near Lingones (the modern Langres in northern France), when he was attacked by a band of Alamanni. The barbarians had crossed the Rhine without any Roman alert, and Constantius may have been wounded in the sudden onslaught. He had been travelling with a relatively light military accompaniment, and both he and his surviving force were soon under siege in Lingones, with the invading Alamanni now able to prepare to surround and attack the seriously discomfited Constantius. The author of the sixth panegyric recalls that Lingones was the site of a victory made notable even by the wounding of the emperor.[31]

We have labelled this episode 'of uncertain date' because of significant controversy. Eutropius clearly thought that it occurred in the late 290s; some modern scholars have been persuaded by a study of imperial titles to date it later, perhaps 302. 'Certainty is unattainable.'[32]

Word had somehow been able to reach Roman garrisons in the vicinity of the peril to the emperor, and he was able to rejoice at the sight of a large relieving force. What history knows as the Battle of Lingones ensued, in which the Romans were victorious with a heavy barbarian slaughter and the rescue of Constantius. The battle is thus illustrative both of the hazards in the Rhine region, but also of the efficient response of Roman military might. When we hear that some sixty thousand barbarians were slain in the struggle, we may wonder if the casualty figure was embellished. But it is clear that a great victory was obtained, and the Roman army had illustrated again that it could credibly defend its borders and inflict a devastating toll on any would-be invaders or raiders.

The near disaster for Constantius, however, was treated rightly as a sign that better work needed to be done to fortify the Rhine frontier. There would be a second battle against the Alamanni, the so-called Battle of Vindonissa. This engagement took place near the modern Windisch in northern Switzerland, where a legionary camp had been established, the remains of which constitute a significant archaeological site. We are not sure of the date of this engagement – it may have been as early as 298, or as late as 302. We are also at a loss in terms of appreciable detail about the clash, save the key fact: the Romans once again won a great victory against the Alamanni, and were able to strengthen the border still more, with the infliction of another costly defeat on the barbarians. Constantius was amply proving his ability to manage his challenging sector of the empire, and while no one could erase entirely the threat posed by the Germanic tribes, Constantius was more than competent in his response to the problem. The sixth panegyric makes mention of Vindonissa, and of fields covered in corpses. Some have connected this account with the prior episode at Lingones, where sixty thousand were said to have fallen. The sites are about a hundred miles apart; it is most likely that we have two closely connected victories that have become somewhat conflated (Eutropius may have mentioned Lingones alone because of the memorable story of the rope rescue). Lastly, the panegyrist mentions an obscure episode from this period in which a band of Germans tried to cross the Rhine over ice to an island in the river, only to be stranded by a thaw and to be attacked by Constantine with naval units. The Germans were forced to decide which of them would be taken into captivity, and which would have to return home to report the whole shameful episode.

The Franks continued to be another threat, and Constantius fought against them as well around 300. There is some evidence that he tried to secure a more lasting peace here by encouraging Frankish settlement as tenant farmers in areas of Gaul that had been devastated by frequent war and other depredations.

If we can believe our trusty sixth panegyric, Constantine also managed to arrive at some indeterminate point in Hibernia – i.e. Ireland – and in *ultima Thule*, a mysterious land often cited in Latin literature that has been identified with the Shetland Islands or even Iceland.[33] There is no good reason to believe that Constantine managed to voyage as far as Iceland; in our view the Shetlands is the likeliest location for Thule, or perhaps the Orkneys if one has a less adventurous imagination. A Hibernian visit is more realistic than a Shetlands sojourn and cannot be ruled out. For the panegyric, there is even mention of the mythical Isles of the Blest alongside the Caledonians and the Picts, with invitation of the gods to join their number. We are reminded again of why historians have treated these texts with such reserve. Still, the imperial lot of Constantine and his father in Britain allowed for ready production of such florid, laudatory prose: this was the edge of the Roman world.

As the century turned, there was much to be proud of in the work of the tetrarchy. Matters had devolved to a relatively stable state, despite the obvious need for expensive vigilance on the lengthy borders of the empire. If anything, this was the high point of the Roman military complex, the vast army that was needed as a permanent standing force to respond as quickly as possible to any threat along the frontier. While the Roman empire was not at the greatest extent of its land mass that it had briefly obtained under Trajan, it was largely intact compared to that high water mark – and the most conscious and deliberate effort in centuries (if ever) had been made to secure its borders.

Chapter 6

The Persecution of the Christians

I n the eastern theatre, we have already outlined the impressive Roman achievements in Persia that followed Diocletian's successful settlement in Egypt. What we have not detailed yet is how Diocletian and his colleagues came to focus on Christianity as one of the more pressing internal problems of the empire. There is controversy concerning how exactly what came to be known as the Great Persecution was launched. We have mentioned the dramatic case of the Theban Legion under Maximian. Diocletian has usually been cast as a religious traditionalist who was devoted to the Roman gods and the customary rites of Roman cult practice.[1] But there is good reason to believe that for the entirety of the first fifteen years or so of Diocletian's reign, Christianity was not something that weighed much on the imperial mind. Certainly the emperor was occupied with numerous and weighty other problems. But there may be some truth to the report in some sources that it was Galerius and not Diocletian who had particular feelings of animosity towards Christians. If Galerius were the instigator of what would become organized and aggressive religious persecution, Diocletian was hardly to be expected to serve in the role of defender of religious minorities. No doubt he shared any negative appraisal of Christianity that was held by his imperial colleagues.[2]

The year 299 may have been the occasion for the first significant stirring of a movement toward suppression. It was a year of marked foreign policy success, which would now see movement toward what would be a less than auspicious internal government action. We hear of a sacrificial ritual performed for purification and divination, and a report from pagan priests that there was impurity in the imperial household even – that is, the presence of Christians on the staff – and trouble forecast for the future, should the Christian problem not be addressed in the name of reverence and respect for the ancient religion. Soon the word was sent out to every military commander: religious rites should be performed for the expiation of any impurity, and to appease the traditional gods of Rome.

The military order concerning the performance of sacrifices may date to as early as 298; the period 298–9 seems to mark the commencement of what would become a more systemic tetrarchal response to the continuing spread of Christianity. The ecclesiastical historian Eusebius blames the *magister militum* or 'Master of the Soldiers' Veturius for being the progenitor of what we might term the Christian crisis in the army, demanding that the Christians in the army sacrifice to the emperor lest they forfeit their position and rank.[3] The clear implication of what evidence we have for Christian persecution in this age is that the root problem was the sacrifice rituals for the emperor and state that involved invocation of Jupiter and traditional Roman gods. Especially given Diocletian's expectation of *adoratio* and his association with Jove, any refusal to participate in the state cult could be taken as a personal affront to the emperor, and as a threat to the stability of his reign. If Eusebius is right that the persecution commenced in the army, all of this makes more sense. The barracks emperors of the third century derived their power from the army and not the senate. The army was the single most important institution in Roman society. For the army to be populated with men who were unwilling to sacrifice for the health of the emperor and his safety because their religion did not allow rituals in honour of other gods was unacceptable. For a Christian army man to assure his superiors that he wished the emperor all good will and no harm was not sufficient. His loyalty was questioned the moment he declined to participate in what was seen as the normal practice of state religion. Roman legionaries venerated even the standards of their unit; to refrain from cult practice because of one's monotheistic beliefs would be seen readily enough as a threat to security.

Christian martyrdom stories from the era of the tetrarchy, we should note, certainly predate the Great Persecution. Saint Marcellus was reported to have been a centurion with *Legio VII Gemina* in Spain who was killed at Tingis (modern day Tangiers) after he refused to participate in sacrifices to the gods during the birthday celebrations in honour of Maximian in 298; the veracity of details of the legend has been questioned in part on account of the detail about the legion's identity appearing only in later versions.[4] 'In the late 290s we first hear of incidents which, though recorded as glorious martyrdoms, were peripheral brushes with the law and can in no sense be called persecution.'[5] But Eusebius, in short, may preserve a valuable piece of information: from the perspective of the tetrarchs, at least, the Christian problem started in the army – the last place where quasi-divine emperors would want monotheists. For even if Diocletian did not really think that he was a god, he was not likely to be tolerant of someone who was unwilling to burn incense to Jupiter or Hercules.

We have seen again and again that the tetrarchy faced one crisis after another in the maintenance of empire. It is commonplace in times of chaos and uncertainty to witness religious revival and warning, and to hear the argument made that the gods and supernatural powers are angry with humanity. There is another consideration to be made here. Diocletian, we have seen, was a man devoted to order and codification, to having rules written down carefully and then duly obeyed. He disliked ambiguity and lack of standardization. He was fond of bureaucracy and layers of highly detailed and organized administration. Christianity was, in this sense, simply another area of Roman life that had thus far eluded definitive rubric and legislation. There had been previous persecutions of Christians, to be sure – but there had also been long periods of de facto toleration of the religious practice. Many an emperor had not bothered to worry very much about the question of Christianity. It is no accident, we would argue, that the tetrarchy began moving towards a systematic persecution of Christianity at exactly the time when the border crises and various military and political settlements of empire were drawing to a close. It was in this sense simply another item on the agenda list, another problem that required some memoranda of order and response.

The timing of the persecution seems easily explainable. The question of whether Galerius or Diocletian was more responsible for the direction taken is the consequence of our aforementioned sources that blame the former.[6] These sources are Christian, and unsurprisingly they wish to identify a specific target for blame and censure. It is possible that the sources settled on Galerius because he was the newer figure in imperial government. If Diocletian had already been in power for some fifteen years, the argument would go, why only now did he decide that Christianity needed to be persecuted? Galerius would thus be a logical candidate to blame for the sudden eruption of antipathy against the monotheistic religion.

Again, there is ample justification for why Diocletian would have ignored the problem until now. It was nowhere near as pressing as the other concerns that had occupied his attention thus far. To call Diocletian religiously tolerant until 299 is to underestimate the degree to which he was busy with other concerns. It may be that Galerius was more aggressive and scrupulous in carrying out the agenda of bullying Christians – but it is likely that Diocletian and he were of one mind on the matter. Diocletian was an administrator by nature, a man who enjoyed agendas and the marking off of one item after another on a list. Christianity was not so much something to be tolerated until 299, as it was something to be addressed once Sarmatians on the Danube and rebels in Britain and Egypt had been handled. 299 was a year of tremendous successes (especially in Persia), and that alone may account for why the problem would be addressed systematically only now.

One consequence of delaying confronting a given problem is that the problem is likely to get worse over time. Christianity was spreading, to be sure, and increasingly there were government officials and members of the imperial household and entourage who were exposed to it and attracted to it, not to mention soldiers in the army. It was no longer an obscure offshoot of Judaism that was the province of mostly poor members of the lower classes of society. It was becoming a serious movement that had roots even relatively close to the emperors. The story of the Theban Legion points to the spread of Christianity in the Roman military, which would be a particularly easy source for the idea that it was the wrath of the neglected pagan gods that was to blame for any shortcomings or disasters on the military front.

And, as we have seen, it was not novel to persecute Christians. It had happened under Nero, in the very earliest days of the church at Rome.[7] It had happened under Domitian, Trajan, Decius, and Valerian – to name but a few. Indeed it was one of the features held in common by the reigns of both the 'good' and the 'bad' emperors. Christianity, after all, had never been a legal religion, merely an occasionally tolerated one. And in the tetrarchy, tolerance for breaking the law lasted only as long as it took for previous instances thereof to be corrected.

As we have seen, it would be no surprise if the first organized actions against Christianity came with respect to the imperial household and the army. Christianity was by nature a secret religion, practised away from the public eye to avoid drawing attention to illegal acts of worship. One way to determine and to expose who exactly was a secret Christian was by compelling people to participate in sacrifices to the pagan gods. A Christian would avoid such practices even under pain of death. Christianity was ardently monotheistic, like its parent religion Judaism. There was no question of religious tolerance and pluralism here: a Christian was not permitted to call on foreign gods, who were viewed as if demons. If you wanted to ferret out who the Christians were in a given group, a most effective way was to demand religious rites to the pagan gods. Indeed we shall see that one of the problems that would confront Christian religious authorities was what to do in the case of professed, baptized Christians who violated their baptismal promises by engaging in such sacrifices. Were they able to be reconciled to the religious community and the body of faith? What if it had been a member of the Christian clergy even, a bishop or presbyter who had engaged in such an act of idolatry?

We do well to remember, too, that Christianity was one of many religious sects that had spread in the sprawling Roman empire. It was the most enduring and widespread of those sects, to be sure – but the tetrarchy witnessed other religious persecutions as well. Manichaeism was one of those other religions that aroused the concern of Diocletian. It was much younger than Christianity – its founder Mani is said to have lived in the mid-third century in Persia, perhaps c. 216–276 – thus putting his death only a decade or so before the accession of Diocletian to the purple.[8] Mani's religious movement had been tolerated, it seems, under the great Persian monarch Shapur I (who was no doubt more concerned with his military adventurism than with the new sect in his realm). Manichaeism was never as successful as Christianity or, for the matter, Zoroastrianism – but it seems to have held an appeal from the start to the higher echelons of Persian society. Whatever success Mani had, however, was short lived. The winds in Persia often shifted from one imperial reign to another, and Mani is said to have died awaiting his death under Vahram I. Manichaeism was one of many religious movements in history that was rooted in the belief that its prophet or teacher was the last and greatest of such men in history.

Manichaeism had much in common with Christianity, and indeed Jesus was venerated by the Manichaeans as a prophet – though the Manichaean views on Jesus were not remotely orthodox by Christian standards. The religion was based on the notion of a cosmic duality of light and darkness. Light was associated with the eternal and the divine, and darkness with the corruption of earth. The two elements were engaged in an age-old struggle, one rooted in the gradual process of the removal of light from the world and its ultimate freedom from the stain of the dark. Soon enough Christian writers would be concerned about the movement; the great Saint Augustine of Hippo was attracted to Manichaeism in his youth as part of his roaming from one philosophical and religious movement to another before settling on Christianity and receiving baptism.

Manichaeism had been born in Persia, and it would spread west even to such places as Egypt. Opposition to the religion by the tetrarchy would come in obvious response both to its challenge to traditional Roman religious practices, and to its origins as a Persian sect – there was no way that a novel Persian religion was likely to be tolerated for long in Diocletian's Roman Empire.[9] And so there is no surprise about a well-documented incident that occurred on the emperor's watch during a visit he made to Egypt. Further, Diocletian may not have been particularly interested in discerning distinctions between Christians and Manichaeans.

Diocletian had left Egypt in 298 after quelling the tax rebellion, and he had proceeded east to confront the Persian threat with Galerius. The year 299, we have observed, had been one of triumph and consolidation on the foreign affairs stage. Diocletian was based in Antioch (the modern Antakya, Turkey, very close to the Syrian border) from 299 to 302, but he travelled to Egypt during the winter of 301–302. In March 302 we have record of a problem with a group of Manichaeans in Alexandria, one that Diocletian would respond to by decreeing the burning of both the leading adherents to the sect, and their religious writings. To be a Manichaean would now mean death if you were of lower rank, and hard labour if you were more noble in station.

The persecution of the followers of Mani could be explained by the recent Persian war, with Diocletian determined not to allow a native Persian sect to begin to infiltrate the Roman Empire. The Romans were by nature and culture inveterate and unapologetic traditionalists. Traditional Roman morality and religious practice was deeply suspicious of anything novel. Novel things from Persia were doubly suspect. The Persian element to the movement was of special concern in the immediate aftermath of the great war, and in any case once again we see the checking off of items on a list – in this case, attention to religious order and even something approaching uniformity, at least in terms of what practices would be permitted in public.

The Manichaeans were handled in 302 in Alexandria, and Diocletian returned to Antioch and made his first dramatic moves against the Christians. In other words, there would have been a period in around 298–9 of initial persecution, followed at an interval of some three years by the outburst of concentrated fury. It is from this period that we hear of the martyrdom of Romanus of Caesarea.[10] He was a deacon of the Christian faith, who was accused of interrupting pagan religious rituals and sacrifices with the word that the gods of the Romans were idols. This was a good example of the difference between the private and the public realm of Roman religious tolerance. Romanus was a brave and daring spokesman for his faith, and he attracted attention by his disruption of the services. Soon enough he was arrested and would be sentenced to death. We do not know exactly the date of Romanus' execution, though it was c. 303. Our knowledge of the episode is due to Christian sources, which make Romanus a native of Palestine and an exhorter of his fellow Christians in the aforementioned matter of the expectation that everyone would sacrifice to the pagan gods to satisfy the imperial demand for greater fidelity and devotion to the traditional liturgical rites of Rome. The reason for the question about the exact date of his death is that he seems to have been imprisoned for some time before at last he was killed. His tongue is said to have been cut out after his initial arrest – a good example of the gruesome tortures that early Christian sources report about the fate of the martyrs.

But how did it all start in the first place, in say 298? Lactantius relates that Diocletian was a nervous man, much given to fear for the future.[11] This was no doubt true. During sacrifices, the *haruspices* or soothsayers reported that the entrails of the customary slaughtered animals revealed no signs for the future, just after Christians who were present made the sign of the cross. Tages, the chief soothsayer, repeated the pagan rites and reported finally that there were profane people present who were obstructing the liturgy. Diocletian was driven to rage and ordered the punishment of the Christians, and so in turn he made his order to the armies about the need to root out those who defiled the sacrifice rites. Diocletian proceeded to Bithynia for the winter, which is where and when Galerius arrived and inspired him to be harsher in his prosecution of the sect.[12]

The main controversy that we find in this period is the question we have briefly sketched regarding the relative zeal with which the Christians were targeted for persecution by Diocletian and Galerius. The early Christian writer Lactantius is the main source for the argument that Galerius was the driving force behind the persecution, with Diocletian's Caesar urging that the Christians should be killed, while the Augustus was of the view that it was sufficient to deprive Christians of their rights, and certainly to keep them out of the army and government service.

Again, it seems most likely that the two men were of one accord in the matter of whether to persecute Christians. There may have been a difference in the question of how severely to punish Christians (either recalcitrant ones or not), but there is no persuasive reason to believe that Diocletian was somehow pushed into a more intolerant position by Galerius. Diocletian had been willing to order the burning of the leading adherents of Manichaeism in Alexandria, along with the scriptures of the sect; there is no reason to believe that he would have urged leniency for Christians, who were no doubt increasingly viewed as an internal threat to the stability of the empire. Clearly the period from 302–303 was spent in determining an exact strategy to be followed, (indeed, this process likely commenced as early as 298–9) in accord with the usual tetrarchic practice of producing a legalistic, highly detailed and codified plan. The results of that deliberation appeared on the Kalends of March 303, in the issuance of Diocletian's first law regarding Christianity. The date was deliberate: it was the time of the festival of the Roman god Terminus.[13]

Lactantius and Eusebius, we have seen, are the two main surviving sources for the early stages of the persecution (i.e. the events of 298–9). Lactantius tells the story of the interrupted sacrifice; Eusebius refers to an issue in the army. These were either the same event or separate ones. We are inclined to believe that there were indeed discrete incidents of similar import.[14] There were Christians in the army, and in the imperial household. The Christians were of one mind in belief and practice, and the same narrative played out in both places. The end result was the same.

The publication of the law was preceded by the usual sort of pogrom and rapine that accompanied religious persecution. Diocletian ordered the burning of Christian scriptures, and a church that had been recently built at Nicomedia was destroyed. The decree issued about the religion stated clearly that all places of Christian worship were likewise to be burned to the ground, and that Christians were no longer allowed to meet in public for their liturgies. Lactantius was a witness to these initial events. The first edict, Lactantius reports, was torn down by an angry Christian, who insulted the emperor and his triumphs over Goths and Sarmatians. He was promptly arrested and burned alive.[15] Christianity had another martyr, immolated for his act of vandalism and defiance.

There is arguably no surprise that this would be a logical moment at which to commence a persecution of Christians – the foreign crises of the eastern theatre had been settled from Nubia to Armenia and Iberia, and the Christians were a leading domestic concern by this point for an empire that was determined to restore some sense of common identity with the resurgence and amplification of the traditional cults of Rome. There is also no surprise in the report that soon after the decree regarding the burning of Christian places of gathering, a fire mysteriously gutted part of the imperial palace at Nicomedia. Soon enough, the Christians were blamed, accused of being incendiaries.

This was a scenario strongly reminiscent of the episode of the so-called Great Fire of 64 CE, when Nero eventually hit on the Christians as likely scapegoats for the devastation in Rome.[16] If a fire really had destroyed part of Diocletian's palace, we cannot speculate with any confidence on the cause or culprit. Disgruntled Christians may have been responsible; a careless slave could have been the unwitting arsonist. Whatever the truth of the matter, the same outcome resulted as in 64: the Christians were now to be attacked with even greater vigour. Not surprisingly, Lactantius claims that it was Galerius who put the idea in Diocletian's head that the Christians were guilty – though if there had been a fire, Diocletian would not have needed his Caesar to suggest the possible cause. Indeed, Lactantius asserted that the fire was a 'false flag' operation conducted by Galerius' own men, with the intention of increasing Diocletian's wrath against the Christians.[17] Was Galerius exercising perverse cleverness and awareness of Neronian history in his actions? Indeed, did he know about the events of Nero's reign? Whatever the truth of the matter, the metaphorical flames of persecution spread as fast as the burnings at the stake of hapless victims.

There were numerous martyrdoms that occurred in Nicomedia from February through at least of April 303. We are told that a second fire broke out in the palace only about a fortnight after the first – Galerius is said to have left the city, convinced that the Christians were too great a threat to his personal safety. Diocletian followed soon after, with both men destined for Rome. Other edicts would also follow. In the summer of 303, Diocletian ordered that Christian clergy were required to sacrifice to the pagan gods under pain of torture and jailing. The third edict came on 20 November 303 as part of the twentieth anniversary, or Vicennalia, of Diocletian's being acclaimed as emperor. That edict promised amnesty to any Christians who performed the usual sacrifices to the pagan gods that were considered to be proof that one was not, after all, a religious dissident. A fourth edict came in 304, which was the key decree in terms of saying that everyone in the empire was expected to participate in the traditional sacrifices of Roman religion, under pain of torture and execution.

The persecution that was unleased at Nicomedia in February 303 was not a local one. It was supposed to be enforced throughout the empire. In point of fact, of the four tetrarchs, it would be Constantius who is said to have been the least energetic in the execution of the edict. Part of the reason for that may have been the fact that his region contained the fewest Christians. He was also said to have been sympathetic to Christianity, according to tradition because his first wife Helena was Christian – scholars question the veracity of this and related anecdotes, mostly on the basis that they may have been later fabrications developed once Constantius' son Constantine became Rome's first Christian emperor.[18]

Certainly more Christians were killed in the east than anywhere. The fact that Diocletian issued four edicts in all can be taken as evidence that the persecution was not exactly as successful as the emperor had intended. For one thing, there was the question of enforcement. Second, there was the fact that making martyrs of one's enemies rarely serves to further one's goal. Third, there was the fact that Christianity was sufficiently widespread at this point that there was a certain safety in numbers, at least for the less conspicuous devotees of the religion.

Some of the victims of the Great Persecution are among the most famous of early Christian saints. Agnes of Rome, for example, is one of the most traditionally popular ancient Roman martyrs. Her story is a good example of the scholarly evaluation of hagiographical literature. In the reforms of the Roman liturgical calendar in the years after the Second Vatican Council, efforts were made to submit the question of the observance of the feasts of certain ancient martyrs to rigorous scrutiny. Agnes was one of those retained, indeed obligatorily remained, because of ancient surviving evidence for her early veneration by Christians, with attestation of the name, date, and place of her killing. Agnes was said to have been born in 291 to the Roman nobility, and to have refused a marriage arrangement out of a desire to preserve her virginity out of a sense of Christian virtue. She was slain in Rome in January 304 and is considered to be one of the best attested of the martyrs of the Great Persecution. Because all of our evidence for her very existence comes from early Christian sources, there have been questions about the details of her story, even of her very existence. But the antiquity of the cult is beyond question, and most scholars acknowledge the veracity of the basic outline of the story. Agnes was venerated as one of the virgin martyrs, and many of the accounts of female martyrs report a similar pattern of a woman of noble lineage who was sought in vain in marriage, only to refuse out of a desire to maintain her virginity. Virginity was valued highly in early Christianity as a quasi-ascetic calling, and was considered to be a more heroic and noble vocation than marriage (largely on account of certain teachings of the apostle Paul). It is likely that there were cases of girls who had been betrothed who then resisted the marriage arrangement out of religious faith, thus betraying that they were likely Christians.

The stories of the martyrs in our Christian sources constitute a frightful catalogue of torture and cruelty: 'even allowing a margin for invention, what remains is terrible enough.'[19] In an age marked by gladiatorial slaughter and by frequent, brutal military engagements, it is within every bound of believability that the Christians were subjected to vicious tortures. And history is replete both with examples of the merciful and of the sadistic, of the disinterested and the zealous. There is no question that the lot of Christians varied from region to region, depending on the fortune of which local officials were responsible for implementing the imperial edicts. Constantius would be celebrated in later tradition for his tolerance, largely on account of the subsequent history of his son Constantine – but there is no doubt that he was not among the more fanatical or even workmanly in the practice of rooting out Christianity.

Williams makes a plain verdict on his senior colleague Diocletian: 'There is no doubt that Diocletian had control of every major policy in the Empire until 304, and has the major responsibility for the persecution until that date. I believe he was guilty of great cruelty, and of a political error ... even by the standards of his age, not ours, the later stages of the persecution were shameful.'[20]

The bishop of Rome at the time of the persecution was Pope Marcellinus, and he offers an interesting window into the time of crisis. His papacy had commenced in 296, several years before the persecution commenced. Marcellinus was said to have been among those who betrayed their faith by agreeing to offer the requisite pinch of incense, as it were, to the pagan gods, only later to have repented of his action and to have been slain as a martyr. 'The Bishop of Rome, Marcellinus, surrendered the scriptures.'[21] Marcellinus was not venerated universally at first, on account of the question of his alleged defection from Christianity. Later writers – among them the famous Saint Augustine of Hippo – denied the veracity of the reports, and Marcellinus is venerated by contemporary Christians among the popes and martyrs. The case of Marcellinus would be an influence on the eventual rise of a schism within Christianity known as Donatism (the name refers to one Donatus, a bishop who espoused the teachings of the sect).[22] The Donatists were extremists. For them, the very validity of a Christian sacrament rested on the personal worthiness of the minister. Sacraments like baptism and the administration of Holy Orders were subject to the problem of the identity of the priest or bishop that conferred them. If a bishop had been one of those who had handed over the sacred scriptures of Christianity to the imperial authorities, then his sacraments would be considered invalid.

Donatism had one serious problem: an individual Christian was at the mercy of knowing the actions and indeed soul of the minister who ministered to him. The problem of rigorist interpretations of Christian law and morality was not new. When Decius had launched his similar persecution of Christians earlier in the third century, the Novatianists (named after the Christian thinker Novatian) had argued that those who lapsed from the faith could not be readmitted. If you made your sacrifice to the pagan gods, there was no mercy for you, and no return to the practice of Christianity. The Donatists viewed themselves as the true Christians, the ones who were fully embracing and practising the tenets of the faith.

Their ardent devotion to their beliefs was a contributing factor to their longevity – there would be Donatists for centuries. This was one of the most significant schisms in Christianity at this time, and it would prove to be one of the more enduring. It was a natural enough consequence of the Diocletianic persecution. Christians had been confronted on a mass scale with the threat of death, and there must have been many adherents of the faith who agreed to make their token sacrifices to the pagan gods, or to turn over religious books.

Noteworthy to mention here in passing is that Marcellinus was preceded in his pontifical office by Pope Saint Caius, who was said to have been a native of Salona in Dalmatia like Diocletian – indeed there is a report that they were of the same extended family. Caius was pope from 283 to 296, and he is traditionally venerated as a martyr, though he died before the commencement of the Great Persecution, with the result that some have questioned the veracity of the report of his violent death. His story is linked to that of Saint Susanna of Rome, who was said to have died as a martyr in 295 because she refused to marry a relative of Diocletian. The legend of Susanna is not considered nearly as reliable as that of Agnes, and so many critics have concluded that there likely was a martyr of the name and age, but that the details of the story have been embellished or in some way fabricated.

It is impossible to determine how many were slain in the Great Persecution. Christian liturgical books and martyrologies are replete with the names of the dead. There must have been a considerable number of those who suffered less severe penalties. What is clear is that the persecution efforts did not succeed in eradicating the religion from the empire, and likely strengthened it. Diocletian and his imperial colleagues had achieved impressive successes in the business of defending the borders of Rome and of stabilizing the government and administration of the empire. But in terms of any wish to see Christianity eradicated from the borders of Rome, there would be ultimate failure.

There were four edicts of Diocletian in all; it is a matter of controversy whether all four were implemented in the areas where Maximian and Constantius were responsible for oversight.

We may focus attention on one of the more interesting and yet problematic sources of information regarding the reign of Diocletian and other tetrarchs, a work that we have mentioned thus far only briefly: the so-called *De mortibus persecutorum* of Lactantius, the author's treatise on the deaths of the persecutors.[23] This is a brief work that has occasioned considerable controversy. It purports to tell the story of how those who tried to persecute Christians met their own host of troubles, a sort of 'reaping the whirlwind' analysis of history by way of tendentious tract.

Lactantius breezes through earlier history in six chapters, before focusing on Diocletian as the source of all of Rome's later problems. In Lactantius' analysis, Diocletian was a disaster precisely by virtue of his decision to create a tetrarchy. Lactantius argues that the establishment of a government of four men triggered an arms race that virtually guaranteed civil war. Lactantius indicts Diocletian for extreme greed and avarice, to which he ascribes tax and financial policies that in his estimation were also disastrous. For Lactantius, the persecution of Christians was focused all too often on wealthier individuals who had properties and goods that Diocletian wished to appropriate. We may quote the entirety of Chapter 7, where the Christian polemicist introduces Diocletian and offers several interesting details about his life:[24]

Diocletianus, qui scelerum inventor et malorum machinator fuit, cum disperderet omnia, ne a deo quidem manus potuit abstinere. Hic orbem terrae simul et avaritia et timiditate subvertit. Tres enim participes regni sui fecit in quattuor partes orbe diviso et multiplicatis exercitibus, cum singuli eorum longe maiorem numerum militum habere contenderent, quam priores principes habuerant, cum soli rem publicam gererent. Adeo maior esse coeperat numerus accipientium quam dantium, ut enormitate indictionum consumptis viribus colonorum desererentur agri et culturae verterentur in silvam. Et ut omnia terrore complerentur, provinciae quoque in frusta concisae; multi praesides et plura officia singulis regionibus ac paene iam civitatibus incubare, item rationales multi et magistri et vicarii praefectorum, quibus omnibus civiles actus admodum rari, sed condemnationes tantum et proscriptiones frequentes, exactiones rerum innumerabilium non dicam crebrae, sed perpetuae, et in exactionibus iniuriae non ferendae. Haec quoque <quomodo> tolerari <non> possunt quae ad exhibendos milites spectant? Idem insatiabili avaritia thesauros numquam minui volebat, sed semper extraordinarias opes ac largitiones congerebat, ut ea quae recondebat integra atque inviolata servaret. Idem cum variis iniquitatibus immensam faceret caritatem, *legem pretiis rerum venalium statuere conatus est; tunc ob exigua et vilia multus sanguis effusus, nec venale quicquam metu apparebat et caritas multo deterius exarsit, donec lex necessitate ipsa post multorum exitium solveretur. Huc accedebat infinita quaedam cupiditas aedificandi, non minor provinciarum exactio in exhibendis operariis et artificibus et plaustris, omnia quaecumque sint fabricandis operibus necessaria. Hic basilicae, hic circus, hic moneta, hic armorum fabrica, hic uxori domus, hic filiae. Repente magna pars civitatis exciditur. Migrabant omnes cum coniugibus ac liberis quasi urbe ab hostibus capta. Et cum perfecta haec fuerant cum interitu provinciarum, "non recte facta sunt", aiebat, "alio modo fiant." Rursus dirui ac mutari necesse erat iterum fortasse casura. Ita semper dementabat Nicomediam studens urbi Romae coaequare. Iam illud praetereo, quam multi perierint possessionum aut opum gratia. Hoc enim usitatum et fere licitum consuetudine malorum. Sed in hoc illud fuit praecipuum, quod ubicumque cultiorem agrum viderat aut ornatius aedificium, iam parata domino calumnia et poena capitalis, quasi non posset rapere aliena sine sanguine.*

'Diocletian, who was the inventor of crimes and the contriver of evils, when he destroyed all things, was not able to hold back his hand even from God. He subverted the world at the same time by his greed and timidity. He set up three partners of his rule, with the world divided into four parts, and with armies multiplied, since each of these emperors strove to have a far greater number of soldiers than previous rulers had had when they ruled the empire alone. So much greater was the number of those receiving than of those giving [i.e. taxes], that by the enormity of the impositions the fields of settlers were abandoned because their resources had been consumed, and the cultivated land was rendered a woodland. And in order that all things might be filled with terror, the provinces were chopped up into pieces; many officials and many offices brooded over the individual regions and almost over the individual cities. Here there were basilicas, here a circus, here a mint, here a factory for arms production, here the house for his wife, here one for his daughter. Suddenly a great part of the city was destroyed. All emigrated together with their wives and children, as if from a city that had been captured. And when all of these things had been completed with the ruin of the provinces, he used to say "Things were not done correctly...let it be done in a different manner." Again it was necessary for things to be torn down and changed – things that were destined, perhaps, to fall again. Thus always he was so demented, desiring to equal Nicomedia to the city of Rome. And now I pass over this fact, namely how many perished on account of their possessions or wealth. This was a customary and almost legalized occurrence, given how wickedness became habitual. But in this matter, what was primary was that wherever he saw a more cultivated field or a more ornate edifice, calumny was prepared against the owner, and capital punishment – as if he were not able to seize the property of others without the shedding of blood.'

From the start, Diocletian is labelled as the very source of crime and wickedness. He was not only the *scelerum inventor* – 'the inventor of crimes' – but he was also (alliteratively) the *malorum machinator* – 'the machinator of maleficence'. His evil was such that even the divine was not immune to his intended assaults – such, implicitly, was the extent of his depravity. Interestingly, Lactantius criticizes Diocletian for both avarice and timidity. The former was a common charge levelled against the emperor. The latter points to insecurity and fear, no doubt occasioned by Diocletian's worry that he was always at heightened risk of being undermined or overthrown. But there is also a hint, perhaps, of the insecurity of a man of servile origins who now needed gems and purple to remind him that he was free, and not only free but also the most powerful man in the Roman world. It is noteworthy that Diocletian's critics do not seem to have had the same rich and abundant catalogue of vices and examples of bad behaviour that were the stock in trade for those who condemned a Caligula or a Nero, let alone a Heliogabalus. Diocletian was not, we can be sure, given over to hedonism or to sexual immorality in the way that some his more notorious predecessors had been. Diocletian's vices were of a sort that Dante would punish more severely than the sins of lust of gluttony, some might think, rooted as they were more in avarice than in simpler sins.

For Lactantius, the subdivision of the empire into dioceses alongside the increased number of provinces was meant to be the occasion of increased fear and anxiety among Diocletian's subjects. This is probably among the more questionable of the polemicist's charges, though certainly the mushrooming of administration likely did result in an increased feeling that one's actions – particularly with respect to finance and taxation – were being monitored closely. The real target of the increased number of administrative divisions may have been not so much the general population as the officials who would be less able to contemplate rebellion if they were in charge of relatively small units. But certainly the emperor had more agents in more places, with layers of management that served also to distance the divine emperor from the administration of mundane local tasks. The accumulation of personal wealth is Lactantius' explanation for much of Diocletian's methodology for the maintenance of empire – again, the emphasis on insatiable avarice. Building projects were the occasions for additional manifestations of the emperor's enormous sense of egotism and desire for personal aggrandizement.

Maximian is accorded much the same criticism as Diocletian, with the exception that Maximian was judged to have been less acquisitive than his Augustan colleague, though bolder and more reckless. Constantius is considered laconically to have been worthy of the sole rule of the empire, with no further comment on his character or nature. Galerius is criticized severely, with the charge that he was essentially a barbarian, possessed of a savage and uncouth nature. The comparatively kind treatment of Constantine is reflective of the tradition of his sympathy toward Christianity, while the corresponding indictment of Galerius is indicative of the blame he was given for much of the intensity of the religious persecutions in the east.

But notwithstanding how seriously Galerius was censured, Diocletian was blamed for being the source of the problem. Needless to say, early Christian writers saw in Diocletian another figure of the Antichrist, and they saw the Great Persecution as hastening the end of his reign. At the time of the Great Persecution, he had been in power for twenty years – itself a testament to his skill at survival and administration of government, since most of his imperial predecessors in the third century had enjoyed dramatically shorter reigns. Diocletian was now likely approaching sixty years of age, and there are indications that he was becoming impatient with the prospect of continued rule. Foreign affairs had clearly always been his preferred arena of administration, and the empire was at least reasonably secure. He seems not to have enjoyed Rome, and we know that before the end of 303 he was already out of the city, heading for northern Italy and Ravenna. Lactantius argues that Diocletian was unable to tolerate the freedom of speech and forthright attitude that he experienced in Rome.

When we say that the empire was 'reasonably secure' from foreign peril, we mean that constant maintenance and attention was required. Diocletian would not stay long in Ravenna, proceeding back to the Danube and familiar campaign country, this time to deal with the Carpi. Foreign problems were never absent from the imperial agenda.

It is a matter of speculation as to whether Diocletian and Maximian reached their agreement in Rome concerning how they would jointly retire from office. It is likely that Diocletian was eager to make plans for his abdication, and certain that Maximian was not eager to abandon his post just yet. Diocletian had not seen Maximian in years, and the two men were of different temperament when it came to licentious living and decadence.

In indication of how many basic details of our story are in doubt, some have questioned whether Maximian was even in Rome in 303.[25] The main point of contention on this issue is why the Vicennalia of 303 was not the occasion for the abdications. As so often, certainty is impossible, but a major factor of consideration was probably the reluctance of Maximian to retire, and the possibly related problem of who the new Caesars would be, especially given the Maxentius question.

Diocletian, at any rate, seems to have been offended by the moral climate in Rome, with its libertine air and lack of the practice of traditional Roman moral values.[26] Lactantius had a different view:[27]

Hoc igitur scelere perpetrato Diocletianus, cum iam felicitas ab eo recessisset, perrexit statim Romam, ut vicennalium diem celebraret, qui erat futurus a.d. duodecimum Kalendas Decembres. Quibus sollemnibus celebratis cum libertatem populi Romani ferre non poterat, impatiens et aeger animi prorupit ex urbe impendentibus Kalendis Ianuariis, quibus illi nonus consultatus deferebatur. Tredecim dies tolerare non potuit, ut Romae potius quam Ravennae procederet consul, sed profectus hieme saeviente, frigore atque imbribus verberatus morbum levem, at perpetuam contraxit vexatusque per omne iter lectica plurimum vehebatur.

'Therefore with this crime having been perpetrated, Diocletian, when now felicity had departed from him, proceeded immediately to Rome in order that he might celebrate the day of his Vicennalia, which was going to be observed on the twelfth day before the Kalends of December. With which solemnities having been celebrated, when he was not able to endure the liberty of the Roman people, intolerant and sick in mind he burst forth out of the city just before the Kalends of January, on which day a ninth consulship was bestowed on him. He was not able to tolerate thirteen days, in order that he might inaugurate his consulship at Rome rather than Ravenna. Instead, he set out while winter was raging. Buffeted by chill and rain, he contracted a mild but constant illness. Vexed by that, he was usually conveyed along the entire route on a litter.'

For Lactantius, the problem was the old Roman watchword *libertas* or 'freedom': the senatorial aristocracy in particular may be referenced here. Diocletian had not been the inventor of the practices of de facto regnal rule that characterized the imperial office in his day, but he was by no means ready to refrain from any overt shows of monarchical rule. On the contrary, he increased the image of the emperor as a quasi-divine, otherworldly autocrat. Diocletian had had limited experience of Rome in his life, and had little or no emotional connection to the city. It would have been a strikingly different place from those in which he had lived and worked for most of his life, such that even without the issue of the senate and the notion of republican freedom, Rome was likely an uncomfortable locale. 'The sheer extravagance and frivolity of the city's celebrations jarred on his puritan taste.'[28] Williams is right to draw a distinction between what he terms the 'Roman Idea' and the reality that Diocletian encountered in the city. Indeed, one is reminded of stories of those in the field of Classics and Ancient History who were imbued in the study of Greece and Rome solely from books and the power of their imagination, only then to travel for the first time to Athens or to Rome and to be disappointed by what they encountered. No actual city could compete with their romantic dreams of the classical world. Diocletian seems to have been in that sort of psychological predicament, preferring to dream of Rome rather than to see the real thing. We cannot be sure of the exact nature of his fever and illness, but whatever it was, he was unable to recover quickly, and seems to have been sick for much of the winter and into the spring.

Diocletian's departure for the Danube was another eastward journey, ultimately back to Nicomedia. The campaign against the Carpi was a typical example of the maintenance of empire that was a hallmark of his style of management.

'We have little information about the period between 20 December 303, when Diocletian left Rome for the last time, evidently suffering from a serious illness, and 1 May 305.'[29] Certainly we have little in the way of details about his military engagements, but they were apparently successful and of short duration. The Carpi are a somewhat mysterious people on account of our relative lack of information about them.[30] We are not certain if they were related to the Sarmatians, for example. They were centred in what is today eastern Romania, heading in the direction of Moldova and Ukraine. They were certainly regular players in the drama of the third century, frequently pestering Rome's Danubian frontier to a greater or lesser extent. Like many of the barbarian enemies of Rome, the Carpi were resilient. One can read of repeated victories over them in which they suffered appalling losses, only to return to fight again another day. Like other tribes, they sometimes endured forced migrations in the wake of defeat, destined for resettlement in border areas of the empire that had suffered population loss from war and privations. They vanish from the historical record early in the fourth century CE, for uncertain reasons. It is likely that they intermarried and became absorbed by other tribes, though it cannot be excluded that they were finally more or less annihilated or deported.[31] Some have asserted that they must have remained in the region in some numbers, but if this were the case they were definitely not in any position to constitute a future threat to Rome. The Carpi are best known today by the name of the Carpathian mountains which were once their homeland. They would have the dubious distinction of being the last people against whom Diocletian would wage war. The old soldier had reached the end of his campaigning, with another victory (more or less resounding) in an area of the empire that was of special concern to him. Surely the soon to be retired emperor knew better than most that every victory was merely the restarting of the clock's countdown to when the next border trouble would emerge. If Augustus could emphasize that he had brought peace to the Roman world, Diocletian's message would be that likewise he had given the gift of peace, though at the price of a very expensive, never-ending maintenance of border security.

'Events in the Balkans are particularly hard to untangle, depending for the most part on imperial victory titles rather than detailed historical accounts.'[32] When these titles are preserved on letters and other records, they can provide an invaluable window into an otherwise lost or shadowy historical record.[33]

It is not certain if Galerius came to assist Diocletian in these military operations. One of the confusing aspects of the tetrarchy is that the four men seemed to enjoy sharing titles, such that if one of them earned a triumphal appellation like *Carpicus Maximus*, it was thought to redound to the glory of them all and to underscore their unity, with all four of them being entitled to use the title – it makes for an interesting twist on the imperial post, with a tetrarch possibly learning one day of a new title that had been bestowed on him for a conflict being waged on the opposite end of the empire.[34] Diocletian is said to have remained ill during this time, such that his health seems to have been significantly compromised by the end of the summer of 304. He departed for Nicomedia in a less than ideal condition, to be sure – by the end of the year there are reports that he collapsed soon after the opening of a circus near his palace during the anniversary celebrations of 20 November. The year 304 had been spent in more or less constant sickness, again of uncertain origin. He was no longer a young man, and he was not much given to rest and relaxation. Twenty years was a significant anniversary, and one that may have weighed on him as he returned to the city where it had all commenced. He had always been devoted to order, and the idea that twenty years was a neat, round figure to mark a reign may have appealed to him.

We have no idea what Diocletian was sick with, but we have no reason to doubt the veracity of the reports. The emperor was seriously ill, no doubt in part from sheer exhaustion. Again, he had taken almost no significant period of rest in his life. He may have already planned for his abdication, but there is no indication that he was malingering or trying to make it seem as if he were sicker than he really was for the sake of finessing his departure from public life. The incessant nature of border problems may have been one of the most pressing reasons for his wish to be finished with imperial management. There was increasing anxiety in his inner circle that he might die sooner rather than later – and after two decades of success, people had come to depend on Diocletian and his presence at the helm.

The winter of 304–305 would be a quiet one for the emperor, one he spent in Nicomedia largely in isolation. One wonders if he had any memory of the fate of Numerian, whose decaying body finally gave away the game that he had died. Rumours began to swirl that the emperor was quite enfeebled, and even that he had succumbed to whatever was wrong with him. This is the stuff of easily written propaganda from Diocletian's Christian opponents about the collapse of his condition as the verdict of God on his unjust religious persecutions. Here is the account in Lactantius:[35]

Sic aestate transacta per circuitum ripae Istricae Nicomediam venit, morbo iam gravi insurgente; quo cum se premi videret, prolatus est tamen, ut circum quem fecerat dedicaret anno post vicennalia repleto. Deinde ita languore <est> oppressus, ut per omnes deos pro vita eius rogaretur, donec Idibus Decembribus luctus repente in palatio, maestitia et lacrimae iudicum, trepidatio et silentium tota civitate. Iam non modo mortuum, sed etiam sepultum dicebant, cum repente mane postridie pervagari fama quod viveret, domesticorum ac iudicum vultus alacritate mutari. Non defuerunt qui suspicarentur celari mortem eius, donec Caesar veniret, ne quid forte a militibus novaretur. Quae suspicio tantum valuit, ut nemo crederet eum vivere, nisi Kalendis Martiis prodisset, vix agnoscendus, quippe qui anno fere toto aegritudine tabuisset. Et ille Idibus Decembribus morte sopitus animam receperat, nec tamen totam. Demens enim factus est, ita ut certis horis insaniret, certis resipisceret.

'Then, after the summer had come to a close, he came via a circuit of the banks of the Danube to Nicomedia, with a serious disease now rearing its head. When he saw that he was being oppressed by this, nevertheless he was brought forth, in order that he might dedicate the circus that he had built, with a year now having passed since his twentieth anniversary celebration. Then he was oppressed with languor, with the result that there was prayer to all the gods for his life, until the ides of December, when there was a sudden lament in the palace, sorrow and the tears of the judges, trepidation and silence in the entire city. Now they started to say not only that he was dead, but even that he had already been buried, when suddenly in the morning on the following day the rumour spread that he was alive, and the faces of those of his household and the judges were swiftly changed. Nor were people absent who suspected that his death was being concealed, until Caesar came, lest there be some revolt by the soldiers. This suspicion was so strong, that no one would believe that he was alive, unless he had come forth on the Kalends of March. He was scarcely able to be recognized, since after almost an entire year spent in illness he had wasted away. He had fallen into his stupor on the Ides of December, and had now regained his spirit, though not totally. He had been rendered unsound of mind, with the result that at certain hours he was insane, and at others he regained his senses.'

Again, we have the condemnatory narrative of the classic critic of the tetrarchs. For Lactantius, Diocletian was barely lucid at points now, given over to fits of insanity and bouts of severe illness. For the defender of Christians, it was the continuing decline of the man who had defied God. Some have wondered if he suffered from dementia or at least the increasingly obvious decline of his mental faculties. He may have had some chronic illness that is impossible to diagnose in the absence of more specific information as to his symptoms. There may be a hint in Lactantius' account of a certain appropriateness in how the people began to spread the rumour that Diocletian was dead, and how there were demands to see the emperor. After all, we may recall the case of Numerian in his carriage, the similar situation at the commencement of Diocletian's reign. Once again there was a case of an emperor who had barely been seen by anyone for some time – in Diocletian's case, far longer than the poet-ruler Numerian had been absent. Even in early fourth century Rome, a world far removed from the contemporary milieu with its merciless constant news cycles and monitoring of the whereabouts of leaders, an emperor was expected to be seen and to be heard. Something was seriously wrong with Diocletian.

Meanwhile there were numerous political and administrative concerns afoot. One of the most prominent was the question of who would succeed to the position of Caesar should an Augustus step down and promote his subordinate. Two more men would be needed to be chosen for admission to the exclusive club of the tetrarchy. There was also the issue of whether

Diocletian and Maximian were both prepared to retire simultaneously – and to stay retired. Maximian had already seemingly stepped down from active engagement, at least on the foreign front. But relaxation – even extended – was not retirement.

Meanwhile the rumours about Diocletian continued to flourish during the fateful winter. Health concerns predominated, though there was also a report in December 304 that the emperor had fallen into a coma, or even that he had committed suicide – an odd development, it could be argued. Perhaps Diocletian had become sufficiently frustrated as to the progress of his recovery from whatever was wrong with him, such that his courtiers began to despair that he might take his own life. It is revealing that when finally we hear that Diocletian did appear in public, all indication is that he looked exceptionally weak. It was March 305, and he was certainly in no condition to prepare for any new campaigns or major initiatives. Barnes concludes: 'His judgment and his will power were now impaired.'[36] Whatever was wrong with his physical health – and we can only hope to speculate in the dark – it was serious and sufficiently debilitating so as to require a season of rest and recovery. Galerius arrived in Nicomedia in that same month, reunited with his Augustus. He was well aware by this point that he was on the verge of being promoted at last to that rank.

Lactantius despised Galerius on account of the active persecution of Christians, and Galerius is cast as the villain at every possible juncture in his account of events. And so we hear of Galerius importuning Diocletian to retire even to the point of threat and recrimination, bullying the older man into surrendering power. Many modern historians find little to no credibility in this account.[37] Lactantius blames Galerius too for the crises that resulted from the choice of the new Caesars who would replace the promoted Galerius and Constantius. On this, the rhetorician had more grounds for complaint – both of the new Caesars would be partisans of Galerius, and anyone could have foreseen the trouble that would ensue, trouble that would be incarnated in Constantine and Maxentius. It does not matter, ultimately, whether Galerius browbeat Diocletian into confirming his wishes. Galerius won the day, and he would live to suffer the consequences of the decisions of that fateful spring.

Again, we may note that the suspicion has been raised that Diocletian was a master thespian, making sure that his planned abdication would seem reasonable and appropriate by convincing people that he was exhausted and physically ill. There is ample evidence that a man can recover his health once he is removed from a stressful situation, and Diocletian was destined to enjoy several years in retirement, whatever illness he had in 304–5 (and possibly beyond) not proving to be an immediate life or death crisis. But likelier is that the whole episode was a genuine case of physical exhaustion, advanced age, and whatever ailment or ailments had befallen the emperor on his winter exertions as he proceeded from Rome to Nicomedia. Diocletian was not the sort who would want to try to remain in power in an enervated state. By the spring of 305, he was ready to retire. Galerius was with him.

Chapter 7

Abdication and the Second Tetrarchy

Great controversy surrounds the events that led to the dramatic scene of abdication on the Kalends of May 305.[1] Lactantius, as we have seen, relates that Galerius was quite insistent about the need for Diocletian and Maximian to retire. His version of events is that Galerius persuaded Diocletian that the time had come to vacate his office, and that he had persuaded Maximian of the same at Sirmium.

We know that there would be a dramatic announcement, on the spot where over two decades before Diocletian had been hailed as new emperor by his troops. Diocletian was in tears, and he declared his fatigue and tired condition. He was ready to abdicate, the first Roman emperor to do so in all of the long history of the empire. It was, no doubt, one of the most dramatic occasions in Roman history.

It is likely that the truth was not so much that Galerius had to work very hard to persuade Diocletian of anything, as it was that Diocletian was experiencing the normal mental challenges and emotions of anyone who was acutely aware that he was doing something unprecedented. Those emotions would have been aroused all the more acutely by the setting, exactly where it had all begun.

We have noted that the principal problem that confronted the tetrarchy was the question of who the two new Caesars would be in the event of an abdication of the Augustuses. The question to some seemed to have an obvious answer. There were only two adult sons: Constantius' son Constantine, and Maximian's son Maxentius. For many in the Roman world, they were the obvious choices for promotion. Of course, the situation was not as ideal as it might have been had Diocletian had a biological son. Constantine was the son of a Caesar, and Maxentius was the son of an Augustus.[2] But especially given the effort that the tetrarchy had taken to share in honours and triumphs, one could argue that there was no serious problem here.

We have also recalled that throughout Roman imperial history, there were two typical modes of advancing men to higher office, including the highest of offices. One was simply to promote one's biological son. The other was to adopt a son, namely the man considered to be best for the job.

In the present instance, to choose two men who were judged to be the most suitable – at the cost of bypassing Constantine and Maxentius – was clearly a potential catalyst for causing enormous trouble, and even the risk of civil war. There had been twenty years of relative stability at the top of the imperial government. There had been usurpers and rebellions, but nothing like what Rome had seen for so many chaotic decades. And there was no civil war among the tetrarchs. They cooperated impressively, especially given the tenor of recent times.

And yet the first test of the tetrarchy's enduring quality would come at this moment in the spring of 305, as promotions were considered. In the end, the two men who were chosen to be the replacement Caesars and Constantius and Galerius were Severus and Maximinus, men who have not yet figured in our story. We may now explore the biographies and backgrounds of the men who would be thrust into prominence as ominous winds blew in the spring of 305.

Severus was born of unknown date in northern Illyria – with place being as unknown as time. He was, to be sure, another military man, entering the Roman army and at some point attracting the notice of Galerius. According to Lactantius, Diocletian was well aware of Severus' reputation, but in a negative way. He considered Severus to be given over to alcohol and gambling, a man of absolutely no merit to be considered for a promotion to Caesar. Galerius pressed hard for his candidate, arguing that he had done well in the work of being in charge of the administration of army salaries – always a major concern for Roman emperors. Galerius won the day, and Severus was nominated to be one of the new Caesars, assigned to serve under Constantius in the west once he took over as the new Augustus.

Certainly Galerius and Constantius would have been given priority in the choice of Caesars over the retiring Diocletian and Maximian, we might conclude. We do not know how the tetrarchy had agreed among themselves to carry out the difficult process of selecting the next members of their number. It is easy with hindsight to think that they should have insisted on a system of unanimous agreement as to who would be best for the position, or some other means to ensure that the choice would result in as smooth a transition as possible. There were no doubt many ambitious men, even leaving aside the question of the two blood relatives who factored into the mix.

In the absence of sufficient evidence, Severus may seem to be a strange choice, and if Galerius had to fight for him with Diocletian, we may have our answer in something of the vicissitudes and commonplaces of human psychology. Galerius wanted someone who owed him a position, someone with whom he had established the fact that he could cooperate and be amiable. Severus met those qualifications. No doubt Galerius also wanted to avoid having a blood son of Constantius with his father in the west, or a blood son of Maximian serving under him – there would be too much of an air of familial dynasty, and Galerius would be the odd one out in the absence of a son of his own in the game. One may wonder just how much of Diocletian's illness and convalescence in the winter of 304–305 was the result of the stress he must have been under regarding the succession. Surely he knew the questions that were soon to come to the fore, and surely he had some sense of the likely resurgence of a very old and often intractable problem in Roman history – what to do about the question of blood relatives versus those considered to be the most qualified for a position.[3] In this case, it is possible that Galerius responded to fears about the familial ties enjoyed by Constantius and Maximian with their respective sons by choosing someone who was not the best man for the job in the conventional sense – namely, who would be best for Rome – but the best man for the job in terms of ensuring the prominence of Galerius in the inevitable jockeying for power that accompanied any transitional period for government.

In the end, Severus would have a little over a year to serve in the west as Caesar, and he would be dead by violence in a little over two years. We mention this fact from the start to highlight just how quickly events would move in the period after the announcement of Diocletian's abdication.

The other Caesar of that spring of 305 was the man who is known best to history as Maximinus Daza (or Daia). Of him we know significantly more than we do Severus. He was born of low birth in what is today eastern Serbia – yet another Balkan emperor, from that modern country that can boast to have been the cradle of so many emperors. He had one advantage from birth in terms of later history – he was the son of Galerius' sister, and thus a nephew to the future emperor. Maximinus had one lucky detail in his biography: he was born on 20 November, the same day that Diocletian marked as the commencement of his reign.[4]

Like so many of the other individuals in our story, Maximinus entered military service and achieved some degree of distinction from an early age. No doubt his most fortunate quality, however, was being a blood relative of Galerius. Nephews were not as significant as sons, but they qualified as being useful elements in something of the construction of a dynastic arrangement. Like Galerius, he seems to have had a real antipathy toward Christianity, which likely further recommended him to his uncle. Severus had more experience than Maximinus in military affairs, but both men were probably more qualified for their roles than hostile sources would indicate.[5]

At this juncture we may pause and consider the crisis that was in the making. Galerius managed – if only we knew exactly how – to connive for the appointment of not one, but two Caesars who were obviously connected to him. We may speculate on something of what happened here. To be sure, Galerius was interested in checking the ambitions of the sons of Constantius and Maximian. His task was made somewhat easier by the fact that Maximian had spent some time in what seems to have been a quasi-retirement, living well in Italy and refraining from participation in military campaigns. We have observed that some considered Diocletian to have been the politically savvy one, the administrator who chose Maximian as his partner to be the military expert. If this were the case, subsequent events would put in question the wisdom of that initial analysis. Maximian had significant difficulties in his military endeavours early in his career. Even if it would be unfair to blame him for the troubles he experienced in exceedingly difficult tasks, the fact remains that the final months of Diocletian's imperial tenure were marked by continued attention to military command duties – we think of the campaign against the Carpi – while Maximian spent years in comparative rest.

There was also proximity. Constantius was the distant one, off in Gaul and Britain. He did not have the ear of Diocletian (or Maximian, for that matter) in the same way as Galerius. If Diocletian were the key figure – the man who, after all, had put the whole system together, the man of twenty years of respected experience as an Augustus – then Galerius needed to convince Diocletian first and foremost of what he wanted, and then most of his task was accomplished.

Diocletian, one gets the sense, was weakened by exhaustion and illness, and had no desire to become a player in what could easily become a civil war. We do well to remember the period after his accession. Diocletian faced Carinus as a foe in what was unquestionably another eruption of civil war. But for twenty years, Diocletian had been able to focus most of his attention on foreign affairs and civil administration. There had been remarkably little in the way of internecine civil strife in Roman history for two decades. The troubles in Egypt were comparatively minor. It had been an extraordinary twenty years, given the propensity of the Romans to fight among themselves for power. Diocletian no doubt had no stomach for civil war, especially not at his age and with his health. One has the impression that he was willing to hand Rome over to his Caesars, ready for them to do their part in the way he had in 284. He had inherited a mess, and they were receiving a stable empire. To the degree that they ruined things, it would be more to their discredit than to his, so long as he stayed out of affairs.

One could counter this line of reasoning by saying that Diocletian should have done more to ensure that the succession would go in a way that was more likely to result in peace and prosperity. Diocletian's exhaustion may have factored into his decision not to do more than argue with Galerius. The very fact that he questioned the appointment of Severus, for example, would be enough for history to remember that he realized the problematic nature of the promotion.

Maximinus Daza would serve as Caesar under his maternal uncle Galerius. In other words, the nephew would remain close with his beneficent relative, and the friend – perhaps better put, the boon companion – would be in the west, possibly mostly to serve to allow Galerius to know better what was going on with Constantius. Maximinus Daza was assigned responsibility for affairs in Syria and Egypt, as arrangements were put in place to set up the new tetrarchy.

So far we have discussed the question of succession in the tetrarchy with respect to Galerius and Diocletian – the rulers with primary responsibility for the east. Galerius' motivations are easy to explicate. They were self-serving and focused more on preserving his own prerogatives than on assuring a peaceful transition for the new administration. They were short-sighted and of almost assured likelihood to fail. Diocletian's response may rest ultimately in the powerful factor of fatigue. But what of Maximian and Constantius?

To understand something of what happened in May 305, we must consider what was afoot – possibly, probably, and certainly – during the immediately preceding years. The key element may have been Galerius' aforementioned meeting with Maximian at Sirmium in 304. Constantius was certainly not there. The situation in Gaul was busy, and so it was within the realm of possibility, even probability, that the western Caesar needed to be tending to military affairs. On the other hand, the question of the succession was crucial.

Did Galerius meet with Maximian alone in order to convince him that Severus and Maximinus Daza should be the next Caesars? Did Galerius merely lay the groundwork for a scenario where first he would convince Diocletian of his wishes, and then he would leave it to Diocletian to convince Maximian?

This latter option is more in keeping with protocol – the two Augustuses were the ones who were supposed to make the decision about the succession. One thing is certain: Galerius was more active and politically astute than Constantius. Galerius clearly took full advantage of his 'senior' Caesar position as the Caesar to Diocletian. He knew that his Augustus was tired and sick. He was active in promoting his desires in a way that Constantius was not, either because of inclination or the exigencies and relative remoteness of his duties in the west. Diocletian may have expressed to Maximian that above all, conflict should be avoided. Of course, a retort to that argument could have been that conflict was all but assured with what Galerius was scheming to implement. But the question was about conflict today versus conflict tomorrow or a year from tomorrow, and the choice there was to delay the inevitable rather than to embrace it.

One of the certainties of history is that on the occasion that Diocletian announced his abdication at Nicomedia – that unforgettable first day of May 305 – Maximian did the same thing at Mediolanum. He agreed to resign, notwithstanding the fact that he had his son Maxentius, who had been passed over for promotion in the same way as the western Caesar's son Constantine. Nicomedia had become not only an imperial capital, we might note, but the senior imperial capital under Diocletian. It had a strategic location, making it possible for the emperor to respond to numerous problem areas with relative convenience. It would hold sway in such a position of honour until the reign of Constantine who would prefer Byzantium, which would be renamed in his honour as Constantinople (the modern Istanbul).

We have noted that the agreement to retire in the first place – whoever the new Caesars would be – had been taken possibly as early as 303. The period 303–4 marked twenty years of Diocletian's rule, and ten of the Caesars Constantius and Galerius. Largely because of later events, there are reports that Maximian had his misgivings about abdication, and that Diocletian needed to persuade him. Certainly it is possible that Maximian enjoyed being Augustus without having to do very much. And it is true that subsequent history would see him engaging in quite vigorous activity on behalf of the cause of his son. The ability of Diocletian to carry the day should not be underestimated. He clearly was able to persuade his colleague to agree to the abdication. The mystery we have not explored thus far is Maximian's logic regarding his son, and the parallel case of Constantius with his.

The key to the mystery may rest in Maxentius' early life. He had been born around 283, not very long before Diocletian had assumed the purple. He was thus now in his early twenties. We have no evidence that he served in any significant military or political position in his youth. There are no accounts of his soldiering, for example, alongside his father on any campaign. There are not only no heroic exploits to report or conventional signs of future glory to relate, but also no unconventional ones. Maxentius' father had more or less retired from campaign life when his son was at a young age, too young to distinguish himself in any way in battle. And he does not seem to have been aggressive in any ambition for political or military distinction as he matured. In short, the only qualification he had for high office was his pedigree. Even Severus – for all his alleged vices of the bottle and the dice – had a more impressive curriculum vitae.

Maximian could have argued for the promotion of Maxentius only on the grounds of parentage, not on the merits of any arguments about who was the better man for the job. As of the winter of 304–305, Maxentius lacked a credible record, and there was also the chance that the army would be disturbed at the promotion of someone in that position. We hear that Galerius hated Maxentius, and had an abiding personal distaste for the young man. This may be true, or it may have been an inference from subsequent events. In any case, while a son was passed over in the decision of Maximian to support Galerius' plan, a man of impressive record was not.

What of Constantius' son Constantine? He posed a different case. He had been born around 272, and was thus a decade older than Maxentius. Constantine actually spent his formative years at the court, not of Constantius his father, but of Diocletian. Part of the point of such an arrangement was to draw together more closely the 'family' of the tetrarchy. We have mentioned Lactantius – Constantine may have heard him lecture, and he certainly received a fine education in the cultural milieu of Nicomedia.

A cynic would argue that Constantine was also something of a hostage.[6] His father was in the distant west, in an area that had been the locus for significant civil uprisings in the rise of the breakaway Gallic and then Carausian empires. Constantine could not both live and serve with his father – there was too great a risk for the creation of a dynasty. He would instead serve in the east under Diocletian and Galerius – and here he would have a military career, fighting on the Danube as well as against the Persians. He had the advantage of a decade in age over Maxentius, and the chance to earn military credibility before the decision had to be taken regarding the succession.

Constantine's greatest problem may have been the fact of his parentage. No matter how well he performed in his military and administrative tasks in the east, he was the son of the western Caesar, and his promotion would have a dynastic air to it. One could argue that the smart course of action might have been to promote Constantine, but to have him serve under Galerius in the east rather than under his father in the west. But the prime concern of Galerius seems to have been to checkmate Constantius, his fellow Caesar. Galerius was determined to prevent his Caesarian colleague from being able to promote his blood son. This determination carried risks – Constantine would obviously be disturbed by the new arrangement, and Rome had ample experience of civil war, including civil war for far less weighty reasons. Williams concludes that Diocletian was not necessarily opposed to dynastic succession, but that he opposed promoting Constantine and Maxentius because of lack of experience, not least in administration.[7] One could counter this argument by saying that

Severus and Maximinus were not particularly experienced either, at least in comparison to Constantine. Possibly the truth lies in the problem of honouring one son and not both, and the conclusion that this would have been a more perilous course than to allow Galerius to have two cronies as Caesars. In our view, it was a colossal blunder of administration. Diocletian's illness and fatigue may have resulted in a lack not so much of foresight, as of energy to argue overmuch with Galerius. Williams rightly notes that 'it seems Diocletian, unsure about the succession question, did not quite know what to do with him [sc.Constantine].'[8]

One clue to the mood of the tetrarchy is that Constantine did not remain in the east for long after the proclamation of the new state of affairs. In the official version of events, Constantius wrote to Galerius and asked for his son to be allowed to return to him, ostensibly on the grounds of ill health. It was a thinly veiled pretext to conceal the truth of the matter: both Constantius and Constantine were clearly seriously discomfited by the new arrangement, perhaps even privately livid.

Constantius was in a curious position. He technically was the senior Caesar, and thus now he was to be the senior Augustus. In other words, he had not been passed over for any position – he was now at the height of his power. He was to retain full possession of his western realm, with the privilege of assigning Severus his tasks under him. But his son was in an obviously suitable enough place to be promoted to Caesar. He had earned far more credit for his military reputation than Maxentius, and he was of an age to be promoted to higher office.

The problem was that the only way ultimately to fight the new tetrarchy plan was to be willing to commence a civil war. There had not been a civil war of any note for some time, and the idea of opening that door again must have weighed heavily on Constantius, indeed on other members of the tetrarchy. The tetrarchs had built their new government and administration on the foundation of fraternal amity. They had presented the argument that the tetrarchy was not only the most efficient way to manage the huge empire, but also the best government in terms of avoiding future civil wars. For one of the tetrarchs now to go to war over the question of the succession would be unthinkable after so much had been accomplished in the stabilization of the empire. Rome had been brought to the brink not of war but of peace, and her borders were more secure than they had been for ages.

Still, the recall of Constantine to his father was ominous. In modern diplomatic terms, it was something akin to recalling one's ambassador in protest. It was a way to save face, to indicate displeasure without severing ties entirely, let alone going to war. It was a warning shot, too – Constantius had made his concession, and it was a huge one. He was now to be an Augustus, and he had more than earned his position by his outstanding achievements in military and administrative affairs in the west. Everyone knew that he had outperformed Maximian. Galerius had never come close to outperforming his Augustus, and this too would have been tacitly known by all.

Was Constantius even consulted about the arrangement? This is a question concerning which we have no definitive evidence. Constantius' weakness here was geography – he was in the most remote position. It seems shocking with hindsight that there was no four-way conference of the tetrarchs (that we know of at least) to settle such weighty issues. On the other hand, the tetrarchy was also founded on the notion that the crisis points of the border needed the ready intervention of an emperor – it would invite chaos if the emperor and his entourage were gone on some long journey. Two of the tetrarchs could be together – but four, no. We might wish to have access to the no doubt voluminous imperial correspondence. Constantine of course would have known more about what was going on because of his residence at Diocletian's court – though one imagines that Galerius worked to have as much privacy as possible with his Augustus.

We may summarize the disaster in the making. Diocletian is the easiest of the four tetrarchs to explain: he was exhausted and sick, and had no desire to maintain power. He was also blessed to be devoid of any concerns about the ambitions of a son. Maximian may not have wanted to retire just yet, but he had also been by far the least active member of the tetrarchy of late, and he had a son who was not qualified to assume any high office except by virtue of his parentage. Galerius had been active under the senior Augustus, and he had a nephew as well as powerful friends in the military. Constantius had powerful friends in the military on his side of the empire, and he had a powerful son.

In the ultimately deadly game that was to be played, Diocletian would receive what he wanted more than anything – retirement. His Caesar Galerius would receive his promotion to Augustus, and would win in the question of the selection of Caesars. Maximian would not fare so well – all he would get was a retirement. Then again, no doubt he was well aware that he had not been so active, and again he could not at this juncture make a strong case for his son's promotion. Constantius would be promoted to Augustus, indeed technically to senior Augustus (even if this latter point meant very little in practice).

Some might think that Constantius and Galerius should have been allowed to choose their Caesars individually. This ran counter to the logic of the tetrarchy and its emphasis on unity and shared polity – there was a palpable fear about creating a situation where there were two empires instead of one. Further, Constantius would have selected Constantine, we can be sure – and that would have created a familial dynasty that would have been utterly unacceptable to Galerius, even in a case where he could have placed his nephew under Constantius while he worked with Constantine.

One wonders in particular what Diocletian thought about the transition on that Kalends of May, given that he had set up the system that was now to have its first test as a viable, permanent arrangement for the government of Rome. If we can believe Lactantius, until the very end everyone believed that Maxentius and Constantine would be the new Caesars. Much of our knowledge of subsequent events from the dramatic year 305 comes with the caveat that Constantine eventually would emerge victorious, and so the history has in large part been written under the influence of his propaganda.[9] We hear, for example, that Galerius agreed to release Constantine to his father only because he had been drinking alcohol and either did not fully realize what he was doing, or was in a jovial mood of concession.[10] Constantine fled in the night, eager to escape before Galerius could change his mind. There is no need for such dramatic explanations of events. Constantius was now an Augustus, and everyone knew that he had made a major concession by not fighting for his son's promotion. The request to have him sent back to his father was one that could not be refused. It makes for good theatre to imagine Constantine on horseback, hamstringing horse after horse in his relentless quest to escape Galerius' sphere of influence – but the reality was likely far less thrilling.

Were there attempts on Constantine's life that spring and early summer, the assassination plots that we hear of from this period? This is more believable. Accidents and illnesses happened with regularity. Constantine's death would have been met with immediate suspicion, however, and Galerius – if indeed he wanted to see the young man dead – was in a difficult position in terms of securing success. Constantine would be sent to his father, and by the summer of 305 he was in Bononia in Gaul. There was tension, to be sure – but there was also an initial absolute acceptance of the decisions that had been made regarding the succession. This was not to be one of those many occasions in Roman history on which civil war broke out at once on account of some perceived or actual slight. 'Everyone observed the letter of Diocletian's settlement. Constantius loyally accepted Severus without demur. The political atmosphere was not unlike that of the passing of Oliver Cromwell.'[11]

Life in the Roman empire did not come to a halt during the difficult and extended process of deciding on a succession. Foreign enemies followed their own calendar. When Constantine arrived in the west, his father was engaged as usual in the business of maintaining his borders and administering his territory. New Augustuses also had an expectation of achieving something of note on their own, something to distinguish themselves in their newly promoted office. In the case of Constantius, there was also the desire to see his son in a position of honour, with a chance to earn valour on the battlefield.

Britain recalls our attention at this juncture. The great island had never been subdued *in toto* by the Romans. There had always been some line of demarcation, the most famous of which was Hadrian's Wall. For a Roman emperor in charge of Gaul and Britain, the conquest of the entirety of Britain was an obvious, if seemingly unrealistic dream.

Constantius in 305 was planning campaigns in Britain, campaigns that may well have been inspired by his desire to carve out some impressive achievement for himself to inaugurate his Augustan reign – with the implicit challenge for Galerius to do something equally great in the east. The Picts lived in northern and eastern Scotland, and they had never been subdued by the Romans – indeed, they were a regular source of trouble and harassment on the northern frontier of Roman Britain.[12]

Constantius' expedition in what is today northern England and Scotland can be associated with the same foreign policy initiatives that had been a hallmark of the tetrarchy – efforts to stabilize and to patrol the borders. It was a constant job, though the advantage of the insular geography of Britain was that one could dream of taking the entire island, thus eliminating the need for a frontier per se. Constantius probably envisaged operations in the far north even before the issue of the succession became a pressing concern. In fact, the idea that he would be preoccupied with events in one of the most distant corners (if not the most remote) of the empire may have weighed on Galerius – Constantius was peripheral geographically, even if he was an anointed Augustus. If Galerius knew about the planned British campaign, did he have a hope that Constantius would not survive?

Constantius had had an impressive career thus far in his military adventures. Scotland and northern England had been especially difficult arenas for previous Roman adventurers, and this time would be no different. We have no clear sense of the campaigns that took place, but we can speculate that the plans had been in place for some time based on the fact that almost as soon as Constantine arrived in Bononia, he and his father were ready to proceed to the English Channel to cross over in execution of the start of operations.

The Pictish campaign may explain some of what was happening in terms of Constantius' participation in the final settlement of the tetrarchy succession scheme. Let us imagine that the soon to be promoted Caesar was busy drafting plans for what would be one of the most challenging undertakings of his tenure. As he received word that the retirements of Diocletian and Maximian were imminent, the pressure would have been significant – especially in light of his son being passed over for promotion. He would have wanted Constantine to be with him for many reasons, and may have preferred to have his son by his side rather than his new Caesar Severus. We cannot be certain of much of what was going on in the analyses and thought processes of the key players, but Galerius likely took advantage of Constantius' being distracted, and both father and son may have wanted to see one another as soon as possible given the inherent hazards of the operations that were being contemplated, let alone the probability that Constantius would have wanted someone he could trust absolutely as his principal aide in the expedition.

Constantine would now see the opposite side of the world. Father and son crossed over to Britain and proceeded to Eboracum. That summer and autumn were spent in active campaigns against the Picts. This was exactly the sort of thing that Septimius Severus had tried to do decades before, the last time that a Roman military force had undertaken serious manoeuvres north of Hadrian's Wall. History was destined to be repeated in a haunting fashion. Like Constantius, Septimius Severus had been an extremely competent military officer, with a formidable record and a good expectation of success given his prior victories. Like his Severan predecessor, Constantius had a son by his side (though Constantine was far different from Caracalla and Geta). Like the history of decades before, so the summer and autumn of 305 would pass with little in the way of significant achievement and success. There would be no great victories, though we hear of no defeats either. This was largely a guerrilla war, no doubt, and the prospect was for a long period of continued campaigning.

Constantius was not a young man. He was now in his mid-fifties, significantly older than Diocletian had been when he had assumed the role of an Augustus. This was a difficult military operation, and there was appreciable stress, no doubt, as to what was going on in the east, especially after the promotion of Galerius' candidates as Caesar. Constantius may have become weaker and more enfeebled as the months passed, but by January 306 he was able to claim with some credibility that he had won a victory over the Picts that merited the title *Britannicus Maximus II* (the first British triumph having been for the suppression of the Carausian/Allectan revolt).

The winter of 305–306 would be spent at Eboracum. The campaign was expected to continue into another season. Whatever victory had been declared in January, it was not complete. While we have no definitive knowledge of what the goal of the operations was, our aforementioned supposition that it was the total subjugation of the island is a reasonable one. At minimum, the Picts were clearly to be reduced to a non-entity on the map of military threats. This was a hinterland that was always liable to be problematic – and expensive to guard – as long as there was a potential threat. The conquest of the island was the ultimate way to try to eliminate the problem, even if the cost of doing so would be enormous, both in execution and maintenance. The logic would be that the price tag would be higher to continue to tolerate militant barbarians north of some fortification – a strategy that had not worked thus far in the long term for Rome.

Constantius died on 25 July 306. He would have been about 56 years of age, and he had a long record of achievement behind him. Constantine was with him. We lack any sense of what the campaigns of spring and summer were like that year. We lack information too as to the cause of the emperor's death, though it was natural and not from the usual twin perils of battle or conspiracy. He had lived for a little over a year and two months as Augustus, and he had spent most of that time doing what he seems to have enjoyed – living the life of a military commander. Given the exigencies of the British operation, there had been no time to come to know or to quarrel with a man he likely had no desire to befriend – Galerius' associate Severus. Constantius had had the advantage of an extended time with the son he had not seen in ages, and he was able to share something of the experience of army life with him. Certainly in those long months in Gaul and especially in Britain, the two men had a chance to discuss the tetrarchy and the status of the empire. Maybe Britain was an escape for a man who had lived so much of his life close to the edge of the Roman world, and perhaps pouring himself into the Pictish campaign was a way to distract himself from the mess of domestic affairs that had ensued with the transition in the tetrarchy. We cannot overemphasize the possibility that Constantius knew that he was sick, and that events were set into motion with deliberate preparedness and swiftness.

It is interesting to compare the situation of Diocletian in 304–305 with that of Constantius in 306. The former was given up for dead or even buried, only to recover and to live for years in retirement. The latter seems to have faded relatively quickly, or at least to have been sick in a more private and better concealed way.

In some ways the events of late July 306 would eclipse those of May 305. That earlier spring occasion had been a day on which Galerius was no doubt smug, confident that his political initiatives had secured what he wanted in terms of the succession, with Constantine passed over and largely irrelevant. The seasons would match the mood, given that what was to happen in high summer would be nothing less than the precipitous step towards civil war. The spectre of internal conflict had been what kept things more rather than less in check in the spring of 305. But the summer of 306 would be different, as Constantius realized that he would be the first of the four original tetrarchs to breathe his last. His plans would have been made in concert with Constantine, and with no consultation of his colleagues past or present. In that sense it would have been revenge for how Constantius had been left out of so many of the discussions that had precipitated the earlier decisions.

What Constantius did was to recommend to his army that Constantine should be promoted to Augustus in his stead. Thus the man who had been passed over for the position of Caesar would be leapfrogged into the Augustan status. The plan had a certain elegance to it. One could argue that it was not an infringement in the strict sense on anyone else's prerogative. Galerius, for example, was still an Augustus – there was nothing in the Constantius plan that said that his son intended to take sole command of anything. Severus was still (in theory at least) a Caesar, as was Maximinus Daza. The only change was the replacement of the father by the son. It may be significant – highly significant, even – if what Constantius did was recommend the promotion of his son to the army, rather than decree it.

A key figure in the plan seems to have been a king of the Alamanni, one Crocus or Chrocus. He had allied himself with Constantius and come over to the service of the Romans, and he was present during the British campaign.[13] He seems to have declared at once that Constantine was Augustus, and this led to the soldiers declaring the same. Theatre may have been the name of the game. It was orchestrated, we might conclude, and well planned – even if there was tremendous inherent risk. Constantius and Constantine had had plenty of time to develop a scheme, even if it was unclear how sick Constantius was – we do not know if his condition was of long duration, or of sudden onset and swift termination. The former is likely to have been the case – one gets the sense that there was nothing precipitous about what happened.

The risks were enormous. It is true that Britain and Gaul immediately accepted the idea that Constantine was the new Constantius. But Hispania, for example – an area that had only recently been transferred to Constantius' control under circumstances of which the details are lost to history – was not in favour of the plan.

Spain was the least of the problems that emerged from the events in Britain. Galerius had to be informed of what was going on, and informed he was – Constantine sent him an official dispatch, announcing the death of his father and the fact that the army had acclaimed him as Augustus against his will. Again, we may see the script of theatre. It was imperative and the stuff of normal diplomatic language to claim that he did not, after all, wish to be thrust into high office. Only with regret and deep reservation had he yielded to the will of the army.

The moment when Galerius read this letter, or heard it being read to him, must have been one of those wondrous occasions in history. One can imagine the rage with which he digested the news, coupled with the anxiety that now he would need a plan, and that he was in the reactive position.[14] He must have felt that this was revenge for the spring of 305, when he had been the one who saw his plots and plans come to fruition. This was not a rebellion like that of Carausius decades before in Britain. This was the son of an Augustus, who was now informing his fellow Augustus of the death of his father and his own promotion by army acclaim – in other words, the fundamental arrangement of the tetrarchy was still to remain in place, with Constantine simply assuming one of the four jobs.

The problem of the summer of 306 was the same as that of the previous spring. War was the obvious conclusion if one disagreed too stridently or too overtly with the decisions that were taken. Constantius could have gone to war in 305 over the slight to his son, but he did not. He bided his time, perhaps with the awareness that he was in physical decline and would not live for too extended a period. Galerius was now the one who was confronted with a stark choice – would there be war, or would there be continued peace? Constantine was acting as if things were in a state of business as usual, which was a brilliant element of the plan – matters were such that it would be Galerius who was in the position of plunging the empire into its first significant civil war in decades. Constantine took a gamble that Galerius would do something short of a declaration of war. He might not accept the arrangement without caveat or response of his own – but it was likely that he would not resort (at least yet) to armed conflict. There was an element of risk in this, indeed appreciable risk. But men do not usually become Roman emperors without playing a game with fortune.

The events in Eboracum are thus parallel to those of the preceding year in Nicomedia. There is an undeniable brilliance to what was achieved that summer in Britain, especially given the fact that nobody would have been in any mood to contemplate yet another civil war to evict someone from a position that was far stronger than that which Carausius had succeeded in managing for some seven years, and Allectus for another three. One cannot exclude the possibility that Constantine applied pressure to his father to accept the arrangement by which he would be named to imperial power – but we cannot be sure of what was discussed between them.[15]

Diocletian had accepted a second tetrarchy which presented a host of challenges that must have been all too easy to discern from the start. The inherent weakness of a system of four-man rule is that four men must agree on major issues in order to stave off any threat to the integrity of the system. Every moment spent worrying about the danger of civil war was another opportunity for Rome's numerous foreign enemies to take advantage of perceived weaknesses. Constantine was probably one of those men who gave clear indications from the start of the potential for greatness, indeed of his capability of achieving what he would one day achieve – sole control of the empire. Indeed this may have been one of the reasons why men like Diocletian were willing to see him excluded from the leadership dynamic. Certainly Galerius felt threatened by him. And in the immediate, Galerius would need to decide how to respond to a clear provocation.

Chapter 8

Constantine and Maxentius

Galerius was no fool. His reaction to the letter of Constantine was probably as brilliant and delicately balanced as anyone could muster. In short, he conceded to Constantine's position – with an important change that was accompanied by his own gesture of diplomatic courtesy. He agreed that Constantine should join the tetrarchy – but as a Caesar, with Severus as Augustus.[1] However, he accompanied this decision by sending the traditional purple robes of office to Constantine. This meant that Constantine would be receiving official sanction from Galerius for his entry into the tetrarchy.

This was a diplomatic dance, of the sort that one can admire especially from the vantage of temporal distance. Constantine had outfoxed Galerius, and Galerius had engaged in his own vulpine trick – whether it was his own idea, or the suggestion of his counsellors. For the immediate geopolitical moment, Galerius' sanction of Constantine as Caesar meant that any potential problems in Spain were averted. Constantine was also not without continuing work in Britain – the campaign against the Picts either needed to be abandoned, or to be finished successfully.

We have little information about the resumption of operations in northern England and Scotland. Likely now there was to be no grand project of subjugating the entire island, not with the more pressing issues of membership in the tetrarchy. The north of Britain demanded the usual administrative and logical maintenance that accompanied military action, and Constantine was given the opportunity to oversee those projects before he planned his departure for the continent.

The history of what Severus was doing in this early period of his life as Caesar (and then, suddenly, as Augustus) is obscure. There had been little to no opportunity for him to interact with Constantius, but now he had the son of his former Augustus as his own Caesar. Initially Constantine would be busy in Britain, and arrival in Gaul would bring with it its own set of challenges along the Rhine frontier. News travels fast enough to alert potentially hostile tribes of changes of leadership, and the transition periods in imperial rule were always perilous moments in terms of foreign relations.

Diocletian and Maximian must have learned sooner rather than later about what was happening, not to mention Maximian's son Maxentius. While we do not know of their reactions, we do know that the Franks responded to the news of Constantine's accession by crossing the Rhine sometime in the winter of 306–307. It was exactly the sort of problem that had erupted so many times before, and it was a clear test of the new Caesar's ability to respond to the typical crises of border management. Constantine was at Augusta Treverorum, forced to respond to what was a clear act of treachery on the part of the previously pacified Franks. Here for once the historical record tells us something of early Frankish history: we learn of Ascaric and Merogaisus, names rescued from oblivion thanks to the Latin panegyric tradition and work on the manuscript reading thereof. These two rulers are cast in the typical language of panegyrics as having been traitors to Rome who were justly punished – they ended their lives in an amphitheatre, fed to wild animals for the amusement of the crowd.[2] We hear of trouble in this period from the Bructeri as well, another Germanic tribe that launched its own assault over the Rhine near modern Cologne. Constantine successfully fought them as well, building a bridge over the river and quelling yet another threat on the perennially problematic frontier.[3] Every victory engendered more jealousy and resentment in some, even as the border situation was stabilized at least temporarily. The sixth panegyric boasts that the bridge was designed to show Roman power flaunting its might over the Germans, so that the enemy would always assume a suppliant posture. We are told as well that the Rhine was defended by naval units.

What is clear from the history of 305–307 is that Constantine was by far the busiest of the tetrarchs. He was the one engaged in almost constant campaigning, in part the natural consequence of the area that his father had been assigned. Indeed one of the problems that faced Galerius was the fact that Constantius and his son Constantine after him were in power in one of the more challenging regions of the empire. A man based in Gaul could expect a steady stream of opportunities for conquest and the honing and enhancement of a military reputation, and this was something that both father and son used to full advantage.

We have noted that Constantine was more experienced than Severus in army affairs. Certainly he drew on the reputation of his father in consolidating and solidifying his own rule. Constantius had died at a convenient hour for the rise of his son, and Constantine had considerable work to do in maintaining the border of his corner of the tetrarchy. We do hear from later sources that in this early period of his administration, there was little if anything in the way of the persecution of Christians. Later sources – all of them pro-Constantinian, to be fair – paint a picture of religious toleration, a picture that likely is influenced by the fact that Constantine was destined to be the first Christian emperor of Rome. If his mother Helena were Christian, the tolerance that has been ascribed both to Constantius and to his son makes sense. It may also be the case that neither member of the dynasty had any particular concern, at this point at least, with religious affairs. Galerius was more passionate about the persecutions, to be sure – and Diocletian and Maximian had no real patience or tolerance for the Christian faith. Constantine's ire was roused more by barbarians across the Rhine than by any religious practitioners within his corner of empire.

Constantine may not have been zealous in religious matters, but he was possessed of an early and abiding interest in public works and building projects. His capital of Augusta Treverorum would be, in his estimation, a showcase of Roman amenities and splendour. There would be a significant amount of money and labour invested in the renewal of the city and its fortification, vulnerable as it was to relatively sudden barbarian incursions and threats to its security.

While we have no certain knowledge as to what the retired tetrarchs were doing in this immediate period, we do know that one man was thoroughly incensed by the promotion of Constantine – Maximian's son Maxentius. He had been passed over, and no doubt at some level felt that even in the absence of his own record of achievement, he deserved better as the son of a tetrarch. He had been shut out of government plans, and resentment was building for many months. On the chessboard of Roman imperial considerations, Galerius, Severus, Maximinus Daza, and Constantine should have been relatively content. In an ideal arrangement, Diocletian and Maximian could be depended on to provide elder statesman advice to their successors in power. Maxentius was the obvious candidate for dissatisfaction and a grudge, and it is possible that even with awareness of this likelihood, nobody considered him to be that much of a threat. There was a gamble here, and it was a reasonable one. The young and unproven former prince would seem to have limited options to satisfy his yearning for vengeance against perceived slights.

One wrinkle that had been occasioned by the rise of Constantine was the fact that Maxentius could now claim that the son of a tetrarch had been elevated. This argument neglected the fact that Constantine actually had a record of military service. Lactantius would have us believe that Galerius liked neither Constantine nor Maxentius, and that Diocletian was at least convinced that Maxentius deserved no promotion on account of his lack of experience. Maxentius spent the period after his disgrace living near Rome. He was wealthy and had no particular occupation – the perfect recipe for the development of an increased sense of entitlement.

Was Maxentius seeking to court local favour in this period? Almost certainly. Was Maximian quietly interceding with potential friends on behalf of his son? Possibly.[4] Was Diocletian involved in any machinations? Almost certainly not. Of course, Maxentius had no military resume and thus no armies. He lacked the customary route to usurpation of a title or of power.

The catalyst for the son of the onetime tetrarch to make his bid for power was a by-product of the continuing efforts to standardize administrative systems and to ensure that financial and organizational arrangements were managed under one practice. Connected to this rationale was one of the flaws of the tetrarchy that someone assembling a list of criticisms of the system could adduce: Rome had always been neglected. Maxentius was wise to settle into his exceedingly premature retirement near the city, the heart of the empire for so many centuries, a great and storied locale that in recent years had been relegated to a distinctly second if not fifth class status. Tax regulations were a source of anger throughout the city once the tetrarchs announced the determination to treat Rome like any other part of the empire. And what was left of the once much vaunted and unimaginably powerful Praetorian Guard in Rome was to be disbanded – after all, there was no real need for it any longer. The Guard had always been a relatively privileged organization in contrast to the legions, but the heyday of its awesome power seemed to have passed.

Officers from the Guard were not alone in being ready to voice their opposition to recent developments, and Maxentius was a logical venue for venting. The son of Maximian was bitter and resentful about his own treatment at the hands of an imperial government that seemed to devote most of its attention to foreign affairs and border defence, all the while expecting the son of a tetrarch to have no position of authority, and the people of Rome to be treated as if they were, after all, like everyone else in the empire. Diocletian's decision to leave Rome relatively ignored had resulted in unforeseen consequences.

Italy had not been privileged in any way in Diocletian's much publicized novel division of the empire into dioceses and provinces. Indeed, Italy was treated as if it were simply one of many regions of the empire, without any special claim on favour or prerogative. One could speculate that Diocletian was partly a product of his own non-Italian origins. There was the practical consideration that the empire's problems demanded concerns outside of Italy more often than inside. But certainly there were consequences to this policy of not treating Italy any differently from other regions, and Maxentius had capitalized on them.

It was not entirely clear what anyone could expect Maxentius to do in the current situation, indeed what the disgruntled youth could hope to achieve for himself. Constantine had benefited from the fact that his father had actually died, thus opening one of the four positions in the tetrarchy. Whether Constantine was an Augustus or a Caesar was a point of semantics more than anything, especially in a system with four capitals and four imperial courts. The only way Maxentius could enter the system would be if someone else died or abdicated, or if the tetrarchy became a pentarchy.

The recognition that the son of the dead tetrarch was now himself a tetrarch seems to have convinced at least some of the authorities in Rome that Maxentius too would soon be named to the same honour, even if perhaps a little prodding were necessary. Those who were eager to have Maxentius as their leader engaged in the obvious strategy of seeking out the retired Maximian, who was in leisure and rest at Lucania in southern Italy. Maximian was clear (whether disingenuously or not) that he was not interested in resuming his position in any way. It is not certain what advice if any he had to give regarding his son.

Maxentius opted in the end for a middle road. He was possessed of a tremendous ambition to become one of the imperial class, but he was clearly worried about what to do and how to do it without provoking an immediate state of civil war. He chose not to consider himself to be a Caesar or an Augustus. That said, he agreed to be recognized as having imperial power by those who were inviting him to accept it – the authorities in central and south Italy, Sicily, Sardinia and Corsica, and Africa.

Maxentius was playing an exceedingly dangerous game, and likely he knew it. One Augustus and one Caesar were no fans of his – Galerius in particular seems to have had a strong distaste for him, and Constantine was no friend. The views of the other two tetrarchs are unknown, but one imagines that they viewed any 'fifth' member of their exclusive club as a threat. Maxentius' threat came partly from his paternal association – though it was an ominous sign that the father was not willing to step back immediately into a position of authority to aid his son. We cannot be sure what Maximian was telling Maxentius in this period, but anyone who viewed what Maxentius was doing as a rebellion was able to take note that Maximian was not aiding him overtly. Second – and perhaps, one might have thought at least initially, more importantly – there was clearly brewing discontent in Rome and its environs that had now burst forth on the occasion of the tax law changes and the threat to the Praetorian Guard. Rome was once again a locus for imperial problems. The situation of the father and son in Eboracum in the summer of 306 had been very different from the present Roman drama. Galerius had been willing to accept Constantine as a valid usurper (to employ an oxymoron); Maxentius was a step too far.

Maxentius may not have assumed the title of Caesar or of Augustus, but it is possible that the style he did assume – *princeps invictus* – caused its own problems. 'Unconquered prince' must have caused some snickers in imperial capitals – when exactly had Maxentius left the nursery to engage in battlefield exploits and to earn triumphs? *Invictus* was accurate enough – Maxentius had not yet been conquered, and almost overnight he had taken control of a significant portion of the empire – but the hour was premature for any overweening sense of pride and self-satisfaction.

Galerius, for one, was not remotely impressed by the young upstart, and he refused to accept the usurpation and claim of Maxentius. Certainly one factor that weighed on Galerius and his colleagues in the tetrarchy was the fact that Maxentius did not command very many soldiers. Remnants of the Praetorian Guard did not qualify as formidable opposition in the face of disciplined, veteran legions. It was easy to underestimate Maxentius and, further, Severus was all too readily overestimated as a potential counterbalance. Galerius would need to make his own preparations soon enough to respond to the threat.

Galerius and Maximinus Daza were in firm control of the east, and Severus was Augustus in the west, with Constantine nominally serving as his Caesar, even if in effect one could consider Constantine's corner of the realm to be his own. The plan that was put into effect in response to Maxentius' action was to have Severus advance into Italy to put an end to the reign of the would-be pentarch. Italy fell to the preserve of the western Augustus, and the task thus fell to Severus to end the greatest domestic threat to the peace and orderliness of the tetrarchy in its twenty-some years of existence.

The first months of 307 thus saw the renewed spectre of civil war, and on Italian soil. Severus must have had significant misgivings, but he was buoyed, one might think, by the fact that Maxentius had far fewer troops. In the end, it would be his own troops who would pose the greatest threat to him.

The problem that confronted Severus in Italy was that most of his soldiers had served under Maximian in his tenure as tetrarch. Maximian had earned their trust and loyalty, certainly far more than Severus. If we can believe the criticisms of Severus that are said to have concerned Diocletian at the time when Galerius insisted on his promotion, then we can imagine easily enough that Severus had little respect among his soldiers, at least in comparison to the retired Maximian.

It would have been extraordinary if Maximian had planned in advance for the likelihood that Severus would proceed to confront Maxentius, well aware that they would defect to his son in deference to him. That is, in fact, what happened – Severus suffered nothing less than a mutiny, one in which he was faced with defections en masse to the cause of his opponent. Maxentius suddenly had an army. There is some evidence, too, that Maxentius may have added encouragement to the defections by means of the time-honoured tradition of bribery. Severus, one has the impression, did not command loyalty or devotion, and Maxentius' money was a more persuasive incentive.

Not everyone abandoned Severus – he and the remnant of his army ended up retreating to Ravenna. For not only did Severus face the loss of most of his force to Maxentius, but he also witnessed the return from retirement of Maximian, who now cast his lot into the contest of luck. Maxentius is said to have sent the purple robes of imperial power to his father, hailing him as Augustus 'for a second time' – an interesting appellation. It is not entirely clear what exactly Maxentius – or his father – expected was supposed to happen in terms of the management of the tetrarchy. Clearly the father and son did not expect to aspire to joint rule of the empire. It is more likely that they intended to take control of the west, probably at least the territory that was the preserve of Severus and not that of Constantine (at least not for the time). Maximian had been the western Augustus, and the newly proposed arrangement essentially was that which some had expected to have seen enacted in the first place – Maxentius would be promoted, with the obvious difference that now he was to be in charge (at least nominally, one might think) – with his father as the junior partner who was actually senior, a venerable man whose position was novel: an Augustus, after a fashion at least.

One is invited yet again to imagine what these potentates expected to see happen. Severus was in a dire position, essentially open to being besieged in Ravenna with his depleted and perhaps demoralized force. Maxentius is said to have given his word that Severus' life was not at risk. We should not be surprised that it was Maximian who conducted the siege of Ravenna – the troops who had defected were, after all, loyal to him far more than to the inexperienced Maxentius. Severus had no chance militarily of engaging with Maximian, and his surrender came quickly enough. Galerius' friend – the man he had insisted should be promoted to Caesar to serve under Constantius in the west – became the first member of the tetrarchy arrangement to be deposed. The map in the west had become considerably simpler, and without an eruption of serious violence or civil war.

Severus had been something of the odd man out given the circumstances of the death of Constantius and the accession of Constantine. While Severus was nominally and ostensibly the superior tetrarch in the west, Constantine had the impressive record and association with his venerable father, and the advantage of relative remoteness on the map. Just as Carausius had been able to survive for years as the leader of a de facto empire within an empire (and we may compare the parallel case of the Gallic Empire), so did Constantine constitute a formidable power and potential threat to any adversary. The current civil conflict was – at least for the moment – a western problem. Subsequent events in the current crisis would illustrate that Maximian and his son had the idea to take power in the west, with some sort of accommodation to be reached with Constantine. Maxentius, for example, could be recognized as the legitimate Augustus in the west, with Constantine remaining as his Caesar. Maximian could have his hitherto unique title of 'Augustus for a second time'. The east was a problem, to be sure, given the hostile relations between Maxentius and Galerius – but one wild card was Diocletian, who had been a friend and colleague of Maximian for so long. Perhaps he could be convinced to aid in saving the day, notwithstanding his wish to remain in retirement.

For now, Severus had surrendered, and he was placed under what can only be called a state of arrest. It was the spring of 307, sometime in March or April. The now deposed Augustus was delivered to southern Italy, where he was retained under close guard in a villa. He was the easier of the problems that confronted Maximian and Maxentius – Constantine would be more difficult, one might have thought. Civil war was a horror that few were willing to countenance if it could be avoided. One wonders how much of the rebellion of Maxentius had been planned in advance, and to what extent. The troubles in Rome were timely. Seething resentment on the part of son and – especially as time passed, father – would have leapt at the opportunity afforded by current discontent. Severus had never proven himself to be a particularly formidable foe, and that fact would have emerged with increasing clarity as the months passed. Constantine was busy with barbarians and building projects. The east was a hostile place for Maxentius, but Galerius and Maximinus Daza were also not in the business of interfering in western affairs unless it was necessary. For all the talk of unity in the tetrarchy, the model had been cast for the eventual division of the empire into more separate eastern and western dominions. There was, after all, only so much one could manage without incurring significant risks.

Galerius and his Caesar had not meddled in the business of the west thus far, but the Roman Empire was, after all, still one empire. The Maxentius rebellion was far too serious a crisis to leave unaddressed. Galerius quickly settled on a policy of active response: he would be willing to bring forces to Italy to end what he viewed as a usurpation of power. No doubt Severus had been kept alive thus far precisely to use as a bargaining chip, not to say hostage: he was Galerius' friend, and another useful tool in Maxentius' ambitious drive for empire. Soon enough Maxentius would determine that he had outlived his usefulness – the son of Maximian rarely lost an opportunity for rashness and change of intention.

Maximian, we have noted, had been in retirement in southern Italy. Diocletian had been enjoying the same rest from labours in Dalmatia, in the palace that today is the principal archaeological and tourist site of the modern Croatian resort town of Split on the Adriatic coast.[5] Diocletian had rarely lived so relatively close to his onetime colleague. There is some evidence that the two men were in regular contact with each other, and one does wonder how Diocletian received his first reports of the crisis unfolding in Italy. Did he ruefully recall how he had warned Galerius about Severus? Was he shocked that his long-time associate in power would participate in a civil war to see his son installed in power? Did he imagine now that Constantine would be the most reliable force to bring order to the empire? Was he mostly consumed with a sense of distress that his system seemed to be in real danger of unravelling after twenty and more years of relative internal stability, and the achievement of so much to shore up the long-troubled borders of empire? In the end, was he confirmed in his resolution that retirement had been the right decision?

Galerius was in a difficult position, not least because of the imprisonment of his friend Severus. He did, however, take the momentous step of proceeding to Italy. Severus' ultimate fate is surrounded by some controversy. The most likely account of his fate is that once Maxentius learned that Galerius was prepared to challenge him with military forces in Italy, he ordered the killing of Severus. The former emperor may have been given the customary chance to commit suicide.[6] The story that he never survived the siege of Ravenna, and that he met his death there in the spring rather than the autumn of 307, is less credible. Ravenna was fortified, and the surrender of Severus would have allowed for the avoidance of a long and potentially bloody siege (besides the aforementioned fact that Severus was arguably more useful alive than dead). Once Galerius had proven that Severus was not a factor in keeping the eastern Augustus out of Italy, it is not difficult to conceive that Maxentius would have ordered his death. The son was more impetuous than the father, and Maxentius may have gambled that Galerius would avoid an overt civil war. It was a risky exercise of reasoning.

Severus died with a young son to survive him. Perhaps miraculously, Flavius Severianus would manage to travel safely to the east and the court of Galerius. His story will be resumed later, as an interesting footnote of sorts to the drama unfolding in the west – proof positive that it was exceedingly perilous to be the son of a tetrarch.

At some point, Maxentius assumed the title of Augustus openly – the death of Severus certainly confirmed that there was a vacancy in the tetrarchy. Maxentius' willingness to forego the title as part of his attempted appeasement of Galerius had borne no fruit, and so there was now no reason to engage in pretence. Maxentius and his father were in control of Italy during that long summer of 307, no doubt consumed not only with the shoring up and consolidation of the administration and defence of Italy and the adjoining territories they held, but also in some attempt at negotiation and communication with other players in the game of empire. Here the only logical and indeed possible source of fruitful negotiation was with Constantine. Galerius was too hostile to Maxentius, and he had made it abundantly clear that there would be no room for negotiation with him. Armed conflict was something that the eastern Augustus was willing to resort to in the effort to depose Maxentius. No doubt Maximian's involvement made matters more complicated on any number of levels, but the authority of the retired Augustus was not sufficient to ensure that Maxentius' usurpation would be tolerated.

In several regards the tetrarchy succession arrangement had now broken down. If Maxentius could decide to carve out a territory for himself, what was to stop some other ambitious commander or political figure from doing the same? Maxentius and his father would no doubt argue that their situation was different, and that they were merely engaging in rectifying what should have been arranged more suitably in the spring of 305. But Maximian had agreed to the exclusion of his inexperienced son at that time, and had retired. To argue in favour of changing the terms of the succession settlement now could be taken as opportunistic and inappropriate. In response, Maximian could argue that Constantine had behaved inappropriately with his father in the matter of the latter's illness and eventual succession. If Constantine had been overlooked in 305, only later to find his situation rectified – then so too could the overlooked

Maxentius be restored to what was his due. The crucial difference there of course was that Constantius had died, thus leaving a spot in the tetrarchy open by virtue of natural causes. That spot, however, was not supposed to be filled by the acclamation of soldiers and Alamannic kings serving with the Roman forces in Britain. There was a fair amount of bitterness afoot over how Constantine had entered into his office, most of it centred on Maxentius and his friends.

In short, as in most political situations of this magnitude, there was room for legitimate complaint and counterargument. Maxentius' inexperience was still the proverbial elephant in the room, and the need for his father's presence and approbation only served to underscore that inescapable fact. Nobody could have expected that Maxentius would be able to serve on his own – he needed his father to validate his reign. That brought unquestionable rewards, but also its own problem – without Maximian, Maxentius was no Constantine. Essentially the son owed his army to his father.

Maximian would make his appeal to Constantine. This was the case of a retired Augustus reaching out to the son of a deceased Caesar who had been promoted not so long before his death to Augustus. One could write the appeal based on even a cursory knowledge of events: civil war was to be avoided at all costs. Probably a strong emphasis was placed on the fact that Maximian and Maxentius had no designs on Constantine's territory. With Severus dead, the argument could be made that Maximian and his son were merely taking over the new slot that had been opened – even if that slot now accommodated two instead of one. One imagines that there may have been discussion of the fact that Severus had been an Augustus, at least in name. Here, the weight of Maximian's veteran status as a retired Augustus would be a factor – clearly at least in gravitas he outranked Constantine – and there was the fact that Constantine had not exactly been living and behaving as if he were the Caesar to Severus' Augustus. On the contrary, Constantine had been doing his own thing in Gaul and Britain, more or less running his corner of the tetrarchy as his own fiefdom. While business continued as usual in Constantine's corner of the tetrarchy, Maximian needed to negotiate with him in person regarding the war that was breaking out.

Severus had failed to quell the Maxentius rebellion, and Galerius' initial attempt to bring an army into Italy would fail as well.[7] Galerius had two official reasons for massing an armed force to enter Italy: first, to avenge Severus, and second to end Maxentius' revolt. Italy was of course already largely fortified – Galerius would have no easy task in assaulting the towns and cities that had gone over to the son of Maximian. Further, Maxentius would be able to employ bribery a second time to bring more soldiers to his cause. No doubt distaste for civil war was a factor in the unwillingness of some Roman soldiers to fight against their brothers. Italy was a particularly unpleasant locus for any sort of internecine struggle. Galerius was far more fortunate than Severus, however. He was able to maintain most of his military force as he retreated and regrouped. Realizing that he faced an extremely difficult situation, and probably with the awareness that there was no guarantee that he would not become a second Severus, Galerius quietly began to pursue negotiations to see if there was some accommodation that could be reached – though the negotiations were focused on emphasizing how Galerius respected Maximian. The father carried the weight of venerable fame, not the son. Time and again in this tense period, the wisdom of the decision to pass over Maxentius in the succession scheme must have been validated, notwithstanding its necessary linkage to the similar passing over of the far more qualified, temperate, and competent Constantine.

All offers of settlement were rejected. Especially after the death of Severus and the initial significant setbacks that Galerius had suffered, Maxentius was no doubt emboldened. He was always given to impetuosity and to a sense that he was able to achieve huge gains, and the present instance was no exception. A wiser course might have been to try to capitalize on the universal wish to avoid a full-scale civil war, and to pursue whatever negotiations could succeed with Galerius. But for the moment, Maxentius firmly maintained his position that the only acceptable course of action for Galerius was to return to Nicomedia and his eastern realm. Italy was his.

Maxentius was going to prove to be a more difficult foe than Galerius had wished or even expected, but the eastern Augustus was now on western soil, determined to remind both father and son that Rome was still an integral empire. That determination was not to come to any immediate fruition. The defections from his army were a constant threat as long as his men remained within reach of Maxentius' bribes. Even a carefully managed retreat from Italy was at risk of turning into the slow and steady loss of an army, as Maxentius spent more and more money on seeking to build his own forces at the expense of Galerius. Maxentius may have calculated that time was more on his side.

Galerius' efforts to avenge his friend Severus and to end the Maxentius problem once and for all were meeting with failure and torpor at every juncture. Galerius eventually allowed his men to plunder the countryside as they wished – it was one of the only expedients by which he could maintain some degree of control over his increasingly restless and rebellious men.[8] Maxentius refused to engage Galerius in negotiation or in open battle – no doubt he worried about his prospects of success, and there was the advantage of not being seen as the active party in civil war battles. Galerius was in crisis.

Obviously the best news that the frustrated eastern emperor could receive was that Constantine would complicate the map and spoil the plans of Maxentius and the father who was likely pulling the puppet strings on behalf of his son.[9] Maximian had much work to accomplish with Constantine. In the end the negotiations of 307 were successful. First we may consider why there would have been relative ease in signing a deal (beyond the omnipresent concern about avoiding civil war, or at least about avoiding being the one who would be blamed for the outbreak of civil war). Maximian no doubt wanted peace in the west in order to be able to focus on the immediate crisis – war with Galerius. Constantine was interested in maintaining order and peace in the west, but at the best possible price for his own concerns and interests. In the present case, he had in Maximian someone who was willing to make significant concessions to appease the son of Constantius.

One of the main difficulties in the establishment of any rapprochement between Maximian/Maxentius and Constantine was the question of what to do with the highly volatile situation in which Galerius was clearly opposed to coming to terms with the young man he viewed as a rebellious upstart in the west. The tetrarchy had been founded on the notion of unity and the integral nature of the Roman Empire. Galerius could not be expected to be willing to tolerate any sort of permanent division of the empire – the likelihood of war was stronger than ever in the recent history of the Diocletianic settlement, and it is something of a miracle that matters did not devolve into even greater chaos than they did (as often, many would credit Diocletian with some of this stability – even in retirement, he stood forth as a powerful remora against internecine madness).

The arrangement agreed upon by Maximian and Constantine was in some regards a striking picture of diplomacy and political acumen. On the question of Galerius, the answer was elegant in its simplicity: Constantine would remain on the side lines as a neutral figure in any conflict that might arise between Galerius and the problematic father and son in Italy. Constantine would not be expected to aid Maximian and Maxentius, but he would also refrain from any assistance to Galerius. There would be no influx of Constantine's formidable forces into Italy to check Galerius. Constantine likely had no interest in such a precipitous action, and such a move would serve also to weaken his own borders in the face of barbarian incursions. Constantine would not be fighting anytime soon, and Maximian did not have to worry about the threat of an alliance between the far west and the east, with his son and him trapped in the middle.

It was a balancing act, to be sure – but one that removed a significant piece from the chessboard. The problem inherent to the agreement, one might argue, was that Constantine also made a decision that would be interpreted by all as a clear sign of alliance with Maximian, at least – he agreed to marry Maximian's daughter Fausta. This was an old-style dynastic arrangement of uniting families by nuptials – and it was the sort of gesture that could be expected to infuriate someone like Galerius. The military neutrality issue was one matter – and a weighty one – but Constantine was now openly tying himself to Maximian by a marriage bond. At the very least it was a convenient expedient. If there was any question as to the legitimacy of Constantine's claim to a share in the tetrarchy, it was now being ratified and sanctioned by his family link to Maximian. Constantine would repudiate his wife Minervina and accept the alliance with Maximian that was ratified in the wedding to Fausta.

But there were significant difficulties. Constantine had technically been a Caesar in the settlement that had been reached after his own quasi-rebellion in the wake of the death of Constantius. Severus had been Augustus, but now Severus was all too dead – and so as part of the bargaining with Maximian, Constantine was accorded the title of Augustus. This was an interesting diplomatic sleight of hand. It was not the case that Maxentius, for example, was now envisaged as serving under Constantine as his Caesar. It was more akin to a situation in which Constantine, Maximian, and Maxentius were all associating themselves with Augustan imagery, with the west all too manifestly considered to be its own realm, separate from Galerius' east. At some level the great eastern potentate must have been eager to wait and to see what would happen in the resolution of the problems in the west, even as he knew that he needed to take decisive action to strengthen his own position.

Here we may note another panegyric that provides invaluable information, if once again we must note the usual caution that must be exercised in assessing what we learn. The seventh panegyric was delivered in 307 in celebration of the nuptial union of Constantine and Fausta that marked the alliance of Constantine and Maximian, and the recognition of Constantine as an Augustus. The panegyric is important for historians in part because it provides some information on the question of the agreement of Diocletian and Maximian to abdicate voluntarily. The text – together with that of the sixth panegyric – is our source for the story of the agreement of the Augustuses to step down. Lactantius, in contrast, argues that Galerius forced Diocletian into retirement, and that the crucial first transition of the tetrarchy was dominated by Galerius' machinations to secure what he wanted.

Panegyrics would by their very nature put forth the best face on events, especially on troubled circumstances. Abdication would be presented as the wise and prudent wish of those who were not wedded to power. As often, certainty is impossible, especially when both the panegyrics and Lactantius' work are clearly prejudiced (albeit in very different ways). No panegyric would ever claim that Diocletian and Maximian had been forced to leave office. Galerius may have been eager to see his seniors retire, but his eagerness may have been in accord with Diocletian's own state of fatigue.

A good example of how lavishly mendacious panegyric praise can be may be found in the remark that Maximian was the first to bring Roman standards across the Rhine in combat against the barbarians, complete with the assertion that it was false when previous claims were made for commanders of old. Maximian is presented as being another of those figures to whom Rome could now make appeal to stay with her and not to leave the scene of action, so much did the empire depend on him.

But no amount of rhetorical laudation could erase the knowledge of the tensions and problems that were afoot. We can speculate on some of Galerius' thoughts in the face of the crisis in Italy. Severus' death had removed his one friend in the highest levels of western imperial rule. Constantine was unwilling to become involved in the current fight, but he was also agreeing to marry Maximian's daughter. Galerius may have felt that his previous generosity was being left unrewarded or unappreciated. He had, after all, agreed to recognize what he viewed as Constantine's usurpation of his father's realm. He was livid about the promotion of the man he had wanted nowhere near the tetrarchy. When Constantine and his sick father had orchestrated the sudden elevation of a new Augustus/Caesar, Galerius had ended up sending purple robes instead of preparing for war. Perhaps in recognition of that, Constantine would not expose himself to the charge of being ungrateful to his benefactor and fellow imperial potentate. On the other hand, Galerius no doubt expected that gratitude in the present circumstances demanded nothing less than that Constantine join with him in eliminating the Maxentius problem.

The situation that confronted the tetrarchy as 307 turned to 308 had never been more unstable. Maxentius had shown how easy it was to become an emperor, and we have noted the increasing anxiety that any ambitious and talented military commander might decide to try to test the waters of his own imperial usurpation. It can be highly problematic to speculate on the psychological relationships and machinations of family members, but the current crisis almost compels some consideration of what was going on between Maximian and Maxentius. The former had not had any craving for retirement the way his colleague Diocletian had. Diocletian embraced retirement; Maximian tolerated it, and not for so long. We may recall the difficulties that Maximian had faced in the execution of his onerous duties in the early years of his participation in the tetrarchy. We have noted that in some sense he had retired from active duty long before Diocletian, preferring to live a life of luxury in Italy to winning military glory on the borders. It was almost as if now he were trying to establish a new chapter in his autobiography, with a second career as a tetrarch – free of the influence of Diocletian, independent and now the superior member of the ruling elite. We need not imagine that the two men had tensions in their relationship that could be traced back to the earliest days of their cooperation. Maximian was simply one of those men for whom retirement did not come easily.

Further, Maxentius was no Maximian, and almost certainly the father knew it all along. His experience was nil. His temperament was undisciplined. Maximian secured significant concessions for the family with Constantine, but we may speculate that his time in negotiation with the son of Constantius had put into sharp relief the differences between Constantine and his own offspring. While precise details elude us, it seems that not long after his return to Italy in the wake of his successful settlement with Constantine, civil war of the most intimate sort broke out: Maximian was soon enough in disagreement with his son, disagreement that became serious conflict. The son may have chafed at being subordinate to his father in everything but official title and position. The father may have decided that Maxentius was a liability to his own status and reputation.

Relations between Maximian and son deteriorated rapidly in that crucial winter. By the spring of 308, the situation was so critical that Maximian was prepared to take the decisive step of seeking to end Maxentius' participation in what had become a pentarchy. The winter of discontent ended in a definitive break in family harmony, a break that would only be resolved – perversely – after the death of Maximian, when Maxentius would use family loyalty as a convenient pretext to seek hostilities with Constantine. No doubt there was blame on the side of both father and son. Maximian and Maxentius would demonstrate none of the *pietas* that Constantius and Constantine were reputed to have shared, though in that case the father had died of illness, and the son was not compelled to share his power with his sire.

Maximian had been instrumental in securing his son's position, and no doubt he assumed – not without reason – that he would be able to take away that which he had given. Maxentius had not distinguished himself with any noteworthy deeds in the months since he had assumed power. Maximian was the man with the name and the reputation behind him. It was likely a shock to the old man that when he tried actively to depose his son by what can only be called an attempt at a paternal coup, the army remained loyal to Maxentius. One might even imagine that after having been the recipient of sufficient panegyrical praise, Maximian was beginning to believe the rhetoric about his own glory and ability.

Certainly he was reaching the conclusion that his son was a liability. But the old man's time had in some sense passed, and Maxentius was able to retain the faith of his soldiery. One has the sense that whatever the details of the breakdown in relations, Maximian either did not have the opportunity to plan for the schism with his son, or he assumed that he was the puppeteer and would have control of the armies merely for the asking. He might not have expected that they would remain at his son's side. Lactantius compares Maximian to Tarquinius Superbus, the last of the kings of Rome, expelled from the city and forced to flee his now former place of power.[10]

This loyalty may have been rooted in nothing more than the fact that Maxentius had been the one making sure that his men were well paid. It may have been occasioned by shock that Maximian was so readily willing to try to remove his son from power. But whatever the rationale, Maxentius fared far better than Severus and Galerius in the matter of holding on to his army. Maximian was soon persona non grata, the family feud now a conflict with global ramifications, as the father departed from Italy. Eventually he would make his way to the man with whom he had so recently spent time in negotiation – Constantine. There is something of an air of desperation here, one might easily conclude – but even if it was desperation, it was rooted in good sense regarding what few options Maximian had. Williams compares Maximian to King Lear.[11] But before he took refuge at one of the only places where he could safely rest his head in respectful welcome, there was other business to attend to, with Galerius and the retired Diocletian.[12]

We may indulge here in speculation – and we must emphasize that it is speculation rooted in analysis of the historical record, but without any evidence to support the theory. It is possible that the Maximian-Constantine negotiations that were sealed by the celebration of the marriage of Constantine and Fausta at Augusta Treverorum in March 307 were also the occasion for Maximian's increasing realization that his new son-in-law was far more qualified and competent to be the western Augustus than his own son. This is not to insinuate that Maximian departed from Augusta Treverorum ready to see to the deposing of his son, but rather to suggest that the father left Gaul having decided that he had reached the limit of his patience and tolerance for Maxentius. It may have been something of a tinderbox, with the son not even aware of how close he was to being put aside in the deadly game of imperial political machinations. This was a classic instance of *deterior* comparison: Constantine made Maxentius' faults all the more apparent, merely by being Constantine. At the same time, Constantine was a port in a storm, and Maximian was in need of shelter. The time would come all too soon when Maximian would turn against his saviour. It is likely that the retired Augustus was never entirely comfortable depending on the protection and largess of his junior.

Maxentius had won a significant victory in retaining the loyalty of his troops, but it was a temporary boon. His main problem was that now he had everyone else in the pentarchy upset with him or at best not willing to fight on his behalf or to argue in support of his cause. He had wanted power, and now he had it. He was in complete charge of his destiny, his father now gone from the scene and his men waiting for their orders. Here was a moment where his utter lack of experience in military command (especially in comparison to his rivals) would be a crippling liability. Maxentius now had an opportunity to exhibit not only the daring that had characterized his life, but also resolute resolve mixed with good sense as to a plan. But neither virtue seemed to be at hand for him. Soon enough events would spiral entirely out of control for him, as other tetrarchs made decisions on his behalf.

We have no record of the negotiations that went on between the imperial players in 308, but we do know that by the end of the year there would be a conference to discuss what ought to be done to maintain the tetrarchy and to avoid seeing everything descend into the chaos of civil war. The conference of Carnuntum would provide a blueprint, and in the end it was a plan that spelled significant trouble for Maxentius. It would be the last major chance for Diocletian to participate in the affairs of state. If we can believe rumour and record, even at this late stage there was strong support for having the veteran tetrarch return to power at least in some way, once again to exercise his ability to fix a mess. But vegetables would win the day over renewed imperial rule.

Chapter 9

Diocletian's Last Efforts at Legacy

The one man who had studiously maintained his independent retirement had been the one who had given birth to the entire system: Diocletian. He wanted no part of the current drama, and yet he was motivated not to see his tetrarchy arrangement fall apart so soon after it had been established.

The year 308 would be the occasion of Diocletian's return from retirement, if only to participate in the conference of state at Carnuntum regarding the status of the men who had claimed some share in the rule of the empire. It was to be the sort of conference that the exigencies of war and communications had made all too rare an event. It is difficult to imagine at such a temporal remove how unusual it was for Rome's leaders in this period to meet together to negotiate.

In the immediate aftermath of the breakdown of relations with his son, Maximian had fled Italy and had proceeded to consult with Galerius, with whom his relations were not exactly warm and friendly. It would be fascinating to know exactly what the discussions were between the two men, but in light of subsequent events it seems that one point was not in dispute – the empire was on the verge of civil war, and a solution must be found. That solution would come in part by consultation with Diocletian, who was visited by Galerius after Maximian's journey east. The agreement was secured that the three men – officially, two retirees and one Augustus – would meet.

Lactantius has a darker version of events, claiming that Maximian went to Galerius only under the pretence of wishing to reach some sort of accommodation, but actually with the intention of murdering him.[1] This story holds little credibility, even for the daring and bold Maximian. In Lactantius' judgment, Maximian planned to kill Galerius so that he could usurp his share of the empire, as a counter to his having been driven out of Italy by Maxentius and the forces loyal to him. For reasons that the rhetorician does not make clear, the assassination plan was foiled, and Maximian proceeds to Constantine, ready to try to use subterfuge and trickery to undermine him. Lactantius does note that Diocletian was present with Galerius during Maximian's visit; this is the kernel of truth in the narrative. Carnuntum would be the meeting at which Maximian would learn what his former colleague thought of his recent actions.

This would be the celebrated conference at which Diocletian would be in the enviable position of a retiree who was invited to resume the power from which he had voluntarily abdicated. Everyone, it seems, was willing to see Diocletian resume his authority. This was the occasion for the famous story of the cabbage that Diocletian cited as an example of his peace and serenity: if Diocletian's vegetable that he had planted with his own hands could be seen, there is no one who would suggest that he could ever wish to surrender his garden tranquillity for the never-ending tensions of ambition and high office. Diocletian offered a study in contrast to his colleagues in the tetrarchy past and present – he was seemingly preternaturally immune to ambition or desire for resuming power.

Carnuntum was a storied place in Roman imperial history: in 193 it had been the site where Septimius Severus was acclaimed as emperor. *Legio XIV Gemina* was stationed there (still named in the *Notitia*), though as with most of the legions we have little in the way of definitive evidence of activity after the age of Gallienus.[2]

Officially, at the commencement of the conference, Galerius was Augustus in the east, with Maximinus Daza as his Caesar. That arrangement would continue. In the west, Severus had been Augustus, with Constantine as his Caesar. With Severus dead and Maxentius in rebellion, the status of the western tetrarchal appointments needed to be clarified. November 308 would be another of those decisive months in the history of the now seriously troubled tetrarchy.

'The inherent problem with collegiate government was that it depended upon the actual successes of the members of the college and their ability to agree, to make the images of fraternal emperors embracing each other the basis of government.'[3]

One matter was clear: Maximian was to stay retired. The presence of Diocletian as senior statesman must have made a strong impression on his former Augustan colleague. Diocletian likely argued forcefully that the original retirement agreement should have been respected. Maximian had been rejected by the very troops who had been so loyal to him. He had no armies to speak of, no basis of popular or military support. Arguably he was lucky still to be alive. A second retirement was the only viable option. We develop a clear sense from study of the available evidence that Maximian was blamed for the current mess. He had clearly given his son the necessary encouragement to pursue his reckless course of action, and now the very treatment of the father by the son proved just how unstable and unreliable Maxentius was. 'Of all the players on this crowded stage, Maxentius was in many ways the most dangerous.'[4] And whatever else happened, there would be no place for Maximian in the future government of the tetrarchy. The discussions may have been harsh in import, but friendly in tone and manner. Maximian knew that he had no real chance of regaining power in the absence of intervention from his old colleague. Diocletian was not about to make a foolish mistake in his pleasant old age – one imagines that he was eager to return to Salona with every passing hour he spent at Carnuntum.

There would be nothing for Maximian at Carnuntum. He may well have felt that the whole affair had been an embarrassing waste of his time. If there was anything positive that he could think had resulted from the conference, it was the perverse pleasure of knowing that Galerius and Diocletian were as hostile to Maxentius as they had always been inclined to be. Maxentius would find no favour, support, or help from the three men on the Danube. He was to be treated as a usurper, with the implicit understanding that he would be forced out of power.

Constantine, it was decided, would remain as the western Caesar. We may wonder why it was not decided to promote him to Augustus and to make a decision as to a new Caesar. Part of the answer to this excellent question may lie in the origins of Constantine's own place in the tetrarchy – he was, after all, a usurper himself in the eyes of some. Galerius had been no friend of his, and the eastern Augustus considered that he had made a significant concession already merely in ratifying what he had not countenanced or desired. Further, Galerius had a tendency to like to reward and to promote his friends, and the death of his friend Severus in the present crisis allowed him the chance to introduce another friend of his into the game – Valerius Licinianus Licinius.[5]

Licinius was yet another Balkan military man, born of low birth probably around 265. He rose to become one of Galerius' men, a trusted member of the inner circle who was involved in the failed negotiations with Maxentius in 307. Licinius would also be assigned the responsibility of managing affairs for Galerius in the east while he was absent in Italy trying to quell the Maxentius revolt. And it would be Licinius who would be proposed as the new Augustus in the west. Licinius would be responsible for the management of Italy and Africa once the current crisis had been resolved.

We see here a reminiscence of the Severus episode, though without the negative press about licentiousness and drunkenness. Licinius was being advanced simply because he was a crony of Galerius, and his appointment in the west would ensure the unity of the tetrarchy by restoring Galerius' influence by once again having his friend in power as the western Augustus. Constantine had room for complaint in the initial tetrarchal transition plans that had resulted in the promotion of Severus, and he had a similar cause for argument now. Once again though he was willing to tolerate the Galerian proposal. In this we would argue that Constantine displayed wisdom and foresight. He had built a reputation for himself concerning his tolerance to all with whom he entered into negotiations. His patience, however, was not without limit. The present situation was unquestionably a serious blow to his prestige. He had in effect been demoted. The east, meanwhile, would be dominated by Galerius, a man Lactantius never fails to savage as being among the most vicious of rulers.[6]

'Diocletian had meanwhile returned to his cabbages.'[7] Everyone who has ever written commentary or scholarly criticism of the age has noted that Diocletian must have been rueful about the demise of the system that he had put into place with such painstaking care.

Maxentius was soon in the position of many an imperial ruler, whether usurper or legitimate leader. Cracks began to form in the edifice of his rule. Of course, the biggest of these cracks had been the break between father and son, but soon others began to question the wisdom of following the young would-be Augustus. One such man is shrouded in some mystery simply because of a dearth of historical sources regarding his actions – Lucius Domitius Alexander. We have mentioned that one fear in the wake of the Maxentius rebellion was the idea that anyone could declare oneself emperor. Alexander was an official in Roman Africa who did just that, apparently in the wake of his refusal to agree to Maxentius' demand that he send his son as a hostage to Rome to ensure his loyalty to the Maxentian regime.

Africa was a breadbasket, and Maxentius needed to maintain the province in his camp. Alexander was not willing to engage in hostage negotiations, however, and soon enough his soldiers acclaimed him as emperor – at least as emperor in Africa. There is some speculation that the origin of the Alexander revolt was actually the breakdown of relations between Maxentius and his father early in 308. According to this theory, Alexander and his men were not willing to submit to Maxentius – they were loyal to Maximian. The forced departure of the father from Rome meant that Alexander was now in a position to declare openly that he did not support the son, and so Maxentius would now face a secession from his fledgling secessionist realm.

In addition to this serious public setback, Maxentius also suffered the loss of his teenage son to natural causes in 309. Valerius Romulus had been born around 295 and was thus 14 or 15 years of age. He was proclaimed a god and given a splendid tomb on the Appian Way – the former honour perhaps circumstantial evidence of the grandiosity to which Maxentius was prone.

After the fateful November conference of 308, as the year turned, the unavoidable problem was how to wage war against Maxentius not only successfully, but with an eye to avoiding the spectacle of civil war in Italy. Maximian was no longer welcome anywhere around his son, and early in 309 he proceeded to Constantine. The two men had clearly developed a good relationship, and in some sense both were now disaffected – the older onetime tetrarch by his exclusion from power, and the younger by the series of slights that had most recently seen him effectively demoted, compelled to serve at least de iure if not de facto under the supervision of Galerius' friend Licinius. Maximian and Constantine had ample opportunity to share in bitter and resentful complaints.

Most would agree that Constantine had some room for complaint in the present situation, and his complaint was strengthened by virtue of the fact that another disaffected individual in the increasingly tempestuous mix was a man about whom we have said little thus far – Galerius' Caesar, Maximinus Daza. It is always a challenge to keep ambitious men appeased, and even men of lesser ambition can acquire a taste for power and a desire for increased honour once they have experienced perceived slights. The introduction of Licinius into the tetrarchy had created much the same situation as the previous instance with Severus – there was discontent on leapfrogging someone to the Augustus status, literally over the heads of Caesars. The foundation of the tetrarchy was the idea that the two Augustuses would always be replaced by their Caesars, and that the way you entered the tetrarchy was when there was room for the promotion of a new pair of men into the Caesarian slots. That mechanism for smooth government had failed because of disagreement and lingering dissatisfaction and resentment as to the choice of the new Caesars, and now a chaotic system had emerged where men could simply be named Augustuses, with Caesars left as perpetual bridesmaids, as it were.

The solution to the resentment problem was in some respects a classic example of reactionary thought, not to say of making up answers to problems as you proceed on your merry, chaotic way. Why not simply dispense with the Caesar/Augustus distinction, and declare that all four men are Augustuses? The solution was an example of realism, at least. There had always been grey areas of ambiguity with respect to the difference between a Caesar and an Augustus. Constantine may have been bitter about his junior title, but he had a habit of always acting like an Augustus anyway. Naming everyone an Augustus avoided such technical distinctions as being a Caesar versus a 'son of Augustus', a diplomatic turn of phrase that could be as insulting as it was honorific.

The new tetrarchy – leaving aside the question of titles – was thus comprised of Galerius, Maximinus Daza, Licinius, and Constantine. Maximian was in retirement again, but in the frequent company of Constantine. Diocletian had his beloved villa, and once again sought the refuge of retirement after his intervention at the Carnuntum conference. Alexander was in technical usurpation, we might say, in Africa. And Maxentius was in open rebellion in Italy. Such was the situation in the early months of 309.

Wars are rarely easy to plan effectively, especially civil wars. We should not be surprised that there were no engagements in 309, no attempts for example to dislodge Maxentius. Licinius began his tenure in the tetrarchy in possession of the Roman armies in Illyricum, Pannonia, and Thrace – a formidable force with which to move against Maxentius when the time was right. But in both the east and the west, foreign problems did not cease because of the renewed tensions among the sharers in imperial power. The Sarmatians were a continuing threat, as were the Franks –

and Licinius and Constantine would be compelled to respond to both problems.

We may learn much about the character of Maximian from his actions as they unfolded in this period. There is a clear sense that one of the only imperial courts where he was welcome to stay was that of Constantine. Constantine was required to deal with the usual business of responding to barbarian threats, and in the present instance his situation was precarious because he had a hostile Maxentius who could decide to take advantage of the absence of the campaigning Constantine to move against him. At some point Constantine made the fateful decision to entrust Maximian with the task of defending his southern borders while he proceeded to deal with the latest Frankish menace. This would be the step that would lead to Maximian's downfall, and to an even stronger position for Constantine.

On the surface it was a sound idea, at least in some regards. Maximian had had a serious falling out with his son, so there was no reason to suspect that he would suddenly reconcile with him and try to move against Constantine. There was also the practical consideration that Constantine could not move against his foreign adversaries without defending his vulnerable flank.

Maximian would emerge as a betrayer of Constantine, in the last significant development of his variegated life. The year 310 would see the dramatic emergence of a last effort of Maximian to regain that which he clearly had never truly felt comfortable surrendering – imperial power. He had come to the conclusion that he would never be the underling of his son or the second in power to anyone. He probably had decided that sharing authority as equals was also no longer appealing, even if it were tolerable at least as a temporary expedient. At Arelate – the modern Arles – Maximian declared that Constantine had died while on campaign against the Franks, and that he was prepared to be generous with financial awards to anyone who would pledge allegiance to him as the new emperor. He resumed the wearing of the purple of imperial dignity and tried to conduct himself as if he were enjoying the resumption of his former life as an Augustus: 'the incorrigible old Maximian made a last desperate bid for power.'[8]

In some regards this might be the most shocking of the internecine squabbles of the tetrarchy. This was exactly the sort of shameful episode that in quality was the antithesis of what Diocletian practised. The man for whom retirement meant retirement was no doubt horrified when he heard what his former colleague was doing, though perhaps he was not entirely surprised. A case could be made that Maximian wins the prize for being the most duplicitous of the tetrarchs.

It is easy to conclude that Maximian was more ambitious than Diocletian, and that he had a stronger propensity to violence and to betrayal than his erstwhile colleague. By the end of his life one almost has the sense of a man not acting appropriately for his age, of a man seeking to regain lost glory. It is easy to indulge in psychological speculation, and to argue that Maximian had spent his life in a certain state of insecurity, always second to Diocletian in the estimation of many, and with successes on the battlefield proving to be more elusive. Indeed, his greatest hour may have come in Africa, not in Gaul or elsewhere. Diocletian had not had a Maxentius in his family on whom to pin hopes for some sort of dynasty. Maximian did have a son who in theory could carry on his legacy, but whatever defects of character Maximian had were magnified in his son. In the end, Maximian's actions in the immediate moment strike one as being embarrassing and pathetic.

For there is, one might reasonably conclude, an air of desperation in the actions of a man who tries to pretend that his rival is dead. It was a ruse that could not have succeeded for long unless fortune truly smiled on Maximian, and Constantine did fall in battle. The best that Maximian could realistically hope for is that the army under his control immediately declared for him in agreement with his appeal, and then when the inevitable news arrived that Constantine was alive and reports of his demise had clearly been false, then Maximian could aspire to reach an accommodation where he would share power, even if only (as aforementioned) as a convenience in furtherance of any future attempt at sole rule.

Maximian's dreams were shattered quickly. The lie that Constantine was dead was greeted with immediate (and all too predictable) suspicion, and the army was loyal to their commander. Maximian received very limited support, and nothing approaching the widespread acclamation he needed and desired. He was faced with having to exit Arelate, while word was sent quickly to the front to Constantine that Maximian had graduated from retired tetrarch to would-be usurper. Constantine had spent years focusing on his army and on developing a good relationship with his subordinates, and now in his own hour of potential peril he would reap the rewards. Maximian's gamble had been a dangerous, indeed foolhardy one – and Constantine's officers and men were not in a cooperative mood.

The Franks were a formidable problem, but Constantine had no choice but to respond swiftly and decisively to Maximian's actions. Maximian's ultimate destination of flight was Massilia, the modern Marseilles. It was a fortified city, and Maximian could hope to have some chance of resisting a siege, at least for a time. He did not have any capability of fielding an army to engage Constantine.

It was the end game for Maximian, and likely he knew it. His daring escapade revealed something of the familial traits that existed in his son. Constantine was soon outside the gates of Massilia, ready to negotiate – though it seems that this time, negotiation meant that Maximian was strongly urged to end his life. Constantine was able to display many Roman virtues in one episode: he would be able to display *clementia* by not ordering the death of the onetime emperor, but he was also a strong exhibitor of justice and prudence: Maximian could not simply be allowed to escape unscathed.

Maximian took the suicide option in July 310. 'Maximian died unsuccessful and disgraced, without allies or sympathizers, a dangerous, wild old man who had to be put out of the way.'[9] He was the second of the four original tetrarchs to die, and the first of the Augustuses. Constantius had died by natural causes; Maximian would take his own life, possibly by hanging.[10] If this is true, we must note that the method was traditionally considered disgraceful by Roman standards; there is a chance that Constantine had dictated the mode of death – Maximian would be allowed suicide, but not by honourable means since there was nothing honourable in his actions. What mattered was he was dead, his strange obsession with trying to retain some vestige of his former power settled only by his demise. Williams' conclusion is that Diocletian had been the one who was able to keep his colleagues in check by sheer force of diplomatic persuasion and his own ability to share power without difficulty. Maximian was, no doubt, the lesser man – and his disgrace was profound. It is eerie that the last survivor of the original four tetrarchs would be the man who inaugurated the system, and who had resisted all temptation and appeal to rejoin it in one of its hours of crisis. 'Whether Maximian was executed or encouraged to commit suicide cannot be determined. The sources are divided ... and the distinction is not an important one in any case.'[11] Potter argues that Constantine had owed much to Maximian, and that perhaps he had decided that he needed a convenient story to explain his former superior's death.[12]

What has just been related is the first of two versions of the end of Maximian, the first of which was crafted by Constantinian propaganda in light of subsequent events. The second version was the eventual response to the reaction of Maxentius to the news of the death of his father. Maxentius and Maximian had been on decidedly bad terms for some time, but Maxentius could be a weathervane in much the same manner as his father. The suicide of Maximian was received by Maxentius as an invitation suddenly to practice the Roman virtue of *pietas*: the son would now be devoted to the memory and honour of the father with whom he had clashed so severely in life.[13] Maxentius went so far as to talk about avenging his father, and Constantine was the obvious source of his ire and target of his speaking of vengeance. Soon Maxentius was putting the image of his father on coinage, with the deification of Maximian adding to the honour that was to be accorded to the late tetrarch.

A key source for this troubled period is from a familiar corpus of speeches. The sixth panegyric was delivered on the occasion of the anniversary of the founding of Augusta Treverorum. It may date to 310, although we cannot be certain. It is a fascinating exercise to study this speech in sequence after that in honour of the marriage of Constantine to Maximian's daughter. For, now Maximian is dead, the last chapter of his storied life is one of betrayal of his son-in-law. This speech is significant in part for its introduction of something that seemingly came out of nowhere – the idea that Constantine could actually claim his descent from Claudius II, that is from Claudius Gothicus. This genealogical sleight of hand must have had the point of trying to extol the lineage and heritage of Constantine above that of all the other members of the tetrarchy past and present.

The sixth panegyric is also renowned for its account of an alleged pagan vision received by Constantine in the wake of his victory over Maximian, one in which Apollo promised him years beyond normal human measure.[14] The obvious comparison is with the tradition of the later, Christian vision that he was granted on the eve of his fateful engagement with Maxentius at the Milvian Bridge. The Constantinian propaganda machine may well have sought to provide divine approbation, as it were, for the bold fact of the elimination of the second member of the original tetrarchy. If Hercules was seen as a brutish god, one given even occasionally to fits of drunkenness and resultant violence, then Apollo was a divine patron imbued with more culture, learning, the world of arts and music – in short, there may have been a deliberate effort to associate Constantine with new immortal imagery that marked significant refinement over that which had been connected with Maximian. And, too, Apollo was a far greater god than Hercules, a son of Jupiter with more impressive credentials.

By 311, then, Constantine was engaging in his own propaganda about Maximian, both in response to Maxentius' actions, and to buttress his own reputation after his involvement in the weighty business of having clashed with a former Augustus who was now dead. Here we find the genesis of the 'second version' of events, in which Maximian was discovered to have been plotting to assassinate Constantine. Maximian is said to have been given the option of suicide by the clement Constantine, but to have died in disgrace for his attempted murder of his great benefactor and friend. It is possible, too, that he was hanged against his will, not a suicide but a victim of execution. Lactantius describes the plot in lurid detail.[15] Maximian approached his daughter Fausta, the wife of Constantine. He promised her a better marriage alliance if she would aid him in the assassination of her husband. Fausta betrayed her father's plot to Constantine, who helped his wife to orchestrate a scheme involving a hapless eunuch as bait for Maximian's nocturnal assault on Constantine's bed chamber. In dramatic fashion, the would-be imperial assassin has his fleeting moment of triumph when he stabs his victim – only then to have the horror revealed to him, that his target is alive and well, and that his daughter had proven to be a new Hypermnestra, loyal to her spouse and not to her murderous sire.[16]

The time-honoured custom of *damnatio memoriae* was now practised by Constantine on Maximian: his name and image were to be obliterated.[17] Diocletian had returned to his retired life after the council at Carnuntum, and he learned of the downfall of his veteran colleague. Hauntingly and perhaps poignantly, we are told that when Diocletian learned of

Constantine's actions with respect to Maximian, he dutifully proceeded to take down all of the representations of his onetime friend that were on display in his villa. Diocletian was the man of order and responsibility to the end, and he knew Maximian better than anyone. The dyarchy of Diocletian and Maximian had been highly respected and venerable. Even after so many acts of reckless desperation aimed at regaining his old power, Maximian's name must have commanded some honour, perhaps enough to warrant propaganda and embellishment to improve the role of Constantine in his end.[18]

Lactantius in his lurid account of the deaths of Christian persecutors records that since there were many joint images of Maximian and Diocletian, the latter man suffered the disgrace of seeing his own picture torn down in many places, a circumstance that occasioned his resolve to end his life. Lactantius was of course interested in showing how every emperor who persecuted Christians met with some appropriate just deserts; in the case of Diocletian, the greedy and avaricious emperor suffers an ignominious end as a private citizen who had been cast down into obscurity from his once lofty height. We may quote the text:[19]

> *Eodemque tempore senis Maximiani statuae Constantini iussu revellebantur et imagines ubicumque pictus esset, detrahebantur. Et quia senes ambo simul plerumque picti erant et imagines simul deponebantur amborum. Itaque <Diocletianus> cum videret vivus quod nullium quam imperatorum acciderat, duplici aegritudine adfectus moriendum sibi esse decrevit. Iactabat se huc atque illuc aestuante anima per dolorem nec somnum nec cibum capiens. Suspiria et gemitus, crebrae lacrimae, iugis volutatio corporis, nunc in lecto, nunc humi. Ita viginti annorum felicissimus imperator ad humilem vitam deiectus a deo et proculcatus iniuriis atque in odium vitae deductus postremo fame atque angore confectus est.*

'In the same time the statues of the old man Maximian were torn down by order of Constantine, and his images were removed, wherever they had been painted. And because both old men had often been depicted together, the images of both of them were put aside. Therefore, when Diocletian while he lived saw happen what had befallen no previous emperor, he was afflicted with a double sickness and was resolved to die. He threw himself here and there, his soul in tumult through sorrow, and he took neither rest not food. There were sighs and groans, frequent tears, constant tossing of the body, now on his couch, now on the ground. There he who had been the most blessed emperor for twenty years was now thrown down to a humble state of life by God, and trodden down by injuries and led to hate his life at last he died on account of starvation and distress.'

It is classic Lactantius, drawing on all the great moments of reversal of fortune from classical history and literature. It is not the suicide story involving poison on account of fear of mistreatment and abuse from other tetrarchs, but a tale of physical illness and the infirmities of old age, coupled with an awareness that his fortunes had changed dramatically – for the Christian writer, it is almost as if Diocletian had sold his soul long before, and the devil had come to claim his due.

Meanwhile, in the east, another dramatic development was afoot, as if fortune were now stage manager of the end of the tetrarchy. Galerius had failed in his early efforts to try to settle the Maxentius problem, and now he found himself increasingly enfeebled and beset by illness. Around the time that Maximian committed suicide, Galerius was physically sick and at the start of what would become a pronounced decline. He was fortunate in that in the game of power in which there had been as many as six emperors at once, he was arguably *primus inter pares* – 'the first among equals'. Indeed, immediately after the narrative of Maximian's sorry end, Lactantius notes that the vengeful eye of God turned its gaze toward Galerius, ready to punish him for his manifold wickedness.[20]

Our knowledge of the final period in Galerius' life is clouded by the emphasis in Christian sources on how the end of his reign witnessed the hand of God, one might say, in the matter of the persecution of Christians. We are told that near the end, as he realized that his illness was terminal (whatever his affliction may have been, we do not know for sure), Galerius rescinded the edicts on the persecution of Christians and introduced an official decree of toleration for the faith, with the request that the Christians join the rest of the people of the empire in praying for his recovery. The plea was unsuccessful, and Galerius died soon thereafter in April (or possibly May) 311. His death meant that Diocletian was now the only survivor of the original tetrarchy – fittingly, its founder was the last one alive, and its founder was the one who was steadfastly faithful without stain or blemish to the system he had crafted.

Christian sources speak of the horrible suffering of Galerius, with ghastly symptoms that have led some to speculate that he suffered from some form of abdominal cancer, or perhaps cancer of the genitals. But certainty is impossible, and the hostility of the sources may account for a certain embellishment and overdramatization of the story of his end. The account in chapter 33 of Lactantius' history of the death of the persecutors is full of putrefaction and worms, failed attempts at treatment and noisome maladies. For Lactantius, the judgment of God had been pronounced on one of the staunchest foes of Christianity. Diocletian's demise did not permit such a gruesome catalogue of macabre details, but Galerius' final illness allowed for an unforgettable depiction of divine vengeance.[21] The Christian heretic Arius would also be described as suffering a disgusting end that seemed to incarnate his vile teachings. Galerius' rescinding of the edicts of persecution of Christians may have been a superstitious, last hope in the face of a painful terminal illness.[22] April 311 was a time of renewed vigour for Christianity, as the religion enjoyed a novel legal status, and as the clock struck on the man who had been associated with the most severe reprisals against its practice.

An interesting footnote may be added to the story of Galerius' death. He had built a mausoleum for himself at Salonica, which may be seen today as the tourist attraction known as the Rotunda of Galerius, an edifice later converted into a Christian church in an ironic turn of events. But Galerius was buried at Romulianum, his birthplace – his grand tomb was destined never to be used for its intended purpose. Lactantius is careful to note that Galerius did not live long enough to celebrate the twentieth anniversary of his reign, which was due to come on the next Kalends of March – a final blow to the pride and prestige of the man who had wreaked such havoc for the Christian community.

The death of Galerius constituted an immense blow to the tetrarchy. Officially in the west, Licinius and Constantine were in power, with Maxentius managing to hold on to his share of the imperial puzzle. In the east, there had been Galerius and Maximinus Daza. Maximinus saw an immediate opportunity to seize as much power as he could in the east. One might say at this stage in the history of the tetrarchy, there was greater emphasis on the squabbling and in-fighting of the remaining potentates than on any organized effort to maintain the Diocletianic system. Maximinus moved quickly to try to seize the entirety of the east for himself, which brought him into conflict soon enough with Licinius.[23] The two men were able to reach an accommodation before war could erupt: Maximinus would share the east with Licinius, with the former responsible for the Asian section of the vast region, and the latter for the European. This arrangement dramatically improved the power of Maximinus, who was now the sole lord of an impressive Asian realm – and it did the same for Licinius, who was now also in possession of far more land than he had ever been primarily responsible heretofore.

There was now a simplified map, to be sure, with a sort of uneasy tetrarchy re-established. The illegitimate figure remained Maxentius, who had managed to survive longer at this point than anyone might have predicted. It is perhaps not a surprise that Maximinus and Maxentius would improve their relations by developing a friendship. They may have felt insecure and resentful versus the more powerful and accomplished Licinius and Constantine. Unfortunately for the tetrarchy, there was little in the way of active cooperation in these months between the ruling four – and so there was room for the pursuit of alliances to try to checkmate others. It would appear that the friendship that emerged between Maximinus and Maxentius was in direct consequence of similar close ties that began to bind Licinius and Constantine.

Lactantius loses no chance to note that Maximinus was no friend of the Christians, Galerian deathbed edict notwithstanding. In a perverse gesture of clemency, he is said to have spared the lives of Christians, but to have ordered their mutilation.[24] The rhetorical skills that Lactantius had mastered were never more actively exercised than when he described the tortures suffered by Christians. Contrary to the intention of the author, this indulgence in verbal artifice and excess has meant that many scholars have dismissed the tales of persecution as being grossly exaggerated.

Part of the origin of the problem that had emerged by this point were the careful decisions of Licinius that had been undertaken when first he took his place as the western Augustus. In such a role he might have been expected to move quickly to dethrone Maxentius. But he refrained from civil war, looking only hastily to the west once Galerius was dead, fearful lest Maximinus should take everything.

We have not mentioned the usurper Domitius Alexander in some time. He managed to retain power for a short while, until Maxentius was able to send men on his behalf to put an end to the rebellion. Those forces succeeded, and Alexander was murdered by strangulation sometime c. 309–311 – the surviving evidence does not allow us the ability to be more specific. In the vexed and violent history that was coming into being for the tetrarchy, it was one of the few achievements that Maxentius' record would be able to boast.

War could have erupted between Licinius and Maximinus because of the question of dividing Galerius' piece of empire.[25] We have seen how that potential conflict had been avoided by negotiated settlement. Maxentius was in as tenuous a position as he had always been, despite his ability to resolve the Alexander problem – it does not seem that Alexander (who was allegedly advanced in years) ever took a particularly active part in strategizing and securing his position on a large scale. Maxentius, for his part, fortified Italy as best as he could to prepare for the possibility of conflict with Constantine.

As if to demonstrate that knowledge of when to exit the stage was another of his signature traits, Diocletian died on the very eve of the maelstrom that was to envelop his beloved tetrarchy. Perhaps on 3 December 311, the great restorer of Rome breathed his last.[26] There would be some who claimed that he had committed suicide, overcome as he was with profound distress that the system he had founded was unravelling before his eyes. Others have asserted that he was in a state of true Lucretian serenity, as it were, having abandoned concern for the by now seemingly interminable crises of empire. He was the last survivor of the original tetrarchy. 'Writhing in pain and tormented by delusions he eventually succeeded in starving himself to death.' According to Lactantius, this was God's revenge for everything Diocletian had done to the Christians. The date of his death is unknown. The month and year most often reported is December 311, but it is also possible that he died in 312 or 313.[27] We are thus uncertain of both the birth and the death year of Diocletian. Unlike Galerius, Diocletian would at least be buried in the mausoleum that he had constructed for that purpose in his palace. Today it is a Christian church, and Diocletian is among those fortunate men of history whose burial place has largely been spared the ravages of time, notwithstanding the wars and violence that would plague the Balkans down through the ages.

Chapter 10

The Aftermath

Maximinus was incensed by the relationship between Licinius and Constantine at least in part because he was fearful that he was being shut out of negotiations and deals. In a related sense, he was worried that decisions were being made without the involvement of all of the legal members of the tetrarchy. The ties between Licinius and Constantine were solidified in the winter of 311–312 by the marriage of Constantine's half-sister Constantia to Licinius. Constantia had been born sometime after 293, and at 17 or 18 years of age she was now a key part of the continuing chess game. The nuptial arrangement was reminiscent of the way in which Maximian had proposed the union of Constantine with his daughter Fausta to solidify the bond between Constantine and Maxentius. Now it was Maxentius who was the likely, ostensible target for any new campaign. The fact that he was increasingly publicizing his view that Constantine had murdered his father Maximian did not help matters.

The corresponding, parallel friendship between Maximinus and Maxentius was sealed not with any marriage, but with a legal understanding. Maximinus would agree to recognize Maxentius as a legitimate ruler.

Maxentius had survived for some time now without any existential threat to his empire within an empire. Constantine knew that war was inevitable, and he prepared to launch his invasion of Italy with a target date for zero hour in the spring of 312. He would proceed over the Cottian Alps from Gaul into Italy, taking something like a fourth of the entire military force at his disposal – apparently something like forty thousand men. Segusio (the modern Susa in the Piedmont) was the first of the 'towns of Maxentius' that Constantine would have to take by force. Constantine prepared for a siege and was able soon enough to capture the relatively small settlement. His men were restrained from any lust for plunder after their first victory – Constantine had more important tasks ahead, and he had no desire to spread unnecessary or bad feelings among the people he planned to rule.

We may note here that one of our principal sources for information on the events of the crucial year of 312 is the twelfth panegyric, which was delivered not very long after Constantine's final victory over Maxentius.[1] The text is priceless for historians in the hunt to explicate exactly what Constantine did as he entered Italy on his way to Rome. So too is the fourth panegyric authored by the rhetorician Nazarius.[2] Even his purple prose admits that Segusio was an easy victory.[3] Indeed he focuses on how Constantine was most worried about saving the city from conflagration, such that he expended more energy in defending it than in taking it.

Although the first Italian town Constantine arrived at on his campaign had closed its gates to him initially, others would not react in the same way. Overall, the operations to seize northern Italy were not particularly taxing.

This is the period in which the record of Constantine's deeds first begins to take on something of a supernatural quality. Since later he would be the object of hagiographical veneration, and his ultimate successes and victory have cast a long shadow over the account of his life (especially in this crucial period in which he began to consolidate his power), we must exercise more than our usual caution with evaluating the credibility of what we hear. The story goes that all of Constantine's advisors were strongly urging caution, while their Augustus was seemingly preternaturally confident in his ultimate victory, with the result that his men were fortified in their courage.

Soon enough, Constantine scored his first victory over an armed force loyal to Maxentius. A cavalry unit that was stationed near Augusta Taurinorum (the modern Turin) was enveloped by Constantine's force and defeated. Tellingly, the city opened its gates to Constantine, acclaiming him as saviour and emperor. It was a harbinger of future success, especially in the refusal of the city to give any refuge to the surviving forces of Maxentius. Neighbouring towns soon learned of the advance, and they sent word to Constantine that he would receive a welcome from them.

For military historians, Nazarius' account of this cavalry engagement offers an interesting detail in passing. Constantine's men are arrayed on the plain, in the uncertainty of the tense moment as they face the forces arrayed in defence of the city. Some of the defenders are *clibanarii*, the celebrated horsemen entirely clad in armour – a device the Romans borrowed, it seems, from eastern troops. The Latin word is derived from *clibanus*, an 'oven' – it was as if these men were encased in the same sort of iron container one might use to bake bread (in the heat of battle – especially in eastern locales – they must have appreciated the image all too well). Constantine is depicted as directing the attack on this imposing force. Details are as usual somewhat wanting: Nazarius says simply that Constantine directed his men to draw open their lines to pull in the horsemen, who were then hemmed in and closed up by the enemy; the very rigidity of the iron mail hampered any easy manoeuvring once they were caught in the trap.[4]

Northern Italy would not be taken without further resistance, but Constantine had minimal difficulty (at least relatively speaking) in securing it. The engagement near Augusta Taurinorum was the first of two major clashes in the north, with the second coming near Verona. This was the more serious battle, with the principal casualty being Ruricius (or Pompeianus, or Ruricius Pompeianus), Maxentius' praetorian prefect and leading military commander.[5] (Death, the panegyrist Nazarius says, is all that could in the end subdue his mad fury.) It was preceded by the flight of a cavalry force at Brixia (modern Brescia), which served only to enhance the force at Verona.[6] The list of cities that soon surrendered to Constantine grew longer, as Mutina and Ravenna yielded to the new order.

Maxentius did not bother to fortify or to try to contest central Italy in the wake of the loss of key territory. Rather, he planned for a siege of Rome, confident that he could resist Constantine long enough for his enemy to give up trying to take the mystical if not administrative capital of the empire. In the end, there would be no siege. Maxentius could not afford to risk internal revolt in Rome, and the populace was beginning to show disturbing signs of extreme fatigue with him. We hear of crowds insulting the emperor at the games, shouting that Constantine was coming and that he would conquer. Maxentius had often avoided direct engagements, and had an embarrassing lack of experience of military matters. Leaving aside the mission for which he did not travel in person – the quelling of the Alexander revolt in Africa – Maxentius had very little credibility in army affairs. Now was his chance to be a Caesar, let alone an Augustus. There would have to be a pitched battle for control of Rome, and this would be the determining engagement in the most serious 'hot war' that had erupted in the civil strife that had hamstrung the tetrarchy.

28 October 312. Mythology as well as history have clouded the climactic engagement of the war between Constantine and Maxentius. The tale is well known not only in the annals of Roman history, but in Christian lore. Constantine is said to have received a vision by which he was inspired to have his men decorate their shields with Christian iconography. The ensuing battle – known to us as the Battle of the Milvian Bridge – was a total victory for Constantine, one in which Maxentius was drowned in the Tiber amid the rush of his retreating forces.[7]

The alleged mystical vision that Constantine received became a key element in the path toward the legalization and promotion of Christianity as the state religion that would follow soon a part of the Constantinian programme.[8] Scholars have tried to explicate what actually happened on the eve of the battle, including via analysis of the cult of *Sol Invictus* – 'the Unconquered Sun' – and the possible syncretism of that pagan deity with Christ. Constantine certainly provided inspiration to his men via the symbolism emblazoned on their shields, but they benefited more practically from the fact that he was a far more skilled and talented commander than Maxentius. A cavalry charge seems to have caused initial shock to Maxentius' line, and an ensuing assault by Constantine's infantry led to the disastrous retreat in which the son of Maximian lost his life. It is significant to note that Maxentius almost certainly had a much larger force than Constantine – perhaps twice as many men. Constantine's leadership and tactical skills stand forth as being a key element (if not the decisive one) in his achievement. Nazarius unsurprisingly notes that Constantine was in the thick of the battle at the Milvian Bridge, dispelling any hope on the part of his listener that he might tell us something about the disposition of his troops – after the customary *praeteritio* regarding such details, he tells us merely that all the men stood around Constantine, so active and vigorous was he in the fight.[9] One wonders if in reality the battle was anti-climactic: Maxentius' hour had long past, as the swift fall of his holdings in the north of Italy had made all too clear.

It was finally finished, half a dozen years after it had commenced. Maxentius was no longer a player – he was a decapitated corpse, having been fished out of the Tiber to suffer post mortem disgrace. His father Maximian had met his end in ignominy as a suicide at the suggestion (not to say command) of Constantine, and now the son who had tried too late in life to practice *pietas* was dead in battle just on the threshold of Rome, his attempt to take a share in the empire ultimately reduced to failure. The tetrarchy's members and aspirants suffered diverse fates; the father and son who had clashed so often in life were joined in death by their shared ignominy.

The desecration of Maxentius' corpse included the delivery of his head to Carthage as grisly proof to Africa that the leadership of the empire had been altered.[10] Carthage had been the site of the recently suppressed Alexander revolt, and it is clear that Constantine wanted to ensure the loyalty of the 'third continent' of the empire, without having to engage in any lengthy campaigns. Constantine had attained complete control over the west, the first man to do so since the establishment of the tetrarchy. He had no Caesar or colleague of any sort in rule in the west – only his eastern colleagues.

There were now three emperors, not four. The tetrarchy was now a triumvirate, one might say, with Maximinus Daza in the east, Licinius and Constantine in the west. Constantine had progressed methodically and successfully from the time when he and his father had their discussions in Britain, when Constantius knew he was dying and the topic of the hour was how to secure a place in imperial power for his son. It was a stunning turn of events in some regards, all things considered – and one that Diocletian had not lived to see. His system had been on artificial respiration, and was now in many regards dead. On the other hand, Constantine had proven himself to be both a competent commander and an effective administrator, and his reign would bring immense stability, notwithstanding the further wars that would ensue before the empire would be reunited under one man. Diocletian may not have been entirely displeased at the turn of events, especially considering that Constantine's rise brought stability to what had become an increasingly chaotic mess.

Maximian had suffered *damnatio memoriae*, and now his son would suffer the same. The name of Maxentius was expunged wherever it could be. Constantine was soon acclaimed by the senate not only as an Augustus, but as the greatest Augustus – Maxentius had ended his years in power with increasingly eroded support, and Constantine seems to have been received as a legitimate liberator and saviour of Rome.

At this juncture the relationship between Constantine and Licinius was also a stable and supportive one. Constantine had much to do in the consolidation of his power in the west, and he had no pressing business to worry about in the east, where Licinius and Maximinus Daza respectively managed their European and Asian eastern territories. Constantine did arrange to meet with Licinius at Mediolanum, the conference that would be held in 313 and that would become most famous in subsequent history for its decisions regarding Christianity.

Politically, the principal reason for the Mediolanum meeting was to confirm and strengthen the existing agreement and alliance between Constantine and Licinius. The marriage of Licinius and Constantia had been arranged, and there were discussions to be held about the next steps that should be taken with respect to the maintenance of what was left of the tetrarchy. Christian sources make much of the conference, which they credit with what has become known as the Edict of Milan or the Edict of Toleration. From an end to persecution, Roman social practice would move to a state not only of tolerance, but eventually adoption of Christianity as the religion of empire.

One key factor to consider in this matter requires a look back at Diocletian's institution of the Great Persecution a decade earlier. A case could be made that Diocletian failed in two main areas in his administration of the empire. The more serious failure was with respect to the maintenance of the tetrarchy's succession scheme. For all its stability and success, the tetrarchy did not survive its first transition to a new pair of Caesars and Augustuses. Diocletian does not share sole blame for the failure, and it is easy with the benefit of hindsight to critique his dealings with Galerius and his general unwillingness to push too hard in opposition to the appointment of Severus in particular as a new Caesar.

His other failure was in the matter of how to deal with Christianity in the empire. The Great Persecution largely had failed to achieve its ends. In some regards Christianity had become appreciably stronger, tested and proven in the crucible of martyrdom. The empire faced significant threats, especially externally. The social upheaval caused by the persecution of the Christians had not won any measurable benefits for the empire domestically, and there had never been a time when all of the tetrarchs were equally zealous about enforcing the decrees. Galerius had probably been the most eager to see the religion extirpated from Rome, and Constantine the least motivated – possibly if not probably because his own mother was a Christian, as the tradition reports. Indeed, there is something of a parallel between the tradition of Constantine's Christian mother and Galerius' pagan one.[11]

The agreement reached by Constantine and Licinius at Mediolanum would not be accepted with complete unanimity and assent of the will by the third player in the imperial power dynamic – Maximinus Daza. He was the glaring omission from the conference. On the one hand, he was on the other side of the Bosporus in Asia, while the eastern empire had European territories with land borders with the 'western' realms of Roman territory. On the other hand, there had been clear tensions between Licinius and Maximinus that had resulted in near armed conflict. Constantine was allied to Licinius with the strength of a marital bond; there were no such ties to connect either man to Maximinus.

Maximinus no doubt felt that he was at risk of having his Asian miniature empire threatened by the Constantine-Licinius alliance. Licinius could be expected to have designs on the east. We have noted how Maximinus had decided to make common cause with Maxentius, though it was unclear how exactly he could move to help his new ally in any appreciable way. He could certainly strike at Licinius, but this would change nothing in the matter of the conflict between Maxentius and Constantine. His problems with Licinius, moreover, were independent of his dealings with Maxentius.

Maximinus did engage in military build up and preparation, however, if only for the sake of being ready to defend his piece of the empire. The fact that he decided to take the precipitous step of moving into Licinius' territory during the Mediolanum conference is no surprise, one might think. He may have felt slighted by his lack of an invitation, and it was the one moment when he could move with his opponent out of the field, as it were. Maximinus seems to have had about seventy thousand men. But, as often, it is difficult for us to say exactly what his intentions were. Did he plan to oust Licinius entirely from his command, and to occupy his territories integrally? Did he have less ambitious aspirations? In either case, he made his move to advance into Europe across the storied Hellespont, and he did so with great haste, clearly hoping to take advantage of Licinius' distraction and to do as much as he could to secure territory before his rival could organize a response. One problem was that this course of action required a rapid march through difficult terrain in Asia Minor in winter. It was a challenging logistical expedition, and by the time Maximinus had arrived in Asia Minor, it seems that his men were exhausted and frustrated by the difficulties of transport.

News sometimes travels quite fast, even in the challenging communications circumstances of the time. Licinius was with Constantine at Mediolanum when the reports began to arrive that Maximinus had broken the agreement between them, indeed that he had begun an invasion of Europe. Licinius began his own rapid, reactionary response, hastily exiting the conference and proceeding east, mustering his forces as best as he could along the long journey. The clash that would ensue when the two armies finally met is known to history as the Battle of Tzirallum. Like the engagement at the Milvian Bridge between Maxentius and Constantine, Tzirallum was a lopsided encounter. We are uncertain of the size of Licinius' force, but it was appreciably smaller than Maximinus' – perhaps by more than half. Certainly Licinius had had a less arduous journey than his rival, for all his haste.

We know next to nothing about the strategy and tactics of the battle, which was fought in eastern Thrace on 30 April 313. The key detail is that Licinius won a decisive victory, and Maximinus was forced to flee and to attempt to regroup his shattered force. In Christian sources Maximinus is criticized for having ignored the Edict of Toleration, and for maintaining his persecution of the religion; now we learn that he reversed that course – certainly his plate was full with other concerns.

The eastern Roman empire was now in civil war, and Licinius faced the challenge that his opponent had significant land and resources to ensure the likelihood of a long struggle. The victory at Tzirallum had been impressive, but Licinius still had much work to do, with no assurance of victory (let alone a swift one). Maximinus returned to Asia, staying first at Nicomedia and then at Tarsus.

In August, the worries and anxiety of Licinius were put to rest by the death of Maximinus, perhaps if not probably from natural causes. Christian sources are not without the speculation that the justice of God struck him down, angry on account of his history of persecution.[12] Some have argued that he may have suffered from Graves' Disease, largely because of his appearance on a statue from Egypt that is sometimes identified with him. Lactantius has a characteristic account, in which Maximinus suffers a ghastly botched suicide after attempting to take poison. Chapter 49 of his account of the deaths of the persecutors comes near the end of that work, and it reads as something of a crown to all the previous records therein of the just fates of those who harassed Christians. It deserves to be quoted as a good example of Lactantius' prose at its polemic best:[13]

Sequenti autem Licinio cum exercitu tyrannum profugus concessit et rursus Tauri montis angustias petiit. Munimentis ibidem ac turribus fabricatis iter obstruere conatus est et inde detrusus perrumpentibus omnia victoribus Tarsum postremo confugit. Ibi cum iam terra marique premeretur nec ullum speraret refugium; angore animi ac metu confugit ad mortem quasi ad remedium malorum, quae deus in caput eius ingessit. Sed prius cibo se infersit ac vino ingurgitavit, ut solent ii qui hoc ultimo se facere arbitrantur, et sic hausit venenum. Cuius vis referto stomacho repercussa valere non potuit in praesens, sed in languorem malum versum est pestilentiae similem, ut diutius protracto spiritu cruciamenta sentiret. Iam saevire in eum coeperat virus. Cuius vi cum praecordia eius furerent, insustentabili dolore usque ad rabiem mentis elatus est, adeo ut per dies quattuor insania percitus haustam manibus terram velut esuriens devoraret. Deinde post multos gravesque cruciatus cum caput suum parietibus infligeret, exilierunt oculi eius de caveis; tunc demum, amisso visu, deum videre coepit candidatis ministris de se iudicantem. Exclamabat ergo sicut ii qui torquentur solent, et non se, sed alios fecisse dicebat. Deinde quasi tormentis adactus fatebatur Christum subinde deprecans et implorans, ut suimet misereretur. Sic inter gemitus quos tamquam cremaretur edebat, nocentem spiritum detestabili genere mortis efflavit.

'Licinius pursued the tyrant with his army, as he withdrew in flight and again sought the narrow defiles of Mount Taurus. With fortifications and towers having been built, he endeavoured to block the way. But with his enemy rushing in everywhere he was dislodged from there, and at last took refuge on Tarsus. There when he was pressed on both land and sea and could not hope for any escape, with anguish of mind and fear he fled to death as if it were the answer to the ills that God had heaped on his head. But first he stuffed himself with food and drowned himself in wine, as those are accustomed to do who think that this is their last meal. At last he took poison. But the force of the poison was repelled because of how bloated his stomach was with food, and instead it produced a sickness similar to a pestilence, so that his torment might be of longer duration, with his life extended. Then the poison began to rage against him, whose force raged against his innards, such that by the intolerable pain he was driven to madness. For four days he endured such fits of frenzy that he picked up heaps of earth with his hands to devour them. Then after many serious tortures, he banged his head against the walls and his eyes bugged out from their cavities. At last, deprived of sight he began to sense God approaching to make judgment of him, with his white-robed ministers. Then as if driven by his torments, he began to confess to Christ, imploring and supplicating him to take pity. Thus amid the groans that he gave out as if he were being burned alive, he breathed out his guilty spirit by a detestable manner of death.'

One imagines that Lactantius regretted that he could not write such purple prose regarding the comparatively far more peaceful and less dramatic demise of Diocletian; this death scene is more akin to his account of Galerius' end. The 'white-robed ministers' is probably a reference to the martyred saints in glory; the martyrs are depicted often in Christian hagiography as having white robes that are reminiscent of their baptismal garments.

There is an interesting footnote to the demise of Maximinus. One man who was in his entourage has been mentioned before briefly in our story – Flavius Severianus, the son of the dead onetime tetrarch Severus. Severianus did not survive long after Maximinus' death – he was captured and then killed on the orders of Licinius, with the charge being that he planned to try to seize power himself. Certainly it was hazardous to be the son of a deceased tetrarch, and Severus is known mostly because of his untimely end. Severus was not the only prominent casualty of the defeat of Maximinus. There was also the wife of Diocletian, Prisca. For reasons that are not entirely clear, Prisca and her daughter Valeria fled to Maximinus on the occasion of his revolt. Valeria rejected, however, proposals of marriage from him, and in anger he had her imprisoned in Syria.[14] Indeed, 'imprisonment' is an inexact word, since according to Lactantius, Maximinus had Valeria and her mother bustled about from one place of residence to another, harrying them on alongside the slaughter of their eunuchs and the false accusations of adultery against the women who accompanied them. Most prominently, a matron to whom Valeria was devoted was killed on suspicion of having been the one who persuaded Diocletian's daughter not to submit to Maximinus' lusts.[15]

Lactantius was of the view that Prisca and Valeria were closet Christians.[16] Williams is sceptical of this conclusion, relating the memory from his primary Catholic education that some religious sisters expressed the view at the coronation of Elizabeth II that she was secretly Catholic.[17] To the best of my knowledge, no tradition developed among any Christian group that Prisca and Valeria were martyrs or saints.

After Maximinus' death, like Severus, the mother and daughter were taken into custody by Licinius, who had them both killed.[18] We are ignorant of the precise circumstances that prompted these killings; politically it may have been as dangerous to be the widow or daughter of a former tetrarch as it was to be the son. Williams notes that if they were of the Christian faith, they kept the secret well, and even after they were slain under Licinius, no propaganda was employed to note that the inveterate persecutor of Christians was killing them for religious reasons (the idea that Diocletian's own spouse and daughter were not good pagans would of course be exactly the sort of story that would attract Lactantius, and we share Williams' doubt about the veracity of the report). The very fact of their flight to Maximinus – another matter that is of uncertain inspiration – would also have incurred the ire of Licinius. For the moment, the focus of the now sole eastern emperor seems to have been on ensuring that there would be no possible centre of any resistance to his maintenance of monarchy. Lactantius argues that Valeria had assumed that she would be safer in Maximinus' realm than elsewhere, in part because Maximinus was already married and thus would have no designs on her. His lust and wicked character, however, were unable to resist importuning the daughter of Diocletian, who in Lactantius' account was devoted (like her mother) to Christian principles of chastity. According to Lactantius, Valeria was able to send word to her father about her imprisonment; Diocletian at the time would have been in the last months of his life. We are told that Diocletian immediately commenced appeals to Maximian that his daughter be returned to him in Salona, but all requests were treated with silence or disdain.[19]

'This was what his glorious memory had now come to. This was the ingratitude of a ruler who no longer feared him and therefore cynically dropped any pretence of respect or even courtesy. To these men he was just a nuisance, a useless and barely tolerated relic.'[20] It is conceivable that a tradition developed that exaggerated these episodes, the idea being that Diocletian could not be allowed a quiet death in retirement after his role in the great persecution of the Christians. If there could not be some gruesome abdominal or genital cancer, at least there could be the pathetic scene of repeated pleas for the safety of his daughter, all ignored by Maximinus with contemptuous dismissal. Diocletian would win a victory over Maximinus that he would never know about – history would remember him far better, and for far better reasons. For the moment, there is no question that Diocletian's death – whether natural or by suicide – came to a man who, as most of his biographers have noted, had decided that he had lived too long. He resided in something of a gilded cage on the Adriatic, his magnificent palace a refuge in the end from everything save himself and the power of memory. Born perhaps a slave into total obscurity, he had died in luxurious wealth, but a slave of the system that he had established, one that now would not afford him any particular favour or grace. Potter notes: 'It is a sign of the sudden change in Diocletian's own fortunes that the moment of his death, in either 311 or 313, was not marked with any celebration by his successors. The man who had tried so hard to reform the historical record of the Roman Empire simply dropped out of it.'[21] It remains a sad fact that we know of nothing that was done or requested by the retired emperor after his failed appeal for the return of Valeria.

There was another casualty of Licinius' settlement. Galerius had had a son with a concubine who was born around 296 and was now about 17. Diocletian's daughter Valeria later adopted him, given that she had no biological children. If we can believe Lactantius, Galerius had high hopes for the youth, intending even to bestow imperial power on him at some point. But after Galerius' death, Candidianus became another of the refugees at the court of Maximinus, living in fear of Licinius. Again Lactantius is our source that after the defeat of Maximinus, Candidianus tried to present himself at the court of Licinius where, despite an initially warm reception, he was soon killed. He had been betrothed at the time of his death to the daughter of Maximinus, who was also murdered along with her brother Maximus. This was a purge designed to eliminate any possible threat to Licinius, by removing those with family ties to deceased tetrarchs. Galerius had been successful at maintaining a relative state of peace, but now he was gone and with it a significant *remora* to worsening civil strife.[22]

For whatever the exact circumstances of the death of Maximinus, it came as a blessing and boon to Licinius. Like Constantine in the west, he was now a sole ruler, and the Roman Empire had a dyarchy – two men with the division of empire into halves (at least roughly). The year was 313, and at least for a moment, the civil wars were finished. It is beyond the scope of the present study to detail the next phase of the slide into chaos – the decade long struggle between Constantine and Licinius, the almost inevitable clash between the co-rulers of the Roman empire. That civil war would last from 314 to 324, with periods of truce, alliance, and reconciliation punctuated by full-scale conflict. Constantine would emerge the victor, with Licinius destined to face execution in 324, followed by the *damnatio memoriae* that had been the fate of Maximian and Maxentius before him. From 19 September 324 until his death on 22 May 337, Constantine would be the sole ruler of the reunited Roman empire, a more than dozen years reign at the helm of power. The man who had been raised to some share in the purple in Britain in the summer of 306 would spend nearly thirty years enjoying some share of imperial authority, with brilliant military victories both in foreign and domestic struggles. It is a testament at least in part to something of the stability that Diocletian had given to the empire that Constantine had been able to reign so long. Reared in some ways at the very court of Diocletian in the east, Constantine no doubt had absorbed valuable lessons from the father of the tetrarchy. Overlooked in the initial succession scheme, he had emerged as the most enduring of the sharers in Roman imperial power, ultimately serving not only as the most successful member of the tetrarchal arrangement in the wake of its first transition, but also as one of the longest serving rulers of an integral Roman empire.

An evaluation and appraisal of the reign of Diocletian may suitably begin from a study of what he inherited. Compared to the disasters that predominated in the history of the tumultuous third century, Diocletian's tenure was one of stability and indeed renewal and restoration. It is nothing short of miraculous that he was able to manage for two decades. His tetrarchal system was rooted in old models of governance, to be sure, but he invested it with his own novel approaches in a blended harmony. There was a certain elegant simplicity to his proposed 'best practice' for managing the Roman government and its multifaceted problems, and in practice it worked well during the time he was actively involved in its governance.

There are two areas in which we can identify striking failures. First and foremost, Diocletian failed to oversee properly the crucial first transition of the reins of power. It can be argued that he was in a very difficult situation, one in which he was limited in what he could achieve. But the promotion of Severus and Maximinus as Caesars brought with it a cascading host of problems, such that the seeds were sown for the rapid emergence of a series of near and actual civil wars that would plague domestic affairs for two decades. During Diocletian's tenure as a tetrarch, foreign crises were the priority; the civil wars that erupted caused an erosion of the gains that had been secured on the borders. Here it was the tremendous success of Diocletian and his colleagues that helped to secure the safety of the frontier, not to mention the equally outstanding work in this area of Constantine. The arrangement for the first tetrarchal transition solved some points of contention, but raised arguably equally or more serious problems that were easily foreseeable.

Second, there was the area of the treatment of the Christians, one which in the final analysis is probably inseparable from Diocletian's emphasis on the monarchical, quasi-divine nature of the emperor. Diocletian was perfectly comfortable with receiving the adoration of his subjects, with prostration and the trappings of eastern pomp.[23] There was nothing of the style of Augustus in this, of the respect for republican tradition and the avoidance of the emblems of royalty. Christianity posed a monotheistic threat to this emphasis on the divinity of the emperor (even quasi-divinity). Still, it is important to note that Diocletian was not responsible for introducing *adoratio* into Roman imperial life – even if ancient sources are fond of ascribing to him what has probably rightly been called a 'canard'.[24] 'The ancient sources generally attribute to Diocletian a major change in imperial manners … The affected *civilitas* of Augustus, his pseudo-republican theatre of "first among equals", was now abandoned in favour of glitter and ceremonial ... Specific attribution of these innovations to Diocletian, however, is difficult to establish.'[25] Modern sources often follow ancient in making Diocletian responsible for the introduction of such oriental flattery.[26] Even if Diocletian was not the inventor, he was an eager practitioner.[27]

Diocletian's adoption of the practices of court reverence of the emperor and the virtual worship of his person is of interest in light of his own humble origins, with the likelihood that he was the son of a freedman or possibly even a freed slave himself. We have noted how 'From slave to emperor' could, in all possibility, be a subtitle for his life. His humble origins were compensated for in abundance by his indulgence in the lavish honours that he expected as emperor. But he was willing also to surrender it all.

Diocletian was old-fashioned in matters of military discipline and the conduct of traditional Roman morality, and he may have associated Roman mores closely with the practice of Roman religion and cult. Christianity could not be tolerated in a world where Christians refused in principle to participle in a characteristic feature of Roman life. Christianity could not be allowed to possess exemptions from sacrifices in honour of the emperor, when the emperor was someone who expected deferential acts of worship that underscored his otherworldly, godly aspects.

And yet persecutions are prone to failure because of the powerful allure of martyrdom. Diocletian's persecution did not succeed in eradicating Christianity or in driving it into an obscure underground existence. The practice of persecution created social unrest and disturbances in the body politic, which served to weaken the fabric of domestic life wherever the edicts against the faith were upheld with vigour.

Diocletian was probably not tempted to return from retirement, with every new missive and bit of news revealing more details about the troubles that were consuming the empire that he had restored (indeed, we have noted that awareness of serious problems may have inspired his desire to retire while all was relatively calm). He was willing to participate in the council at Carnuntum as his one significant post-retirement contribution to public affairs. Here the agenda items were very different from those that had consumed him at the time of his retirement. By Carnuntum, Diocletian probably saw Constantine as the most Diocletianic of the new tetrarchs, certainly as the most competent and trustworthy of the lot. It is telling that not only would Constantine be the sole survivor of the later tetrarchy, but that he would see Rome's government revert to monarchy, with his own long tenure a hearkening back to Diocletian's long tenure in power.

We may turn specifically to an evaluation of Diocletian as a military commander. Like other so-called barracks emperors, Diocletian had a profound practical understanding of Roman military affairs. He was skilled in the military arts to an impressive degree. His style was more defensive than offensive, more cautious and conservative than reckless and bold. He was a master of fortification and defences, of how to secure a position and to inflict a high cost on any would-be attacker. He was competent at avoiding the exposure of his forces to risk, and at how to engage in patrols and border country manoeuvres. These talents were ideally suited to the work of defending the Danube frontier that he knew best. There is less evidence to suspect that he was particularly adept at guerrilla warfare. In this, Constantine was more diversified given his experience in Britain in particular. Diocletian was willing to expand Rome's borders, but in exceedingly modest ways. He was more interested in the defence of clearly defined geographical fronts, and had no dreams of vast exploratory glory. That said, his eminent practicality led him to remote corners of the empire that had been largely neglected – one thinks here of southern Egypt and the Nubian border.

We have observed that we know very little about the details of the Battle of the Margus, the engagement that marked Diocletian's victory over Carinus. We have seen how that victory may have owed more to the dissatisfaction that Carinus' men felt for their commander than to any strategic or tactical skill of Diocletian. Margus was the most awkward battle that Diocletian would ever fight, since it was his unique experience of a civil war, one in which he was cast in the uncomfortable position of being yet another usurper of someone else's purple. The narrative by which Carinus' own men mutinied against him may well be true (at least in kernel), or it may represent a deliberate propaganda effort to obscure the rebellious aspect of Diocletian's accession. It would be better for the new emperor's reputation to be able to credit his victory not so much to his military acumen, as to the anger that Carinus had aroused in his own men, especially on account of his alleged immorality. According to this line of propaganda, Diocletian was thus not only a saviour, but a restorer of virtue and morals.

In both military and domestic affairs, Diocletian was a quintessential administrator. He enjoyed having expansive bureaucracies that managed numerous aspects of life in detail. In this regard certainly he succeeded in restoring a sense of order where before there had been much recent chaos. He may have overcompensated, with the pendulum swinging a bit too far in the direction of rubric and legalism. Some of the problems that emerged – one thinks of the origins of the Maxentius rebellion – were rooted in a simultaneous relative neglect of the city of Rome, as if in studied determination to remind that legendary city that the capital of the empire was wherever an emperor was, not where the senate convened. Some of this studied avoidance of Rome and relative ignoring of the senate was connected to his strongly monarchical views. Maintaining a senate was respectful of tradition, but senatorial prerogatives were of no interest to the purpled potentate.

The neglect of Rome was accompanied by a standardization effort that sought to bring all the different cities and towns of the empire under one system for matters such as taxation and economic management. This obsession with efficiency brought with it the usual mix of bane and blessing. One weakness of the Diocletianic system was its tendency to be intolerant of exceptions and deviations from a standard. In economic affairs it was an area of weakness, in which the emperor's edicts would soon enough be more or less ignored.

The principal mystery that surrounds the reign of Diocletian may well be its beginning. We have outlined the controversies that surrounded the commencement of his taking power, in particular the question of whether he had any involvement in the demise of Numerian. While available evidence does not permit certainty, on the whole it seems more likely that he was innocent, though after the deaths of Carus and Numerian he was of no inclination to continue his service under Carinus. Perhaps in the virtual triumvirate of the father and his two sons the son-less Diocletian saw the seeds of what he could perfect in his tetrarchy arrangement. His original system was modelled on the notion of the 'best man' practice rather than hereditary promotion, which may have been a factor in his later willingness to reject the sons of both Constantius and Maximian from high office. Diocletian may have realized from the start that Constantine was both a biological son and a best man, but to have appointed one tetrarchal son while overlooking the other would have been an invitation to an instant civil war, as opposed to the slower descent into strife that took place.

Diocletian was possessed of a strong commitment to the unity of the Roman empire, despite his conclusion that it was impractical and inefficient for one man to try to manage it alone. That unity was always somewhat prone to the tendency of being considered theoretical more than practical, as different tetrarchs were ensconced in their own regions of the empire. It is accepted by many that the purpose of the division of the empire into zones of special responsibility was an administrative tool designed to allow for more efficient management of problems (especially on the borders). We have noted too the vulnerability of one man to assassination and overthrow – it is safer to have colleagues in power, notwithstanding the risk of tensions and disagreements between those in leadership. Diocletian probably did not extend his invitation to Maximian to share power, for example, because he was worried that Maximian would move against him otherwise or try to be yet another of the usurpers of Roman history. Subsequent events would show Maximian to be a man consumed by immense ambition and a desire to remain an active player in imperial power, but much had happened in the course of twenty years, and it can be perilous to interpret earlier events in light of decisions that were taken decades later in very different circumstances. It may well have been the case that Maximian was possessed early on of a strong sense of loyalty to Diocletian, indeed a fierce devotion to a man he considered to be responsible both for solving many of the problems of empire, and of ensuring his own power and success. As events unfolded, Maximian likely felt that he and Diocletian should not seek to resign from office so quickly, but his devotion to his long-time friend may have been the deciding factor in his willingness to agree to the joint abdication plan, notwithstanding his displeasure and uncertainty about the decisions regarding the second tetrarchy. The early history of that new tetrarchal arrangement may have convinced Maximian that Diocletian's unwillingness to leave his vegetables and palace at Split should not be the cause of his own hesitation to try to regain some share of power.

Diocletian was a dramatic success and a dramatic failure. He won for himself a secure reign of some twenty years, during which time the condition of the empire improved appreciably, especially in terms of foreign affairs and border security. Given the crises of the hour that confronted the empire in 284, Diocletian was successful in responding to the threats. He was most notably a failure in the matter of the enduring success of his institutions, and this failure was one for which the blame could be shared quite amply (more so than the credit for his success).

The manner of his death is a mystery that cannot be resolved in the absence of new evidence. His predecessors Carus, Numerian, and Carinus suffered similarly ambiguous fates. It is believable that Diocletian committed suicide, perhaps out of weariness for life and fear for the future of his tetrarchal system, rather than because of any anxiety for his personal safety. Illness and death by natural causes are possible, and depending on the ailments of his last years, suicide as escape from suffering cannot be excluded. It would be entirely fitting with his personality that just as he chose when to leave the Roman stage, so he chose when to leave that of life. Lactantius concludes his *De Mortibus Persecutorum* with a condemnation of the usurpation of the names of Jupiter and Hercules by Diocletian and Maximian, noting that the names of those deities were now gone from the days of his Christian, Constantinian empire. He was not aware of the future Julian the Apostate, and of the travails that were still in the future for Christians in the empire.

Diocletian can be named among the greatest of Roman emperors, and without hesitation. In some regards he experienced the fate of Augustus, in that the system he honed and perfected did not succeed altogether as planned. And while Augustus would be but one emperor removed from a Caligula, Diocletian's long tenure as a tetrarch would give way soon enough to the impressive sole rule of Constantine, a man who himself would come to encounter many of the same problems that beset Diocletian and Augustus – the inability to control perfectly what will happen after one's death or abdication.

Despite her very real problems, Rome certainly was in a stronger and more stable position when Diocletian died than when he had assumed office. By that basic criterion of evaluation, Diocletian stands among the luminaries of Roman imperial history. It is a measure of the man that for all his fondness for bejewelled robes and gemmed shoes, he was, in the end, able to resist any siren song to return to purple and power, preferring to stay with his cabbages and to be remembered for being the man who knew both when to walk away, and how to stay in the gardens of grace.[28]

Notes

Chapter 1

1. Suetonius is an enduringly popular author on account of his fascinatingly drafted biographies of the Caesars from Julius Caesar to Domitian, lives replete with gossip and innuendo alongside valuable accounts of events of political, military, and social history. There is an Oxford Classical Texts edition of Suetonius by Robert Kaster, with a companion volume on textual problems (*Studies on the Text of Suetonius' De vita Caesarum*, (Oxford: Oxford University Press, 2016)). Both the Oxford World's Classics and Penguin Classics series offer accessible English translations with notes. The Loeb Classical Library edition (revised 1997–1998, with a new introduction) has especially good annotations. Individual imperial lives have received extended commentaries, with several appearing from the Bristol Classical Press; Donna Hurley's edition of the life of Claudius for the Cambridge Greek and Latin Classics series (*Suetonius: Divus Claudius*, (Cambridge: Cambridge University Press, 2001)) is noteworthy too.
2. Indeed, by Diocletian's time it was customary to swear to the senate and people that one would emulate Marcus Aurelius in particular.
3. In our estimation the best overall scholarly study of Diocletian in English is that of Stephen Williams: *Diocletian and the Roman Recovery*, (London-New York: Routledge, 1997). It was originally published in 1985. Roger Rees' *Diocletian and the Tetrarchy* (Debates and Documents in Roman History), (Edinburgh: Edinburgh University Press, 2004), provides a valuable collection of sources with commentary. Note also the excellent monograph of Simon Corcoran: *The Empire of the Tetrarchs: Imperial Pronouncements and Government AD 284–324*, (Oxford: Clarendon Press, 1996) (revised for a paperback edition, 2000). There is an interesting collection of essays edited by Diederik W.P. Burgersdijk and Alan J. Ross: *Imagining Emperors in the Later Roman Empire*, (Leiden-Boston: Brill, 2018). All of these works are first-line resources for further study of the emperor and period.
4. The term 'Dominate' is derived from the Latin word *dominus* ('master'); it has implications of a servile relationship of everyone else toward the emperor; even if such implications were not always openly expressed, the etymological implications were present.
5. The sole surviving Latin handbook of astrology is the eight-book *Mathesis* of Julius Firmicus Maternus, who flourished during the reign of Constantine the Great and his successors. It is one of the key texts in the study of

astrology in the Roman empire, and provides an interesting window into the place of horoscopes and superstition in late imperial Rome.

6. Cf. J.G.C. Anderson, 'The Genesis of Diocletian's Provincial Reorganization' in *The Journal of Roman Studies*, Vol. 22, Part 1: Papers Dedicated to Sir George Macdonald KCB (1932), pp. 24–32.

7. Cf. the assessment of C.E. van Sickle: 'After Augustus, probably no single ruler of the Roman Empire exerted a more profound influence upon its destinies than Diocletian' (in 'Conservative and Philosophical Influence in the Reign of Diocletian' in *Classical Philology*, Vol. 27, No. 1 (January 1932), pp. 51–8).

8. See further here C.W. Keyes, 'The Date of the Laterculus Veronensis' in *Classical Philology*, Vol. 11, No. 2 (April 1916), pp. 196–201; J.B. Bury, 'The Provincial List of Verona' in *The Journal of Roman Studies*, Vol. 13 (1923), pp. 127–51; A.H.M. Jones, 'The Date and Value of the Verona List' in *The Journal of Roman Studies*, Vol. 44 (1954), pp. 21–9.

9. On these see J.C. Mann, 'The Creation of Four Provinces in Britain by Diocletian' in *Britannia*, Vol. 29 (1998), pp. 339–41.

10. 'The extent of Diocletian's contribution to these changes can be difficult to gauge.' (Rees, *op. cit.*, p. 17).

11. The issue is a matter of weighty scholarly disagreement. Did Diocletian expand the military with the intention of creating essentially two cooperative forces – one based in fixed fortifications, the other for mobile defence? In some regards the disagreement is rooted in an unnecessary dichotomy of alternatives that are not mutually exclusive. See further Williams, *op. cit.*, pp. 246–7 n. 1.

12. See further Nigel Pollard and Joanne Berry, *The Complete Roman Legions* (London: Thames & Hudson Ltd., 2012) p. 95; note also Yann Le Bohec, *The Imperial Roman Army* (London: B.T. Batsford Ltd., 1994) (English translation of the French original *L'armée romaine, sous le Haut-Empire* (Paris: Les Editions Picard, 1989); reprinted by Routledge, 2000), pp. 205–6, with convenient chart of the most famous legions and their known locations in various periods.

13. Cf. Pollard and Berry, *op. cit.*, p. 105.

14. There were thirty-nine when he began his reign. Diocletian and his fellow tetrarchs raised at least fourteen more.

15. Cf. Le Bohec, *op. cit.*, p. 258.

16. For an introduction to this topic note Ross Cowan's *Roman Legionary AD 284–337: The Age of Diocletian and Constantine the Great* (Oxford: Osprey Publishing, 2003).

17. On the *Magna Persecutio* see especially Min Seok Shin, *The Great Persecution: A Historical Re-examination (Studia Antiqua Australiensia, 8)* (Turnhout: Brepols, 2018); also P.S. Davies, 'The Origin and Purpose of the Persecution of AD 303' in *The Journal of Theological Studies*, New Series, Vol. 40, No. 1 (April, 1989), pp. 66–94. On its commencement

note Elizabeth Deplama Digeser, 'An Oracle of Apollo at Daphne and the Great Persecution' in *Classical Philology*, Vol. 99, No. 1 (January, 2004), pp. 57–77.

18. The bibliography on Augustus is immense. The best anglophone comprehensive study of his life and tenure is Adrian Goldsworthy's *Augustus: First Emperor of Rome* (New Haven, Connecticut: Yale University Press, 2014). Lindsay Powell has produced an exceptional survey of the military history of the Augustan Age, with detailed notes: *Augustus at War: The Struggle for the Pax Augusta* (Barnsley: Pen & Sword Military, 2018).

19. As for Augustus, so for Caesar the available scholarship is daunting in its quantity. Among English works, Adrian Goldsworthy's *Caesar: Life of a Colossus* (New Haven, Connecticut: Yale University Press, 2006) may be recommended without reserve.

20. In the Adrian Goldsworthy trilogy on the transition from Republic to Empire, *Antony and Cleopatra* (New Haven: Yale University Press, 2011) is devoted to the lives of the doomed triumvir and his regal paramour. Note also Barry Strauss' monograph *The War That Made the Roman Empire: Antony, Cleopatra, and Octavian at Actium* (New York: Simon & Schuster, 2022) See Lee Fratantuono *The Battle of Actium* (Barnsley: Pen & Sword Military, 2016) (reprinted in paperback in 2022) for a reappraisal of the naval engagement, with detailed analysis of the surviving literary sources.

21. For Livia see the superlative work of Anthony A. Barrett, *Livia: First Lady of Imperial Rome* (New Haven, Connecticut: Yale University Press, 2002); on Tiberius, best is Barbara Levick's *Tiberius the Politician* (London-New York: Routledge, 1999) (reprinted with a new preface and updated bibliography after its first appearance in the 'Aspects of Greek and Roman Life' series by Thames & Hudson, Ltd.).

22. This accounts for the subtitle of Nicholas Jackson's general study, *Trajan: Rome's Last Conqueror* (Barnsley: Greenhill Books, c/o Pen & Sword Books Ltd., 2022). For a standard, scholarly study of the reign, see Julian Bennett, *Trajan: Optimus Princeps* (London-New York: Routledge, 2000).

23. On Septimius note especially Anthony R. Birley's *Septimius Severus: The African Emperor* (London-New York: Routledge, 1999) (a revised version of the 1971 B.T. Batsford original).

24. The best English study is Ilkka Syvänne's *Caracalla: A Military Biography* (Barnsley: Pen & Sword Military, 2017).

25. Recommended reading here is Martijn Icks' *The Crimes of Elagablus: The Life and Legacy of Rome's Decadent Boy Emperor* (Cambridge, Massachusetts: Harvard University Press, 2012).

26. Essential reading here is John S. McHugh's *Emperor Alexander Severus: Rome's Age of Insurrection, AD 222–235* (Barnsley: Pen & Sword Military, 2017).

27. Ancient sources sometimes speak uncritically of Parthians and Persians. The Arsacids had given way to the Sassanians early in the third century ce, with resultant increased headaches for Rome given that the Sassanians saw

themselves as the true inheritors of the great tradition of the Achaemenids. Kaveh Farrokh's *The Armies of Ancient Persia: The Sassanians* (Barnsley: Pen & Sword Military, 2017) offers a massive introduction to the subject; Lee Fratantuono's *Roman Conquests: Mesopotamia and Arabia* (Barnsley: Pen & Sword Military, 2020) provides a brief sketch of the relevant history.

28. For the status of the religion in terms of population and property after the capture of Valerian by the Persians, see David Potter, *The Roman Empire at Bay, AD 180–395* (London-New York: Routledge, 2004) (second edition 2014), pp. 308–9.

29. There are 2001 and 2004 Vatican Press editions of the *Martyrologium Romanum* in the wake of the reforms of the Roman liturgy undertaken after the Second Vatican Council. The earlier, pre-conciliar edition was last published in 1956, with some modest variations introduced in 1960.

30. For a sound and comprehensive introduction to this author see Michael Bland Simmons, *Arnobius of Sicca: Religious Conflict and Competition in the Age of Diocletian* (Oxford: Clarendon Press 1996).

31. Lactantius is absent from the Penguin, Oxford World's Classics, Oxford Classical Texts, and Loeb series. There is a Teubner edition of the Latin text of the *Institutiones*, as well as of the *Epitome* thereof that also survives.

32. Williams opts for 'probably … 243' (*op. cit.*, p. 22).

33. A wonderful and comprehensive introduction to the province can be found in J.J. Wilkes's massive *Dalmatia* (Cambridge, Massachusetts: Harvard University Press, 1969). Intended as part of a series of volumes on the provinces of the empire, the only other book in the set is Sheppard Frere's *Britannia: A History of Roman Britain* (Cambridge, Massachusetts: Harvard University Press, 1991), which remains a valuable guide to a vast subject.

34. Special note should be made of the ninth panegyric on the restoration of schools, which dates to c. 297–9. This is the only one of the surviving imperial panegyrics that is not in honour of an emperor, or at least delivered to one. It provides no information on military events, though it is an important text for information on the state of Roman education.

35. See Pollard and Berry, *op. cit.*, p. 177.

36. On the question of Carausius' initial commission see Pat Southern, *The Roman Empire from Severus to Constantine* (London-New York: Routledge, 2001) p. 332 n. 6.

37. Lactantius, *De Mortibus Persecutorum* 11 refers to the same personality trait, noting that whenever Diocletian did anything positive, it was always on his own initiative and without advice, whereas when he acted for ill, he was sure to call in many advisors and counsellors, so that the blame could be imputed to them.

38. The case of Nerva with Trajan in 96 was not exactly parallel, though according to Lactantius (*De Mortibus Persecutorum* 18) it would be exactly the precedent that Galerius would invoke to encourage Diocletian to abdicate.

39. Victor also makes a perceptive comparison of Diocletian to the republican hero Marius.

40. It also forces a careful consideration of the fact that Maximian might not have shared Diocletian's sentiments about wanting to depart the scene rather than trying to shape future events. Diocletian would have felt that it would be unthinkable for only one Augustus to retire, however.

41. 'Julian in Italy' is obscure. There were apparently multiple usurpers with the name Julian in the time of Carinus (cf. Aurelius Victor, *De Caesaribus* 39.10), Diocletian, and Maximian. But the Diocletian/Maximian Julian is cited as being a usurper in Africa, not Italy, by Victor (cf. 39.22).

42. There is a very useful chart in Williams, *op. cit.*, pp. 228–9 listing all the emperors from Marcus Aurelius to Theodosius, both with their mode of accession and their manner of death. It is a sobering catalogue that illustrates how hazardous it was for purple to be one's favourite colour.

43. The best available edition of Orosius' history is the French Budé three-volume set (with a critical Latin text and facing-page translation), with good commentary. Roy J. Deferrari did a Catholic University of America Press translation in 1964, and A.T. Fear has a 2010 Liverpool University Press English version as well. Orosius is one of those authors who was of immense popularity in late antiquity and into the medieval and renaissance periods, only to have fallen into relative obscurity in later times. For the study of Diocletian he is of limited use, offering little beyond a recapitulation of what can be found in other sources.

44. These were 'tribal inhabitants of the Atlas Mountains with modern Sétif as their main centre.' (Michael H. Dodgeon and Samuel N.C. Lieu, eds., *The Roman Eastern Frontier and the Persian Wars (AD 226–363), A Documentary History* (London-New York: Routledge, 1991) p. 376 n. 31).

45. Those interested in pursuing the controversies about the two editions of Eusebius' work may consult Timothy D. Barnes, 'The Editions of Eusebius' Ecclesiastical History' in *Greek, Roman, and Byzantine Studies*, Vol. 21 (1980), pp. 191–201; and Richard W. Burgess, 'The Dates and Editions of Eusebius' *Chronici canones and Historia ecclesiastica*,' in *The Journal of Theological Studies*, Vol. 48 (1997), pp. 471–504.

46. Anthony Birley has an excellent Penguin Classics edition of the first part only of the collection.

47. We may mention here some useful English-language works of commentary on the fourth century sources we have cited: H.W. Bird's *Eutropius' Breviarium, Translated with an introduction and commentary* (Liverpool: Liverpool University Press, 1993) and J.W. Eadie's *The Breviarium of Festus: A Critical Edition with Historical Commentary* (London: Athlone Press, 1967) are invaluable. Bird has a similar volume *Aurelius Victor: De Caesaribus* (Liverpool: Liverpool University Press, 1994) again offering a translation with detailed historical annotation.

48. This work should be studied closely in conjunction with A.S. Christensen, *Lactantius the Historian: An Analysis of the De Mortibus Persecutorum* (Opuscula Graecolatina) (Copenhagen: Museum Tusculanum, 1980).

49. One of the more interesting, regrettably unanswerable questions about Diocletian concerns the extent of his education in and knowledge of Roman history and literature, not least the Augustan regime and the development of the principate.

Chapter 2

1. We may recommend here Adrian Higham, 'In Search of Diocletian' in *Classics Ireland*, Vol. 4 (1997), pp. 57–65, with good introduction to the enigmas posed by the youth of extremely humble origins who was catapulted to the heights of power.
2. For a useful introduction to the palace, see A.J. Brothers, 'Diocletian's Palace at Split' in *Greece & Rome*, Vol. 19, No. 2 (October 1972), pp. 175–86.
3. Wilkes, *op. cit.*, p. 416.
4. See Ilkka Syvänne *Gordian III and Philip the Arab: The Roman Empire at a Crossroads* (Barnsley: Pen & Sword Military, 2021).
5. Indispensable for the study of these sites is Dragoslav Srejović's *Roman Imperial Towns and Palaces in Serbia (Sirmium, Romuliana, Naissus)* (Beograd: Srpksa akademija nauka I umetnosti, 1993).
6. Lactantius, *De Mortibus Persecutorum* 4 calls him a 'wild beast', and notes that he fell in battle while fighting against the Carpi after their invasion of Dacia and Moesia. Decius is placed by Lactantius between Domitian and Valerian as examples of what happens to emperors who dare to persecute Christians.
7. One of the most famous martyrs of the Decian persecution is the celebrated Catanian patroness against eruptions of Mount Etna, Saint Agatha. Saint Fabian is honoured in Christian martyrologies on 20 January, traditionally together with the Milanese martyr Saint Sebastian, who was said to have been a soldier under Diocletian and Maximian.
8. Cf. Malcolm Todd, *The Early Germans* (Malden, Massachusetts: Wiley Blackwell, 1994) (second edition, 2004), p. 140.
9. Relatively speaking Gallienus has not been the subject of much secondary scholarship; very useful and reliable is Ilkka Syvänne's *The Reign of Emperor Gallienus: The Apogee of Roman Cavalry* (Barnsley: Pen & Sword Military, 2019).
10. See further here J. Fitz, *Ingenuus et Régalien* (Bruxelles: Editions Latomus, 1976).
11. See further J.F. Drinkwater, *The Alamanni and Rome 213–496, Caracalla to Clovis* (Oxford: Oxford University Press, 2007).
12. Williams' opening chapter on the sources of the crisis of the third century provides a background overview of the history of Roman contacts with the Germans, especially from the time of Julius Caesar.
13. Hugh Elton, *The Roman Empire in Late Antiquity: A Political and Military History* (Cambridge: Cambridge University Press, 2018) pp. 21–2 blames the Sarmatians.

14. For a helpful, accessible introduction see Nathanael J. Andrade, *Zenobia: Shooting Star of Palmyra* (Oxford: Oxford University Press, 2018); note also Richard Stoneman's *Palmyra and Its Empire: Zenobia's Revolt against Rome* (Ann Arbor: The University of Michigan Press, 1992); Pat Southern's *Empress Zenobia: Palmyra's Rebel Queen* (London: Continuum UK, 2008).

15. We may recommend for further reading here Alaric Watson's *Aurelian and the Third Century* (London-New York: Routledge, 1999); note also Ilkka Syvänne's *Aurelian and Probus: The Soldier Emperors Who Saved Rome* (Barnsley: Pen & Sword Military, 2021).

16. Much work has been done to study this aspect of the Roman economy and supply-chain issues. See here especially G.E. Rickman, *Roman Granaries and Store Buildings* (Cambridge: Cambridge University Press, 1971); the same author's *The Corn Supply of Ancient Rome* (Oxford: Oxford University Press,1980), which remain the standard accounts.

17. Indeed, it is not inconceivable that Cleopatra's suicide was exactly what Octavian wanted. It satisfied many goals: it eliminated any chance of his appearing harsh in the treatment of a woman who might attract sympathy; it made Cleopatra appear all the more fierce, as an opponent who had been able to escape the hand of Roman justice (Horace calls her *deliberata morte ferocior*, someone who was more ferocious because her death was premeditated by her and not forced); lastly, it avoided him the trouble of any situation where Cleopatra needed to be housed somewhere, like the tradition of Zenobia with the villa and senatorial marriage. She had had a child with Caesar (illegitimate under Roman law or not), and she was far too problematic a figure for the Augustan regime to tolerate.

18. See Mark Hebblewhite, *The Emperor and the Army in the Later Roman Empire, AD 235–395* (London-New York: Routledge, 2017) pp. 1 ff. for the problematic, tense relationship between the emperor and the army, using the example of Probus.

Chapter 3

1. Not surprisingly, Lactantius (*De Mortibus Persecutorum* 6) notes that the blame for his end was his refusal to heed the example of how previous persecutors of Christians had come to bad ends.

2. The best available study of this obscure figure is Caillan Davenport's 'M. Claudius Tacitus: Senator or Soldier?' in *Latomus*, T. 73, Fasc. 1 (2014), pp. 174–87.

3. Watson, *op. cit.*, p. 108 thinks that the idea could have arisen as an element of Probus' propaganda.

4. Depopulation was a critical problem at numerous junctures in the history of the maintenance of the Roman frontiers. Below we shall consider the panegyric of Constantine that offers extended discussion of the hero's work in Gaul and Britain; toward the end of that address, there is a rare precise delineation of exactly which Gallic tribes left behind lands for new cultivation.

5. Elton, *op. cit.*, p. 29 accepts the lightning bolt story without comment.
6. The classic case in argument for the thesis that Diocletian was somehow complicit in a conspiracy is that of H.W. Bird, 'Diocletian and the Deaths of Carus, Numerian and Carinus', in *Latomus*, T. 35, F. 1 (*janvier-mars* 1976), pp. 123–32.
7. David Potter: *Constantine the Emperor* (Oxford: Oxford University Press, 2013) pp. 26–7) observes that Lactantius does not mention Diocletian's slaying of Aper, arguing that if anyone would have mentioned the killing it would have been the emperor's unrelenting critic.
8. So Elton, *op. cit.*, p. 29. Diocletian probably had no interest in excising this particular tradition, in which his sword gleaming in the sun had functioned as something of a lightning bolt in its own right.
9. *Op. cit.*, p. 35.
10. Williams (p. 34) notes simply, 'Whether Diocles actively plotted Numerian's death we cannot know … Perhaps Diocles merely "wished" the Emperor's death; perhaps he simply read the signs and let it happen.' Williams follows the traditional analysis (exemplified by Gibbon's majestic prose) that Numerian was a 'pathetic figure', one who did not deserve his fate and was simply a bookish, poetic man lost in a hopelessly militaristic environment in which he had no hope of survival.
11. *Op. cit.*, pp. 36–7.
12. He may one day during this reign even have been accorded the title of 'Eternal Augustus'; on this see C.H.V. Sutherland, 'Diocletian As "Aeternus Augustus"' in *Museum Notes (American Numismatic Society)*, Vol. 7 (1957), pp. 67–70.
13. Williams (p. 240, n. 38) notes that there is papyrus evidence that he was still known as Diocles as late as March 285 in Egypt. We have no certainty as to when he changed his name.
14. The attribution of the sarcastic Virgil quote to Diocletian may have had a particular point with reference to Numerian, who was allegedly much given to the study and practice of literature. In the end, it was the man of servile origins who was the ultimate reader of Virgil, at least in terms of absorbing the import of the poet's lessons.
15. A useful introduction to what we know and especially what we do not know about this and subsequent Diocletianic and other tetrarchal campaigns is the article of T.D. Barnes, 'Imperial Campaigns, A.D. 285–311' in *Phoenix*, Vol. 30, No. 2 (Summer, 1976), pp. 174–93.
16. Potter, *op. cit.*, p. 276.
17. See further here Hebblewhite, *op cit.*, p. 11.
18. On this see Alexandra Stefan, 'Dioclétian à l'été 285: son deuxième consulat, les sanctions contre la "memoria" de Carin et l'amnistie générale' in *Zeitschrift für Papyrologie und Epigraphik*, Bd. 204 (2017), pp. 265–79.
19. Cf. here C.E. Van Sickle, 'Changing Bases of the Roman Imperial Power in the Third Century' in *L'antiquité Classique*, T. 8, Fasc. 1 (*mai*

1939), pp. 153–70 (with consideration of the period from the accession of Septimius Severus to Diocletian's retirement).

Chapter 4

1. Williams, *op. cit.*, pp. 43–4 shares the widely held view that Diocletian had anticipated the appointment of Maximian for some time, given the speed with which events unfolded.
2. Potter, *op. cit.*, p. 276 argues that Diocletian realized that without any son or family support to back his claim to the purple, he needed to look elsewhere for help.
3. Cf. Williams, *op. cit.*, p. 45.
4. Potter, *op. cit.*, p. 278 discusses evidence for how even as a Caesar, Maximian could act on his own initiatives, at least within certain parameters. The point of the Diocletianic system, after all, was to allow for decisions to be made without having to wait interminably for the emperor to arrive on the scene or to receive his correspondence.
5. Williams, *op. cit.*, pp. 48–9 considers some of the problems. He agrees with the thesis that Maximian was promoted rapidly to Augustus because of the exigencies of the Carausius revolt (i.e. Carausius had declared that he was an Augustus, and so Maximian could not be a mere Caesar as he went to deal with the crisis). This is a sound enough argument, though Carausius' title was based on personal ambition and invention (albeit defended by significant resources in both men and materials), not on Diocletian's and the senate's support.
6. The date is one of the many mysteries of the tetrarchal period. Part of the problem is our equal uncertainty as to the origins of Diocletian's plan, i.e. did he intend always to have a colleague, and if so, of what rank?
7. P.J. Casey, *Carausius and Allectus: The British Usurpers* (London: B.T. Batsford, Ltd., 1994) provides an accessible introduction. Simon Elliott's *Roman Britain's Pirate King: Carausius, Constantius Chlorus and the Fourth Roman Invasion of Britain* (Barnsley: Pen & Sword Military, 2022) provides a comprehensive account, with a focus on the military history. Note also Norman Shiel's *The Episode of Carausius and Allectus: the Literary and Numismatic Evidence*, British Archaeological Reports 40, 1977. More generally on the history of Roman military involvement in the province, see Rupert Jackson, *The Roman Occupation of Britain and Its Legacy* (London-New York: Bloomsbury Academic, 2021).
8. Numismatic evidence survives complete with a Virgilian quotation honouring Carausius as the one who has arrived as a virtual saviour – the text cited from Virgil (*Expectate Veni* – 'Come, o you who have been awaited') occurs in the *Aeneid* with reference to the Trojan hero Hector. The coinage quote is another reminder of the widespread popularity of Virgil in the empire, even in distant provinces.

9. What is certain is that the divine nomenclature was not an original part of the arrangement, but a later addition. An argument can be made for 287; attempts have been made to defend earlier dates.

10. C.E.V. Nixon and B.S. Rodgers, *In Praise of Later Roman Emperors: The Panegyrici Latini* (Berkeley-Los Angeles-Oxford: The University of California Press, 2015) provides an English translation of the complete corpus of these works, together with an extensive historical commentary of great value. The 1964 Latin text of R.A.B. Mynors (originally published in the Oxford Classical Texts series) is also included, making this an especially convenient, essential guide to study of these difficult works. Note also Roger Rees' *Layers of Loyalty in Latin Panegyric: AD 289–307* (Oxford: Oxford University Press, 2002), and the same author's edited volume, *Oxford Readings in Classical Studies: Latin Panegyric* (Oxford: Oxford University Press, 2012).

11. Pat Southern and Karen R. Dixon, *The Late Roman Army* (London: B.T. Batsford, Ltd., 1996) (reprinted by Routledge in 2000), p. 3, comment, 'It is refreshing to note that as well as sickening panegyrics, hostile narratives were also preserved, regardless of the religious convictions of the victim. The Christian author Lactantius blamed Diocletian for all the ills of the Empire, while Zosimus, the pagan, blamed Constantine instead.' For the way in which Aurelius Victor considered Diocletian a positive influence at first in terms of his economic reforms, but then a negative, see Williams, *op. cit.*, pp. 124–5.

12. The vexed questions of authorship and authorial identity are surveyed by Nixon and Rogers, *op. cit.*, pp. 8–10.

13. *Op. cit.*, p. 242 n. 14.

14. Cf. here Bill Leadbetter, '"*Patrimonium Indivisum*"?: The Empire of Diocletian and Maximian, 285–289' in *Chiron*, Vol. 28 (1998), pp. 213–228.

15. The Sarmatians seem to have been fought in 285 and again in 289. See further Williams, *op. cit.*, p. 242 n. 15.

16. 'Chlorus' is Greek for 'pale'.

17. See further Nixon and Rogers, *op. cit.*, p. 112.

18. Williams, *op. cit.*, pp. 63–4 explores why Diocletian pursued a novel system that deprived him of power by increasing the holders of empire. He concludes reasonably that Diocletian wanted to do more than just 'cope' with the problems that seemed constantly to beset the empire. He did not want to be another failed Illyrian emperor, with appreciable successes finally cut short by assassination.

19. Adrian Goldsworthy, *How Rome Fell: Death of a Superpower* (New Haven, Connecticut: Yale University Press, 2009) p. 161.

20. For Galerius see especially William Lewis Leadbetter, *Galerius and the Will of Diocletian* (London-New York: Routledge, 2009).

21. See Williams, *op. cit.*, pp. 65–6 for the question of what exactly the intended division of the empire was. We should remember that Diocletian did not

want four realms, but one polity managed by four men. There was not supposed to be a strict and rigid division of the empire into four sectors, at least not in its original conception. But such a quartering of the empire may have been inevitable once the tetrarchy was established. The logic behind not precisely dividing territory was to be able to emphasize harmony and serene cooperation between the four emperors.

22. Williams, p. 210 credits the tetrarchal 'top-heavy apparatus' with maintaining Roman security in the face of major threats.

23. Cf. here Williams, *op. cit*, pp. 72–3.

24. Williams, *op. cit.*, p. 72 analyses the hopelessness of Carausius' position economically once he lost control of any continental territory. The fall of Gesoriacum and the surrounding area would have spelled doom to his trading capability. An attack on Britain would be difficult, but it was increasingly inevitable – the 'third Augustus' was no longer to be tolerated. No longer would Carausius be allowed to play emperor, as it were, with only coastal fortifications to deter him from any continental assaults (cf. Aurelius Victor, *De Caesaribus* 39.39).

25. Williams, *op. cit.*, p. 73 is sceptical of the story, which he considers a possible 'rhetorical flourish'. But it made good tactical sense to convince one's men that they had no ready means of escape if they decided that things were too difficult as they faced Allectus' land forces.

26. For the place of Londinium in provincial government, see Anthony R. Birley, *The Roman Government of Britain* (Oxford: Oxford University Press, 2005) pp. 11–2. Birley's volume more generally offers the author's characteristically sound and sober appraisal of various problems in the study of Roman Britain, with comprehensive coverage of political and numismatic issues in particular.

Chapter 5

1. Williams, *op. cit.*, p. 80 considers the story to be a likely later invention, on the grounds that it is not found in Lactantius, but rather in the later sources Ammianus and Eutropius. It is true that Lactantius has a hostile attitude toward Galerius (to say the least), but the absence of the anecdote in his works does not necessarily mean that it was not true.

2. *Op. cit.*, p. 84.

3. Alan K. Bowman, 'Diocletian and the First Tetrarchy: IV. The Period of the Tetrarchy, 293–305' in Alan K. Bowman, Peter Garnsey, and Averil Cameron, eds., *The Cambridge Ancient History, Second Edition, Volume VII, The Crisis of Empire, A.D. 193–337* (Cambridge: Cambridge University Press, 2005) p. 81.

4. Williams, *op. cit.*, p. 246 n. 14.

5. Potter, *op. cit.*, p. 288, argues that if the story of the carriage is true, it was designed as an indication to the soldiery that the commander was apologizing for the loss.

6. See Margret S. Pond Rothman, 'The Thematic Organization of the Panel Reliefs on the Arch of Galerius' in *The American Journal of Archaeology*, Vol. 81, No. 4 (Autumn, 1977), pp. 427–54 for a comprehensive attempt to explicate the images.

7. Charles Matson Odahl, *Constantine and the Christian Empire* (London-New York: Routledge, 2010) (second edition of the 2004 original), p. 60.

8. On this topic note Bill Leadbetter, 'Best of Brothers: Fraternal Imagery in Panegyrics on Maximian Herculius' in *Classical Philology*, Vol. 99, No. 3 (July 2004), pp. 257–66; cf. also Brent D. Shaw, 'Ritual Brotherhood in Roman and Post-Roman Societies' in *Traditio*, Vol. 52 (1997), pp. 327–55.

9. Indispensable for the background of everyday life in the region under Roman domination is Naphtali Lewis' *Life in Egypt under Roman Rule* (Oxford: Oxford University Press,1983).

10. 'There were two rebellions in Egypt during the 290s' (Nixon and Rodgers, *op. cit.*, p. 173 n. 82).

11. For a detailed appraisal of the problems, see Williams, *op. cit.*, pp. 244–5 n. 1.

12. Useful here is Bill Leadbetter 'Galerius and the Revolt of the Thebaid in 293/4' in *Anticthon*, Vol. 34 (2000), pp. 82–94.

13. Cf. Williams, *op. cit.*, pp. 119–20.

14. Robert K. Ritner, 'Egypt under Roman rule: The legacy of Ancient Egypt' in Carl F. Petry, ed., *The Cambridge History of Egypt, Volume One, Islamic Egypt, 640–1517* (Cambridge: Cambridge University Press, 1998) p. 24.

15. 'No ancient writer records the name of Lucius Domitius Domitianus Augustus, who first came to the attention of historians with the discovery of coins issued from the Alexandrian mint dated in his second regnal year' (Allan Chester Johnson, 'Lucius Domitius Domitianus Augustus' in *Classical Philology*, Vol. 45, No. 1 (January 1950) pp. 13–21. For extensive consideration of the numerous problems posed by this elusive figure, note J. Schwartz, *L. Domitius Domitianus: étude numismatique et papyrologique* (*Fondation égyptologique reine Elisabeth*, 1975).

16. 'The most dangerous usurpation faced by the tetrarchic government in the east was that of Domitius Domitianus and Aurelius Achilleus in Egypt in the summer of 296 ce. Only the former has left a numismatic record of his brief tenure of power and due to the unreliability of the ancient sources for this period details of the entire episode remain shrouded in uncertainty.' (David Sear, *Roman Coins and Their Values, Volume 4, The Tetrarchies and the Rise of the House of Constantine, AD 284–337* (London: Spink & Son Ltd., 2011) p. 127).

17. See further here A. Omissi, *Emperors and Usurpers in the Later Roman Empire: Civil War, Panegyric, and the Construction of Legitimacy* (Oxford: Oxford University Press, 2018) p. 79 n. 25.

18. So Williams, *op. cit.*, p. 81.

19. One extant source to evaluate on this subject is the fifth panegyric, a speech delivered in thanksgiving to Constantine. 'The speech is one

of our earliest sources for the subject but it must be admitted that its testimony is exceedingly difficult to interpret. We know too little about the "fundamental principles" of late Roman taxation to be sure of our ground.' (Nixon and Rodgers, *op. cit.*, pp. 256–7).

20. For the disturbing effect of such uprisings on the population of Egypt, see B. Garstad, 'Alexander's circuit of the Mediterranean in the *Alexander Romance*' in R. Stoneman, K. Nawotka, and A. Wojchiechowska, eds., *The Alexander Romance: History and Literature* (Groningen: Barkhuis & Groningen University Library, 2018) p. 150.

21. Cf. Ian Hughes, *A Military Life of Constantine the Great* (Barnsley: Pen & Sword Military, 2020) p. 12.

22. The story is another illustration of Diocletian's oft-cited propensity for severity. The sixth century Byzantine chronicler John Malalas relates it in his *Chronographia*, where Diocletian is said to have dug a trench around Alexandria to divert its water, followed by his burning of the city. He gives his notorious equine order, but soon thereafter his horse trips over a corpse. The Alexandrians set up a brazen statue of the fateful animal. Orosius (7.25) does not mention the horse, noting only that after the eight month siege Diocletian gave full vent to his fury and rage, ordering mass slaughter and destruction.

23. On the use of religious and cult sites to create a successful border area with appeal to diverse interests, see Ilkka Syvänne, *Military History of Late Rome, 284–361* (Barnsley: Pen & Sword Military, 2015) p. 213.

24. A useful study here is Alan K. Bowman's 'The Military Occupation of Upper Egypt in the Reign of Diocletian' in *The Bulletin of the American Society of Papyrologists*, Vol. 15, No. 1/2 (1978), pp. 25–38.

25. There is relatively little literary attestation for the Mauretanian campaigns ('Much of the evidence derives from inscriptions' – Williams, *op. cit.*, p. 244 n. 8).

26. For a standard history see further Chester G. Starr, *The Roman Imperial Navy* (New York: Cornell University Press, 1941).

27. Williams, *op. cit.*, p. 75 offers the fair assessment that there was 'apparent tactical unwisdom' in Maximian's being willing to risk ambush and other hazards by pursuing the enemy into their redoubts and hiding places – but otherwise they would re-emerge at some later date, once again to launch hit and run strikes against Roman interests. Maximian was determined to solve the problem once and for all, and he succeeded in securing Africa in what was perhaps his most impressive military achievement.

28. Williams, *op. cit.*, p. 129.

29. Potter, *op. cit.*, p. 327 considers the currency edict to have been 'reasonable' as a response to inflation, and the maximum price regulations a failure. 'In practical terms, the *Edict on Maximum Prices* was an act of economic lunacy' (p. 328). There is a convenient extract from the price list in Williams, *op. cit.*, pp. 224–7.

30. Williams, *op. cit.*, p. 132 offers a characteristically balanced view: Diocletian, he concludes, was not talented economically, and yet his interventions in the Roman economy were necessary, and it is likely that there were significant limits to what anyone could have done to ameliorate the problems of inflation and inequity of economic burdens.

31. *Pan. Lat.* 6.6., on which see Nixon and Rodgers, *op. cit.*, p. 225 n. 25.

32. Nixon and Rodgers, *op. cit.*, p. 226.

33. A good introduction to a difficult topic is Ian Whitaker, 'The Problem of Pythias' Thule' in *The Classical Journal*, Vol. 77, No. 2 (December 1981–January 1982) pp. 148–64. Cf. also H.J.W. Wisjman, 'Thule Applied to Britain' in *Latomus*, T. 57, Fasc. 2 (*avril-juin* 1998) pp. 318–23; Ralph Moore, 'Empire without End at the Ends of the Earth: Ireland and Thule in Roman Imperial Ideology' in *Classics Ireland*, Vol. 26, Ireland, Britain, and the Classical World (2019), pp. 58–85.

Chapter 6

1. Williams (*op. cit.*, p. 27) characterizes Diocletian as 'generally pious in the traditional religion of the Romans: one who would meet the approval of the great Puritans.' While Diocletian's own thoughts on religion cannot be determined with certainty, it is clear that he saw in traditional Roman religious practice a powerful and utilitarian expedient to help to protect the empire. One thinks of Charles Laughton's Gracchus in Kubrick's *Spartacus*, who when confronted about why he was performing a sacrifice although he had reservations about the gods, responded that privately he believed in none of them, and publicly in them all.

2. Williams (*op. cit.*, p. 173) notes 'Our main sources agree that Galerius was a driving force for persecution, whereas Diocletian had misgivings about the policy, if not the principle, of a general war against Christianity. But eventually he was persuaded.' Diocletian was interested in the preservation of order, and while no doubt he saw in Christianity a very real threat to the traditional Roman order, it is likely that he was worried too that a massive persecution would bring its own brand of disorder to the empire.

3. *Historia Ecclesiastica* 8.4. See further here David Woods, '"Veturius" and the Beginning of the Diocletianic Persecution' in *Mnemosyne*, Fourth Series, Vol. 54, Fasc. 5 (October 2001), pp. 587–91.

4. *II Gemina* appears in the *Notitia*, with a base at Legio (modern León in Spain). See Pollard and Berry, *op. cit.*, p. 111. The unit may have been part of Maximian's force for his Mauretanian campaign against the Berbers. We know little about north African legions during the tetrarchy; *III Augustani* is named in the *Notitia*.

5. Williams, *op. cit.*, p. 170.

6. Williams, *op. cit.*, p. 171 is sympathetic to the view that Galerius intended earlier, smaller steps as a prelude to a wider campaign against Christianity

– the mechanism of creeping incrementalism to obtain a preordained outcome.

7. The persecution of the Christians under Nero has become famous in popular culture because of the novel *Quo Vadis* and its subsequent film adaptations. Useful as a convenient and reliable scholarly introduction here is Robert Louis Wilken's *The Christians as the Romans Saw Them* (New Haven, Connecticut: Yale University Press, 1984); note also John Pollini's article 'Burning Rome, Burning Christians' in Shadi Bartsch, Kirk Freudenburg, and Cedric Littlewood eds. *The Cambridge Companion to Nero* (Cambridge: Cambridge University Press, 2017). It is interesting that in the general liturgical calendar of Rome, the so-called protomartyrs of Rome did not receive a universal feast until the reforms after the Second Vatican Council, when the day was fixed as an optional observance on 30 June (i.e. the day following the feast of Peter and Paul, the two most prominent Neronian Age martyrs). A separate feast on 27 June had been instituted only under Benedict XV for use in Rome and its environs, with the martyrs named on 24 June in the martyrology and celebrated on the first free calendar day thereafter. The martyrs of Nero's reign are attested to in pagan (Suetonius, Tacitus) as well as Christian sources (the early fifth century chronicle of Sulpicius Severus); thus they are far better attested than many a victim of the persecutions inaugurated by the tetrarchy. Interestingly, Lactantius, *De Mortibus Persecutorum* 2 does not reference these well-attested martyrs in his account of Peter and Paul and their martyrdoms at Rome under Nero.

8. Potter, *op. cit.*, pp. 298–308 provides a concise and learned introduction to the sect.

9. 'Before 302, Diocletian had outlawed Manichaeans, people claiming to be true Christians and whose origins in Persia, Rome's archenemy, made easy targets' (Elizabeth DePalma Digeser, *A Threat to Public Piety: Christians, Platonists, and the Great Persecution* (Ithaca-London: Cornell University Press, 2012) p. 1).

10. He figures in Eusebius' account of the persecutions.

11. *De Mortibus Persecutorum* 10.

12. Williams, *op. cit.*, p. 171 argues that Diocletian's wrath as reported by Lactantius is completely credible, but that it is unlikely that a general policy of persecution followed on such a relatively trivial episode. We might counter that major events are often triggered by seemingly minor catalysts.

13. The dramatic scene is narrated by Lactantius, *De Mortibus Persecutorum* 12.

14. We concur with David Woods on this point (*op. cit.*, p. 588).

15. *De Mortibus Persecutorum* 13.

16. Cf. here Anthony A. Barrett, *Rome Is Burning: Nero and the Fire That Ended a Dynasty* (Princeton: Princeton University Press, 2020).

17. *De Mortibus Persecutorum* 14.

18. Lactantius reports that Maximian and Constantius were not even consulted about the persecutions, simply informed and given their orders

(*De Mortibus Persecutorum* 15). In Lactantius' estimation, Maximian was by nature a violent man, and thus more than happy to comply; Constantius is credited with agreeing to the burning of some churches to make it appear that he was obedient to the edict, though he preserved the bodies of the Christians, the temples of the soul.

19. Williams, *op. cit.*, p. 179, in response to the scepticism of Gibbon.
20. *Op. cit.*, pp. 183–4.
21. Williams, *op. cit.*, p. 177.
22. See further W.H.C. Frend, *The Donatist Church: A Movement of Protest in Roman North Africa* (Oxford: Oxford University Press, 1952).
23. For the value of this work in constructing a chronology of the age, see especially A. S. Christensen, *Lactantius the Historian: An Analysis of the De Mortibus Persecutorum* (Copenhagen: Museum Tusculanum, 1980).
24. The text is Dubner's (Paris: Libraire Victor Lecoffre, 1891). There have been many editions with extensive notes; we may recommend in particular Alfons Städele, *Laktanz: De mortibus persecutorum: Über die Todesarten der Verfolger* (Turnhout: Brepols, 2003) (Fontes Christiani 43).
25. So G.S.R. Thomas, 'L'abdication de Dioclétien' in *Byzantion*, Vol. 43 (1973), pp. 229–47; *contra*, cf. C.E.V. Nixon, 'The Panegyric of 307 and Maximian's Visits to Rome' in *Phoenix*, Vol. 35 (1981), pp. 70–6. Elton, *op. cit.*, p. 33 notes: 'After the acclamation of Maximian in 285, he only met with Diocletian in 288, 290, and 303, while the Tetrarchy as a whole never met as four men in the same city.'
26. Elton, *op. cit.*, p. 35 makes the good observation that Constantius never visited Rome; Diocletian only for his twentieth anniversary in 303; and Maximian only four times, despite being the western Augustus.
27. *De Mortibus Persecutorum* 17.
28. Williams, *op. cit.*, p. 188.
29. Potter, *op. cit.*, p. 334.
30. The standard scholarly reference work here is G. Bichir, *Archaeology and History of the Carpi* (Oxford: British Archaeological Reports, 1976).
31. See further here Thomas S. Burns, *A History of the Ostrogoths* (Bloomington: Indiana University Press, 1984) p. 32.
32. Elton, *op. cit.*, p. 31. Elton concludes that Diocletian 'possibly' engaged the Sarmatians in 285 and certainly in 289, and then again in 306/307; also the Carpi in 296 and 304; and Galerius the Carpi in 301, 303, and 308, and the Carpi and the Sarmatians in 302. Different scholars would quibble about some of these dates, owing ultimately as so often in this subject to the poor state of the historical record.
33. For a good illustration of the point, see e.g. Simon Corcoran, 'Galerius, Maximinus and the Titulature of the Third Tetrarchy' in *Bulletin of the Institute of Classical Studies*, Vol. 49 (2006), pp. 231–40.
34. The Carpi have sometimes been conflated and confused with the Goths, especially in the matter of whether *Gothicus* was ever a title assumed by the

emperor. On this see especially Peter Brennan, 'Diocletian and the Goths' in *Phoenix*, Vol. 38, No. 2 (Summer, 1984), pp. 142–6.

35. *De Mortibus Persecutorum* 17.

36. T.D. Barnes, *Constantine and Eusebius* (Cambridge, Massachusetts: Harvard University Press, 1981) p. 25.

37. Cf. Williams, *op. cit.*, p. 190: 'If Galerius did exert pressure, it was only to hasten the implementation of a step that has already been carefully planned.'

Chapter 7

1. 'Never before had a man at the height of his power voluntarily laid power aside, exploiting the very symbols that he had made those of the imperial office.' (Potter, *op. cit.*, p. 335).

2. He was also married to Valeria Maximilla, the daughter of Galerius.

3. For how the death of Constantius was the problem Diocletian could not prepare for in these plans, see Jonathan Bardill, *Constantine, Divine Emperor of the Christian Golden Age* (Cambridge: Cambridge University Press, 2012) p. 81.

4. Barnes, *op. cit.*, p. 29 notes that superstition may have been a factor in making his selection appealing to the aged Diocletian.

5. Cf. Williams, *op. cit.*, p. 191: 'the two new men were probably capable enough.' Faint praise, we might think, but the real problem was not so much the qualifications of the men (mediocre or not), but the fact that both were Galerian.

6. 'To describe him as an imperial "hostage" as some have done, is quite untrue' (Williams, *op. cit.*, p. 191). But Constantine may have felt at times as if he were, and certainly he had a sense that he was a second-class citizen in comparison to Galerius' associates.

7. *Op. cit.*, p. 191.

8. *Op. cit.*, p. 191.

9. Cf. here Potter, *op. cit.*, p. 335 on the fortune of Constantine in confessing a 'very bookish' religion that ensured abundant historiographical praise.

10. Lactantius, *De Mortibus Persecutorum* 24 relates that Constantius was already seriously ill,

11. *Op. cit.*, p. 192.

12. See Nixon and Rodgers, *op. cit.*, pp. 226–7 for the vexed question of when exactly this campaign was: probably 305 and not 296 (that is, not in the wake of the Allectus rebellion). Nixon and Rodgers wonder if this was a campaign then for 'trophy hunting', rather than a case of the Picts taking advantage of any weakness or distraction occasioned by the Carausius/ Allectus episode. For how 296 was significant in the weakening of the northern frontier, see Peter Salway, *A History of Roman Britain* (Oxford: Oxford University Press, 1993) p. 226.

13. Nixon and Rodgers, *op. cit.*, p. 229 plausibly connect this monarch with the recent victories over the Alamanni.

14. Lactantius, *De Mortibus Persecutorum* 25 relates that Galerius was shown a portrait of Constantine, and that he wished at once to consign it to the flames along with the man who was holding it (in other words, as if he and the image were but further victims of his incendiary rage).
15. Williams, *op. cit.*, p. 194 uses strong language to describe what happened: 'Constantine now took the first step in demolishing the settlement of Diocletian.' This is a reasonable interpretation of events, though the exclusively pro-Galerian arrangement of the second tetrarchy had virtually guaranteed that instability of the transition.

Chapter 8

1. Lactantius, *De Mortibus Persecutorum* 25 notes that the official reason given for the arrangement was that Severus was older than Constantine. Of course, he had been in office longer as well.
2. Potter, *op. cit.*, p. 343 considers this 'an unusual act of savagery in the case of leaders who might otherwise be employed in Roman service or sent back to their peoples bound by promises to support Roman interests.' But clearly Constantine was angry about the constant recurrence of problems on the border.
3. Cf. *Pan. Lat.* 6.12, with Nixon and Rodgers, *op. cit.*, p. 235 n. 6. The panegyrist offers some detail: the Bructeri are said to have been fond of launching raids and then frustrating their pursuers by hiding in the forest. Constantine launched a devastating, massive attack into their territory, burning their fields and destroying settlements and villages. Captives were slain in the amphitheatre, since they were too savage to serve as slaves, and too unfaithful to be trusted as auxiliaries in the army. Nixon and Rodgers note that whatever Constantine did on this occasion, it was successful: 'there appears to have been a lasting peace on the Rhine until the mid-fourth century, punctuated only by intermittent hostilities.'
4. Williams, *op. cit.*, p. 195 notes that Maximian needed 'no second bidding' to return to power.
5. Williams, *op. cit.*, p. 256 n. 1 accepts the assessment that construction on the palace must have commenced in the 290s 'at the latest'.
6. Lactantius, *De Mortibus Persecutorum* 26 says that the only grace he received was the concession of an easy death, and that he opened his veins.
7. In his typical fashion, Lactantius fulminates against Galerius, arguing that he intended to slay the entire senate and massacre the population of Rome (*De Mortibus Persecutorum* 27).
8. Lactantius (*De Mortibus Persectorum* 27) describes Galerius as having been reduced from emperor of Rome to pillager of Italy, intending in part to allow his men to plunder the countryside so that any pursuing force would have no supplies in the field. Lactantius goes so far as to say that Galerius was actually hostile to the very name of Rome, preferring to call himself the emperor of Dacia.

9. The view of Lactantius (*De Mortibus Persecutorum* 28) is that Maximian was childish in his resentment of his son, who held greater power.

10. *De Mortibus Persecutorum* 28.

11. *Op. cit.*, p. 196.

12. For Maximian's itinerary at this crucial juncture see Nixon and Rodgers, *op. cit.*, pp. 238–9, n. 66. A key source here is Lactantius, *De Mortibus Persecutorum* 29. It seems possible that Maximian travelled first to Gaul for unspecified reasons, then to Galerius, and then after Carnuntum back to Gaul and, certainly, to Constantine. Nixon and Rodgers conclude that it is at least plausible that Maximian went to Carnuntum as Constantine's de facto 'mouthpiece'.

Chapter 9

1. *De Mortibus Persecutorum* 29.

2. See further Pollard and Berry, *op. cit.*, p. 191.

3. Potter, *op. cit.*, p. 342.

4. Potter, *op. cit.*, p. 341. Potter argues that Maxentius showed his true colours by his killing of Severus, which proved that he had no interest in diplomacy when brute force would suffice to obtain his ends.

5. For Lactantius (*De Mortibus Persecutorum* 20) Galerius was the classic example of a man who seemingly had prepared for every eventuality ('stacking the deck', as the saying goes), only to find his plans foiled by the hand of God.

6. *De Mortibus Persecutorum* 21–2 gives a grisly catalogue of Galerius' alleged tortures and punishments, not without mention of his fondness for collecting wild bears as the animal most suited to his own nature, so as to provide ursine executions for his amusement. What started as part of the persecution of Christians is said to have spread to the rest of the population, such that there was a collapse of the rule of law.

7. Williams, *op. cit.*, p. 196.

8. Williams, *op. cit.*, p. 197.

9. Williams, *op. cit*, p. 197.

10. Cf. Lactantius, *De Mortibus Persecutorum* 30, who describes the shameful suicide and end of the onetime tetrarch.

11. Nixon and Rodgers, *op. cit.*, p. 246. Their conclusion is that while Constantine was within his rights to slay Maximian, he may have avoided doing so out of political considerations. Certainly it was to everyone's advantage to have the disgraced old man take his own life.

12. *Op. cit.*, p. 344.

13. Lactantius, *De Mortibus Persecutorum* 43 has a convoluted version of events in which there was allegedly an elaborate scheme on the part of Maxentius and Maximian to feign a quarrel, so that Maximian could then proceed under cover of being at enmity with his son to see to the elimination of the other tetrarchs, all so that in the end the father and son could share

the empire. Lactantius notes that this allegation was false; in reality, he says, Maximian had the plan to destroy everybody, and to restore both Diocletian and himself to power. Whatever machinations Maximian was involved in regarding power sharing or usurpation, Diocletian's behaviour at Carnuntum would dash any hopes of renewing his arrangement with his former colleague.

14. Nixon and Rodgers, *op. cit.*, pp. 248 ff. offer extensive commentary on *Pan. Lat.* 6.21.

15. Nixon and Rodgers, *op. cit.*, p. 247 are rightly suspicious of the fact that the plot is not referenced at all in the text of the sixth panegyric. 'It must be said that this elaborate and heavy-handed justification of Maximian's death is puzzling and might lend weight to a theory that Maximian surrendered at Marseilles on conditions that Constantine failed to meet.' At any rate, the story of a plot is found even in pagan sources (Aurelius Victor; Eutropius; Zosimus). The most likely scenario seems to be that Maximian was urged to commit suicide; he was probably more than willing to cooperate; post mortem the stories about what he had done increased in dramatic detail, as needed to silence any criticism or negative reaction to the death of the once venerated tetrarch.

16. *De Mortibus Persecutorum* 30.

17. Williams, *op. cit.*, p. 256 n. 22 underscores that the *damnatio* was not enacted immediately, but only after the break with Maxentius, and that Constantine would later rehabilitate his old enemy.

18. Potter, *op. cit.*, p. 344 makes the same argument for the concoction of a connection between Constantius and Claudius II, all so that Constantine could have an imperial father with an imperial lineage.

19. *De Mortibus Persecutorum* 42.

20. *De Mortibus Persecutorum* 31.

21. On connections between the sufferings of Galerius described by Lactantius and the torments visited upon the martyrs, see L. Stephanie Cobb, *Divine Deliverance: Pain and Painlessness in Early Christian Martyr Texts* (Oakland: The University of California Press, 2017) pp. 101–2.

22. Lactantius, *De Mortibus Persecutorum* 34–5 provides a text of the purported edict, as well as the author's rejoicing on account of the release of Christian friends who had been held in custody for half a dozen years.

23. Lactantius, *De Mortibus Persecutorum* 32 relates the background history of the enmity between Maximinus and Licinius, stemming from Galerius' promotion of the latter. The ensuing squabbling between Maximinus and Galerius is the last episode related before the gruesome narrative of Galerius' final illness and death, such that Lactantius casts the final period of his favourite target's life as being consumed with strife and discord.

24. *De Mortibus Persecutorum* 36.

25. Potter, *op. cit.*, p. 348 states succinctly: 'It was Licinius who was in the most danger.'

26. On the much debated controversy as to the date of death, see for example Byron J. Nakamura, 'When Did Diocletian Die? New Evidence for an old Problem' in *Classical Philology*, Vol. 98, No. 3 (July 2003), pp. 283–9. Lactantius connects the death of Diocletian with events from c. 311 to 313, and is frustrating in his lack of precision – as a contemporary source, he was speaking to an audience that knew far more than we do. There is fifth century evidence for a date of 3 December 316, which is the source for a reliable citation of day and month, with the year subject to some scholarly dispute occasioned by questions of confusion about consular tenures – and so the argument for 3 December 316 is the conclusion of T.D. Barnes in his important study 'Lactantius and Constantine' in *The Journal of Roman Studies*, Vol. 63 (1973), pp. 29–46. Note also the same author's 'Maxentius and Diocletian' in *Classical Philology*, Vol. 105, No. 3 (2010), pp. 381–22. It is certainly most likely that Diocletian was dead by the time Licinius ordered the death of his wife and daughter.

27. Fik Meijer, *Emperors Don't Die in Bed* (translated by S.J. Leinbach) (London-New York: Routledge, 2001) p. 116. Williams (*op. cit.*, pp. 199–200) opts for 312.

Chapter 10

1. It is a testament to how poorly documented even a key year like 312 in the west is that the twelfth panegyric is the best source of information regarding Constantine's campaigns that we possess.

2. On the connection of this panegyric to the images on the celebrated Arch of Constantine, see Potter, *op. cit.*, pp. 353–4.

3. *Pan. Lat.* 4.20.

4. *Pan. Lat.* 4.22–4. Nixon and Rodgers, *op. cit.*, p. 368 n. 97 note the silence of the panegyrist as to whether Constantine also had mailed cavalry.

5. The name is cited as Pompeianus at *Pan. Lat.* 12.8, as Ruricius at *Pan. Lat.* 4.25, and elsewhere with combined name.

6. Cf. *Pan. Lat.* 4.25. Nazarius cannot help but note that the flight of these horsemen was noble, because they were fleeing from Constantine.

7. Lactantius, *De Mortibus Persecutorum* 44 offers a dramatic account. Nazarius at *Pan. Lat.* 4.30 dwells on the slaughter on the Tiber banks and the heaps of corpses, and the 'tyrant' Maxentius, dead in a manner befitting his cowardly and cruel nature. There is even the usual omen of battle that portends doom: Maxentius is said to have arranged his men on the banks of the Tiber in such a fashion that the last ranks could feel the water lapping at their feet, in harbinger of how soon they would be drowned in the fateful river.

8. Lactantius and Eusebius are the main sources for the famous story. Eusebius wrote a *Vita Constantini* after Constantine's death in 337, in which the story is told that the emperor and his men saw a vision of the cross in the sky at high noon, and that further the emperor had a dream that inspired him to

order the cross emblem to be used for shield adornment before the battle (1.28–30) – the *in hoc signo vinces* prediction. Eusebius credits the story to Constantine's own account to him. Nixon and Rodgers, *op. cit.*, pp. 292–3 note that the author of the twelfth panegyric does not report his source for the account of any supernatural vision, so that we remain quite in the dark as to the genesis of what became the defining moment in Constantine's life.

9. *Pan. Lat.* 4.29. Nixon and Rodgers comment on Nazarius: 'His account of the battle of the Milvian Bridge is as empty of substance as it is full of descriptive elements' (*op. cit.*, p. 374 n. 124).

10. *Pan. Lat.* 4.32 notes the appropriate nature of the dispatch of the head to Africa: Maxentius was thus to give satisfaction to the people to whom he had brought so much affliction. Africa, the panegyrist takes care to note, rejoiced in the decapitation.

11. Lactantius, *De Mortibus Persecutorum* 11 describes Galerius' mother and her devotion to superstition and pagan religion.

12. Lactantius, *De Mortibus Persecutorum* 38 relates with characteristic luridness the wickedness of Maximinus with respect to women of the nobility, complete with accounts of how marriages needed his permission so as to allow him to gratify his wicked lusts, and how women who refused to submit to his depravity were drowned.

13. *De Mortibus Persecutorum* 49.

14. Williams, *op. cit.*, p. 199 summarizes what we know of the story.

15. *De Mortibus Persecutorum* 39–40.

16. Cf. *De Mortibus Persecutorum* 15.

17. *Op. cit.*, p. 255 n. 5.

18. Lactantius relates the story of the executions at *De Mortibus Persecutorum* 50–1, with less in the way of sensational details than usual. He notes that Maximinus, for all his cruelty, never proceeded to kill these noble women, who were beheaded at Thessalonica, their bodies ignominiously cast into the sea. They are the final deaths recorded in Lactantius' catalogue of doom, and appear in a sense as if they were martyrs, with Valeria explicitly said to have been harried and finally slain because of her devotion to chaste virtue, and both women because of their noble status.

19. *De Mortibus Persecutorum* 41.

20. Williams, *op. cit.*, p. 199.

21. *Op. cit.*, p. 348.

22. Cf. Potter, *op. cit.*, p. 348.

23. See further here Nixon and Rodgers, *op. cit.*, p. 52.

24. So T.D. Barnes, *Ammianus Marcellinus and the Representation of Historical Reality* (Ithaca-London: Cornell University Press, 1998) p. 178. More generally on the topic, note H. Stern, 'Remarks on the *Adoratio* under Diocletian' in *Journal of the Warburg and Courtauld Institutes*, Vol. 17 (1954), pp. 184–9.

25. Simon Corcoran, 'Diocletian' in Anthony A. Barrett, ed., *Lives of the Caesars* (Malden, Massachusetts: Blackwell Publishing, 2008) p. 236.

26. Cf., e.g., V. Cotesta, *Kings into Gods: How Prostration Shaped Eurasian Civilization* (Leiden-Boston: Brill, 2012) p. 42 (English translation of the Italian original); Meaghan McEvoy, *Child Emperor Rule in the Late Roman West, AD 367–455* (Oxford: Oxford University Press, 2013) p. 44.

27. For the 'culmination of a long process', see H.W. Bird, *Liber de Caesaribus of Sextus Aurelius Victor* (Liverpool: Liverpool University Press, 1994) p. 162.

28. We may quote here the close of the prologue to Williams' magisterial study on Diocletian: 'Its [i.e. Rome's] restorer was a soldier-Emperor of the humblest social origins, Diocletian, who was compelled to dye himself and his successors so deeply in purple that henceforth the Roman Emperor resembled a godlike Pharaoh more than a first magistrate – a figure the Chinese visitor would instantly have recognized' (p. 11). Different students of the age will debate the question of to what degree Diocletian was compelled to adopt his style of rule – certainly the fact that he abandoned it willingly, and remained in retirement despite provocation and invitation to return is important to consider, alongside the theory that Diocletian considered the trappings of office a necessary concomitant of the security of imperial power.

Select Bibliography of Secondary Sources

This list aims to provide an introductory, elementary list of works for further study of the reign of Diocletian, the tetrarchy, and related problems. It includes some useful commentaries on primary sources.

Alföldi, A. *The Conversion of Constantine and Pagan Rome* (Oxford: Oxford University Press, 1948).

Bardill, J. *Constantine, Divine Emperor of the Christian Golden Age* (Cambridge: Cambridge University Press, 2012).

Barnes, T.D. *The New Empire of Diocletian and Constantine* (Cambridge, Massachusetts: Harvard University Press, 1982).

Barrett, A. A. ed. *Lives of the Caesars* (Malden, Massachusetts: Blackwell Publishing, 2008).

Bird, H.W. *Aurelius Victor: De Caesaribus* (Liverpool: Liverpool University Press, 1994).

Bird, H.W. *Eutropius' Breviarium, Translated with an introduction and commentary* (Liverpool: Liverpool University Press, 1993).

Birley, A.R. *The Roman Government of Britain* (Oxford: Oxford University Press, 2005).

Bowman, A.K., Garnsey, P., Cameron, A. eds., *The Cambridge Ancient History, Second Edition, Volume VII, The Crisis of Empire, A.D. 193–337* (Cambridge: Cambridge University Press, 2005).

Burgersdijk, D.W.P., Ross, A.J. eds. *Imagining Emperors in the Later Roman Empire* (Leiden-Boston: Brill, 2018).

Casey, P.J. *Carausius and Allectus: The British Usurpers* (London: B.T. Batsford, Ltd., 1994).

Corcoran, S. *The Empire of the Tetrarchs: Imperial Pronouncements and Government AD 284–324* (Oxford: Oxford University Press, 1996) (revised for a paperback edition, 2000).

Cowan, R. *Roman Legionary AD 284–337: The Age of Diocletian and Constantine the Great* (Oxford: Osprey Publishing, 2003).

Creed, J.L. *Lactantius, De Mortibus Persecutorum* (Oxford: Clarendon Press, 1984).

Digeser, E.D. *A Threat to Public Piety: Christians, Platonists, and the Great Persecution* (Ithaca-London: Cornell University Press, 2012).

Dodds, E.R. *Pagan and Christian in an Age of Anxiety* (Cambridge: Cambridge University Press, 1965).

Dodgeon, M.H., Lieu, S.N.C. eds. *The Roman Eastern Frontier and the Persian Wars (AD 226–363), A Documentary History.* (London-New York: Routledge, 1991).

Drinkwater, J.F. *The Alamanni and Rome 213–496, Caracalla to Clovis* (Oxford: Oxford University Press, 2007).

Eadie, J.W. *The Breviarium of Festus: A Critical Edition with Historical Commentary* (London: Athlone Press, 1967).

Elliott, S. *Roman Britain's Pirate King: Carausius, Constantius Chlorus and the Fourth Roman Invasion of Britain* (Barnsley: Pen & Sword Military, 2022).

Elton, H. *The Roman Empire in Late Antiquity: A Political and Military History* (Cambridge: Cambridge University Press, 2018).

Frere, S. *Britannia* (Cambridge, Massachusetts: Harvard University Press, 1991)

Goldsworthy, A. *How Rome Fell: Death of a Superpower* (New Haven, Connecticut: Yale University Press, 2009).

Hebblewhite, M. *The Emperor and the Army in the Later Roman Empire, AD 235–395* (London-New York: Routledge, 2017).

Jackson, R. *The Roman Occupation of Britain and Its Legacy* (London-New York: Bloomsbury Academic, 2021).

Jones, A.H.M. *Constantine the Great and the Conversion of Europe* (Oxford: The English Universities Press, 1948).

Leadbetter, B. *Galerius and the Will of Diocletian* (London-New York: Routledge, 2009).

Le Bohec, Y. *The Imperial Roman Army* (London: B.T. Batsford Ltd., 1994) (English translation of the French original '*L'armée romaine, sous le Haut-Empire*' (Paris: Les Editions Picard, 1989; reprinted by Routledge, 2000).

Lewis, N. *Life in Egypt under Roman Rule* (Oxford: Oxford University Press, 1983).

Liebeschutz, J.H.W.G. *Continuity and Change in Roman Religion* (Oxford: Oxford University Press, 1979).

Luttwak, E. *The Grand Strategy of the Roman Empire* (Baltimore, Maryland: Johns Hopkins University Press, 1976).

MacMullen, R. *Soldier and Civilian in the Late Roman Empire* (Cambridge, Massachusetts: Harvard University Press, 1963).

MacMullen, R. *Enemies of the Roman Order* (Cambridge, Massachusetts: Harvard University Press, 1967).

Meijer, F. *Emperors Don't Die in Bed* (translated by S.J. Leinbach) (London-New York: Routledge, 2001).

Nixon, C.E.V., Rodgers, B.S. *In Praise of Later Roman Emperors: The Panegyrici Latini with Latin Text of R.A.B. Mynors* (Berkeley-Los Angeles-Oxford: University of California Press, 1994).

Odahl, C.M. *Constantine and the Christian Empire* (London-New York: Routledge, 2010) (second edition of the 2004 original).

Omissi, A. *Emperors and Usurpers in the Later Roman Empire: Civil War, Panegyric, and the Construction of Legitimacy* (Oxford: Oxford University Press, 2018).

Pollard, N., Berry, J. *The Complete Roman Legions* (London: Thames & Hudson Ltd., 2012).

Potter, D. S. *The Roman Empire at Bay, AD 180–395* (London-New York: Routledge, 2004) (second edition 2014).

Potter, D.S. *Constantine the Emperor* (Oxford: Oxford University Press, 2013).

Rees, R. *Diocletian and the Tetrarchy* (Debates and Documents in Roman History) (Edinburgh: Edinburgh University Press, 2004).

Sear, D. *Roman Coins and Their Values, Volume 4, The Tetrarchies and the Rise of the House of Constantine, AD 284–337* (London: Spink & Son Ltd., 2011).

Seston, W. *Dioclétien et la tétrarchie, I: guerres et réformes* (Paris: De Boccard, 1946).

Shiel, N. *The Episode of Carausius and Allectus: the Literary and Numismatic Evidence* (British Archaeological Reports 40, 1977).

Simmons, M.B. *Arnobius of Sicca: Religious Conflict and Competition in the Age of Diocletian* (Oxford: Oxford University Press, 1996).

Southern, P. *The Roman Empire from Severus to Constantine* (London-New York: Routledge, 2001).

Southern, P., Dixon, K.R. *The Late Roman Army* (London: B.T. Batsford, Ltd., 1996) (reprinted Routledge, 2000).

Srejović, D. *Roman Imperial Towns and Palaces in Serbia (Sirmium, Romuliana, Naissus)* (Beograd: Srpksa akademija nauka I umetnosti, 1993).

Syme, Sir R. *Emperors and Biography* (Oxford: Oxford University Press, 1971).

Syvänne, I. *Military History of Late Rome, 284–361* (Barnsley: Pen & Sword Military, 2015).

Syvänne, I. *Aurelian and Probus: The Soldier Emperors Who Saved Rome* (Barnsley: Pen & Sword Military, 2021).

Thompson, E.A. *The Early Germans* (Oxford: Oxford University Press, 1965).

Todd, M. *The Early Germans* (Malden, Massachusetts: Wiley Blackwell, 1994) (second edition, 2004).

Watson, A. *Aurelian and the Third Century* (London-New York: Routledge, 1999).

Wilken, R.L. *The Christians as the Romans Saw Them* (New Haven, Connecticut: Yale University Press, 1984).

Wilkes, J.J. *Dalmatia: History of the Provinces of the Roman Empire* (Cambridge, Massachusetts: Harvard University Press, 1969).

Wilkes, J.J. *Diocletian's Palace at Split* (Sheffield: University of Sheffield, 1986).

Williams, S. *Diocletian and the Roman Recovery* (London-New York: Routledge, 1997).

Index